THE PARADOX OF POVERTY

Ballinger Series in

BUSINESS IN A GLOBAL ENVIRONMENT

S. Prakash Sethi, Series Editor

Center for Management
Baruch College
The City University of New York

THE PARADOX OF POVERTY
A Reappraisal of
Economic Development Policy

PAUL STEIDLMEIER

BALLINGER PUBLISHING COMPANY
Cambridge, Massachusetts
A Subsidiary of Harper & Row, Publishers, Inc.

International Standard Book Number: 0-88730-184-3

Library of Congress Catalog Card Number: 86-26589

Printed in the United States of America

Library of Congress Cataloging-in-Publication Data

Steidlmeier, Paul, 1942–
  The paradox of poverty.

  Includes bibliographies and index.
  1. Economic development. 2. Economic policy.
3. Poverty. I. Title.
HD75.S75 1987   338.9   86-26589
ISBN 0-88730-184-3

CONTENTS

v

LIST OF FIGURES

LIST OF TABLES

PREFACE

For years the international community has been pushing uphill in the battle against poverty and hunger only to find, as a modern-day Sisyphus, that solutions slip away and that the problem seems to get worse with each succeeding development decade.

It is commonplace that growing poverty has gone hand-in-hand with economic growth. It is also paradoxical. The persistence of poverty amid growth has raised a number of questions about both the quality of social science analysis and the role of markets and public policy processes. Development policy today is shot through with many dilemmas of analysis (what, after all, is the problem?) and policy (what can and should be done and by whom?).

The concrete case of hunger clearly symbolizes the quandry. There are few symbols so transcultural and multidimensional as that of sharing a meal, an act of human well-being, fulfillment, and solidarity. The fact that so many in the world today have little or nothing to eat, while others are exceedingly well off, is a profound indictment of the world economic system. It is morally outrageous that millions starve while simultaneously many food markets are glutted with surplusses. It is also economically inefficient.

Who are the hungry? They are those who either do not command the productive resources to produce enough food for themselves or those who do not possess adequate income to enter the market and purchase what they need. Hunger is but one manifestation of indigent poverty and cannot be adequately conceived of in isolation from other basic needs or from an overall development strategy geared to overcome such poverty. But it potently symbolizes the larger problem. The spectre of world hunger and indigent poverty is a powerful drama that calls into question the very foundations of the world economic order on both moral and technical grounds.

THE MORAL QUESTION

In the world today, this drama is very volatile indeed and is marked by fingerpointing and the heaping of blame on various parties, if not by outright violence. To gain perspective, I find it fruitful to turn to literature.

A stimulating representation of this drama is presented in one of the more neglected of Shakespeare's plays, *Coriolanus*. When it was performed in Paris in 1934 at a time of social tension, it caused riots between leftists and rightists. This play, while dramatizing political themes, is not a mere political debate but a tragedy. *Coriolanus* begins with a clash of interests and prejudices between the citizens of Rome. The security of Rome is threatened from without by the Volscians; the common citizenry, who are called upon to defend the city, suffer starvation, and are on the verge of revolt. Ironically, at the same time the city storehouses are bulging with corn. There is a fundamental clash between social reality and peoples' expectations. A crisis is inevitable.

The first citizen opens the scene asking his fellow citizens if they are resolved to stand up for their rights and to even die rather than famish. They reply emphatically that they are. At this point, the worthy Menenius Agrippa cautions them not to be rash and reassures them that the patricians really have charitable care and concern for them.

The first citizen cuts him off:

> Care for us! True, indeed! They ne'er cared for us yet. Suffer us to famish and their storehouses crammed with grain; make edicts for usury to support usurers; repeal daily any wholesome act established against the rich, and provide more piercing statutes daily to chain up and restrain the poor. If their wars eat us not up, they will, and there's all the love they bear us [I, i].

At the heart of the drama is the tragic hero, Coriolanus, who is valiant and noble in war but behaves like a brute beast in civil society. He is full of contempt for the poor. He scorns their fickleness in social matters as well as their cowardice in war. The dramatic action is played out in terms of a root metaphor that is fundamental to political thought in western civilization: the body politic. It is an intriguing metaphor for it suggests unity, solidarity, and common interests, on the one hand, and a social division of labor with different roles, status, and benefits, on the other. The metaphor is creatively shaped by Shakespeare in the development of his different characters. Coriolanus, for example, sees the poor as "scabs" and "measles" that afflict the body politic. Menenius sees political life as an harmonious whole with differences resolved in common interests. And the Tribunes of the people (who are charged with defending the poor) see Coriolanus as a disease that must be cut away ("a gangrened foot," III, ii). The central theme of the drama is that there is a disease in the body politic and tragedy awaits all of its members because they are incapable of acting together for the common good.

Are the poor and hungry justified in their complaints against the contemporary political economic system? Menenius presents a penetrating allegory of "the complaint against the belly." He compares the unrest of the poor citizens to all the body's members rebelling against the belly: "that only a gulf it did remain in the midst of the body, idle and inactive still cupboarding the viand, never bearing like labor with the rest. . . . " (I, ii) The belly defends itself saying that the food it receives it sends through the whole body.

In response to the poor, Menenius weaves a beguiling allegory of mutual self-interest, much as the modern trickle-down theory. Yet Menenius cannot answer the complaint: The belly seeks only to store ever greater supplies for itself and secure the defense of its girth. It stores food rather than send it through the whole body.

A Coriolanus can impudently suggest that the poor do not want to work and fight, that poverty and hunger are their own doing. Yet those like Menenius today (for example, the authors of *The Brandt Report*) have come to realize that the belly cannot stand on spindly legs nor bring food to its mouth with hands that cannot lift their own weight. There is an imperative in order to send food through the whole body.

The moral tragedy of Coriolanus is upon us, as many world leaders are more concerned with defending the city's gates than life within the city. The fundamental crisis in world poverty and hunger is not the lack of the necessary means to overcome the problem but the lack of political will. Political tragedy looms in the failure of civic virtue, the inability of people to galvanize political will to overcome social problems. In this case, poverty.

This moral component of development policy frequently is pushed into the background. In recent statements on the international economy, western leaders (for example, the Trilateral Commission) have laconically underscored the fact that many people in the West are losing faith in their institutions. They locate the causes for this crisis in the failure of western society's problem-solving ability and the shattering of the illusion of "progress" (continual growth plus trickle down). These observers assert that the breakdown of western institutions is manifested in terms of inverted social priorities: expenditures for the welfare state versus productivity, high taxes versus incentives. Linked to this is the decline of the work ethic. In addition, the price volatility of commodity and industrial products hampers capital budgeting and planning.

These observers, however, fail to analyze sufficiently the complaint against the belly. They accept that the poor are members of the body, not scabs as Coriolanus would maintain. But these modern-day patricians view with alarm the proposal that contemporary tribunes of the people put forth: The Coriolanuses in the world are a disease that must be cut away. For such a proposal invites the destruction of the present political and economic system.

The dramatic action of development focuses upon civic virtue and political will. The sheer egoism of the belly reveals the tragedy that is at the root of the loss of faith in national and international systems. Many contemporary policymakers continue to pursue a Coriolanus strategy of providing the belly with ever more provisions, defending its girth in the name of national security. But the challenge goes beyond even mutual self-interest to embrace some sacrifice of self-interest to protect universal economic rights and to fashion a truly common good. The dramatic tragedy centers upon political will; the civic virtue called for is not adequately expressed in either aggregate or group egoism but only in a just society where all are rendered their due in terms of social, political, and economic rights and correlative duties. Development is not value-free. The focus of the dramatic action in the development arena today is upon human dignity and values, upon people participating as *subjects* of their own destiny in collective political moral choice. Development plans must provide for social justice.

DEVELOPMENT, SCIENCE, AND TECHNOLOGY

The paradox of persistent and even growing poverty and hunger amid progress and economic growth calls into question what is actually occurring in development circles. One increasingly finds an awareness that economic development must be rethought on both national and international levels. This involves new methods of social analysis of poverty (that is, the attempt to answer the questions, "what is actually happening?" and "What are the causes?") and creative approaches to social change (that is, "How does one go from present systems to a new situation?"). The two types of questions are interrelated and a faulty diagnosis of the first question (the problem) only leads to confused and unsalutary prescriptions.

There is no shortage of research on poverty, hunger, and development. The technical literature on plant and animal breeding, human nutrition, and economic transformation and development is vast, very specialized, and generally of high quality. At the same time, economic development literature contains shortcomings both in completeness of social analysis as well as in presuppositions regarding social change. The technical literature is characterized by problem-solving approaches based on the findings of oftentimes narrow and rigid empirical method. I am convinced that the root of the development crisis lies not simply in the lack of technology but in faulty analysis of the problem and in unexamined implicit models of social change that underlie policy proposals.

Economic development policy is inherently paradoxical. Much of the theory amounts to learned ignorance. One must begin an approach to poverty and development by questioning accepted methods of analysis. There are many indications in social science and public policy literature that just such an endeavor is underway. Throughout the book, I accord priority to historical, institutional, and cultural analysis. My aim is to set forth the outlines of sound and effective development policy. In my view, adequate policy has a clear normative component; that is, it is value-critical. But it also necessarily must be empirically comprehensive and technologically feasible. And most of all it must be capable of being implemented within a particular sociopolitical milieu.

To date, such a policy has proven to be elusive. I justify yet another treatise on poverty, hunger, and development because I think I present a fresh analytical structure of the problem and a fruitful approach to development in a broader context of social change.

I approach social analysis of poverty and hunger in terms of four variables: (1) population, resources, and scarcity; (2) the promise of technology; (3) power and social organization; and (4) culture. The first two are well known in North Atlantic economic development literature and have been, in fact, overemphasized. Social power and participation has received scant attention, although there are recent signs that this is changing. But culture is hardly ever directly considered in economics literature, which to my mind represents a major flaw in analysis. My research will attempt to be comprehensive by including all of the above four points and integrating them into a complete sketch of poverty and hunger. Necessarily, attention will be given to differences as well as resemblances among different geographical areas.

Economic development is not just a matter of production, marketing, and consumption. It is part of the broad process of social change. Strangely, the sociological theory of social change has received little explicit attention in economic development literature. This point is directly linked to the neglect of power and culture in analysis. Whatever "development" one introduces must build off of the dominant values, institutions, and structures already existing. My research focuses on what development policy and planning frequently overlook: namely, the sociocultural organizations and institutions already in place, which could, for very little capital investment, be used to promote development. I specifically give attention to such things as the role of religious organizations that have grassroots structures. But I also am thinking of systems of informal credit, fruitful methods of traditional agriculture, forms of family, kinship and village cooperation and interaction, education and attitudes towards time, records, and work. All of these issues represent important aspects of policy planning and implementation. They are not only important on the local level but also affect international cooperation for development. My approach to economic development policy, then, lies within a larger historical context of social change.

As seen from the above, I give attention to the integration of social, political, and economic factors in development. Nonetheless, I think that the central action in the drama of development is political. This accounts for my institutional emphasis. My position does not make technical economic analysis or other sociocultural factors less relevant. Rather, I integrate them into a culturally and historically based political economic framework. In so doing, I part company with recent narrow traditions of neoclassical economic analysis. My approach rests on a fundamental reexamination of the adequacy of contemporary divisions of the social sciences as well as of methods used in social analysis and models of social change. Particular emphasis is placed upon the latter and the question of how, in fact, to overcome the present malaise plaguing most developing countries.

This book falls into three parts. In the introductory chapters I set forth the structure of the problem and my method of approach. In Part II, I undertake social analysis of the problem in terms of the four variables indicated above. In Part III, I discuss development policy alternatives in terms of a social change framework.

ACKNOWLEDGMENTS

I owe many people a word of thanks. First of all the many teachers I have had, authors I have read, and students I have taught. This work began nearly ten years ago. I would like to thank the Misereor Foundation of the West German Bishops' Conference for partial funding during the earlier part of my research. I am also grateful to Winrock International for funding, support, and the opportunity to work at Winrock's headquarters, which enabled me to carry this work to completion.

I express my gratitude to the Food Research Institute of Stanford University where many of the questions underlying this study germinated during my graduate years. I am also grateful for the privilege to use the resources of the New York City Public Library, the National Agricultural Library in Beltsville and the Food and Agriculture Organization in Rome. I am particularly thankful to the faculty, administration, and students at the Institute of Agribusiness of Santa Clara University, the Gregorian University in Rome, Woodstock Center at Georgetown University, and Loyola Marymount University in Los Angeles.

In a special way I am grateful to S. Prakash Sethi whose interest in this work provided a catalyst in getting it published. I am also thankful to James O'Connor, Eleanora Masini, Theodore Mulder, Richard Wheeler, and Frances and Simon Williams, and other friends who have encouraged my research and taken time to read parts of the manuscript and offer comments. Needless to say they are absolved from the shortcomings of the book.

I wish to thank Carole Keese, who helped edit the manuscript and guided it through many revisions. Without her dedication and efficiency this project would have lagged far behind. Likewise, I am grateful to Carol Franco, Marjorie Richman, Barbara Roth, and the staff at Ballinger Publishing Company for their cooperation during the process of final editing and publication.

Finally, to my parents and family, my heartfelt gratitude for more things than I can mention. Special gratitude to my brother Leo, who provided me with secretarial services, and to my brother Mark, who has helped handle business affairs, and to all for their love and support.

School of Management
State University of New York
Binghamton

INTRODUCTION

1 POVERTY AND PROGRESS
The Structure of the Problem

There is hardly a problem that has elicited so much compassion on the part of observers as poverty and hunger, especially with regard to the suffering of the most vulnerable groups: children, pregnant and lactating women, the urban unemployed, and the rural landless poor. Many people have apparently been stirred to do something. Atheists and religious people, communists and multinational executives have even spoken of cooperating. Yet in the past years progress toward the eradication of poverty has been slight. At the same time, it has become clear that the means are at hand, even within the scope of today's technology, to resolve the problem satisfactorily and to meet people's basic needs. In fact, it seems that few problems are so close to a potential solution as poverty, whether in terms of technical capacity or the heightened consciousness and motivation needed to mobilize people into action.

Poverty is a troubling paradox. It is so in a moral sense because it gnaws away at conscience: it need not be and should not be. Poverty does not result from blind fate or one's sins either in the present or a previous life. It is an injustice that derives primarily from the failure of collective human responsibility. Poverty is unsettling in a political economic sense because it breeds social instability and diminishes the possibility of improving the general quality of life. Poverty is unsettling in a third sense because it resists "progress." In a manner reminiscent of pests such as the tsetse fly, which have developed genetic mutations and become immune to the toxic substances de-

3

signed to exterminate them, poverty is the problem that will not go away. Despite considerable progress in various fields of science and political economy, poverty, in an aggregate sense, seems to be growing. As Robert McNamara noted some years ago, one of the most salient characteristics of growth in the developing countries is that it is not equitably reaching the poor, and the poor are not significantly contributing to growth (McNamara 1977).

The last few years have been a time of searching reappraisal of international economic and development policies by all concerned parties, no matter what their color on the political spectrum. There is no political economic system in the world today, whether rich or poor, right or left, that is not being buffeted about by rough waters. In many places the basic livelihood of the people is threatened. In other places the desired levels of the quality of life are imperiled. The world in the mid-1980s is only just emerging from the worst recession in decades. Economic dualism is accentuated as the number of the poor grows, unemployment mounts, and deficits persist. All of this makes it necessary to reexamine the structure of poverty in order to acquire a deeper understanding of how to overcome it.

In what follows I first clarify the notions of poverty and malnutrition. Secondly, I present a profile of poverty in the world today. Thirdly, I trace the outlines of the myth of progress, which has embodied people's hopes of liberation from the scourges of poverty and hunger and has provided the guiding vision of development in the modern age. (By myth, I do not mean false or illusory but a primarily narrative vision of reality that serves in this case to present development in terms of the fundamental beliefs and worldview of a people.) Next I contrast this guiding vision with the crisis in development circles today. I conclude with a summary outline of the structure of the problem.

THE GENERAL NOTIONS OF POVERTY AND MALNUTRITION

What does poverty mean? It is helpful to begin with the observation that poor people are not fully able to participate in their society. As Oscar Altimir has said: "On the face of it, poverty is a situational syndrome in which the following are combined: underconsumption, malnutrition, precarious housing conditions, low educational levels, bad sanitary conditions, either unstable participation in the production system or restriction to its more primitive strata, attitudes of discouragement and anomie, little participation in the mechanisms of social integration and possible adherence to a particular scale of values different to some extent from that held by the rest of the society." (Altimir 1982: 2).

How poor is poor? Nearly one-fifth of the United States's population was recently classified as living in poverty, yet many of those so identified have nearly ten to twenty times the income of those classified as poor in the developing countries. In this context, it is helpful to clarify two broad concepts of poverty: absolute and relative.

Absolute poverty is defined in terms of subsistence and is concerned with the provision of the minimum needed to maintain health and working capacity. Its terms of reference are the maintenance of physical health, the development of human capacities, and survival. The primary focus is meeting basic human needs.

In a very penetrating article, Amartya Sen has argued that poverty must be seen primarily as an absolute notion (Sen 1983). In so doing, he distinguishes his view (1) from those who hold strictly relativist views of poverty, or (2) from those who treat poverty simply as an issue of inequality between income groups, or (3) from the more arbitrary "policy definition" approaches to poverty (as seen in government established poverty lines).

According to Sen, the key defining characteristic of poverty is that it is an absolute deprivation of a person's capacities. He means a failure to develop a person's ability to do various things which would ordinarily be within his or her reach. It touches physical, intellectual, artistic, communicative and other functional capacities. Contrarily, Sen notes that an approach to poverty that simply focuses upon baskets of commodities, incomes, and resources will invariably lead to a relative notion of poverty, since the necessities of life and the means to meet them are not fixed. Rather, they are dynamic; they grow and develop and are constantly being reshaped.

I find that Sen's position has close parallel to the work of Abraham Maslow, who some years ago articulated a view of human development in the context of being-needs and deficiency-needs (Maslow 1963). The focus of overall human development is the full self-actualization of the person. The poverty syndrome in an absolute sense is defined as the negation of such a prospect. On the *individual* level this means the deprivation of a person's capabilities to learn, work, be creative, assume responsibility, and so forth. As a *social* syndrome, poverty manifests itself in severely limited access to commodities and resources, illness and functional weakness, vulnerability to contingencies, powerlessness, and isolation.

It is important to mention that in this context many speak of an opportunity-cost approach to poverty. They attempt to measure the social cost to society that permanent poverty represents in terms of lost productivity, the lack of market development, and so forth, which would have resulted had the undeveloped potential of the poor been tapped. This notion is related to Sen's absolute deprivation of capacities. It is intuitively clear but very difficult to estimate in precise terms. Usually the presentation is rhetorical and focuses upon the social benefits that would have been lost had not Newton, Edison, Lincoln, or other leading figures developed healthily. (Obviously the tables could be turned in terms of the social costs of a figure such as Hitler or Idi Amin.) Nonetheless, the opportunity-cost notion remains useful for it underlines how poverty itself breeds more poverty.

How is one to measure absolute poverty (Chambers, Longhurst, and Pacey 1981; Elliott 1975)? The reality of poverty represents a very complex *social* phenomenon. The interrelation between the social and economic elements of poverty remain unclear. As a result, there is no satisfactory *economic* theory of poverty. Consequently, there is no truly precise economic measurement of poverty nor have clear strategies emerged to combat it. More often than not the measures themselves are relative.

Definitions of relative poverty vary. Three notions are most prominent:

- policy definitions of poverty that define a poverty line based on income
- relative disparities between income groups
- the dynamically changing nature of human needs.

Policy definitions of poverty represent a pragmatic effort to set social priorities and to implement policies to meet the set of social goals that a society may establish. Such policies represent what is desired by those who exercise effective social voice. They are designed to be practical and feasible. But they are not necessarily always targeted upon the absolute deprivation that poverty represents nor are they, in the scramble over budget priorities, always sufficient. They usually result in the establishment of "poverty lines," which serve as guideposts to various social welfare benefits. There is an arbitrary character to them rooted in organizational politics.

Poverty lines are not easy to construct. If the goal of such a policy instrument is to capture a household's socioeconomic opportunity set, it is not clear that simply defining the target group as that population below "x" amount of income would do the trick. There is considerable discussion on whether to focus upon income or upon consumption expenditures, on how to handle free, public, and otherwise nonmarket goods and services, and on how to evaluate structural barriers that prevent access to goods and services. Nonetheless, such policy definitions of poverty can be helpful, in a general way, to get a hold on the reality of poverty. For the absolute deprivation of poverty necessarily manifests itself, albeit in relative form, in the realm of an income level and what that income can purchase. Income is a helpful but relative indicator of poverty. Since the 1960s, the United States federal government has employed such a concept in its legislative proposals (United States Government 1976). Periodically, the dollar amount of the poverty line has been raised to reflect rising costs and inflation (at present it is near $10,000 for a family of four). The World Bank in its studies also has projected various international "poverty lines" (World Bank 1979). The absolute poverty line at the World Bank has been pegged at less than $150 per capita, while all those under $400 are classified as "low income poor." Those above $750 are upper income in developing countries; those between $400 and $750 are the middle income poor. Per capita income, however, remains a troubled indicator. Often patterns of distribution are not known, and it is a less relevant indicator in cases of subsistent economies or where noncash transactions predominate. Poverty lines are necessarily relative measures. Neither what is needed to meet one's needs nor the amount of income necessary to purchase it are easily defined.

Poverty defined in terms of inequalities between income groups is concerned with the relative position of income groups to each other. In many studies the relative poverty line is approximately drawn at one-third below the average national per capita income. Poverty in this sense cannot be understood by isolating the poor and treating them as a special group. The composition of society is seen as a strata of income layers, and relative poverty compares how those on the bottom fare with respect to those who are on the top. The focus is on social inequalities, rather than on basic human needs. The chief problem of such a measure is to be found in reaching agreement on what constitutes basic living standards relative to society as a whole. It may readily be seen that those who are relatively poor may not suffer at all from poverty in an absolute sense. Poverty defined as income inequality actually focuses on another issue: What would constitute a just pattern of social *distribution?*

A final aspect of the relative notion of poverty is that human needs are dynamic, changing, and always reconstituting themselves. It follows that what is considered necessary or adequate to meet those needs is also always in flux. This is true both over different periods of time as well as across different socio-cultural settings (Townsend 1979). To return to Sen's capacities, human capabilities can and do have extremely variable resource requirements. Particular goods do not always render the same set of satisfactions to different people nor are they prized for the same characteristics. Furthermore, "basic needs" and "wants" are not always easy to differentiate. Thus, when poverty as the absolute deprivation of capacities manifests itself in the context of income levels, socially defined needs, commodities, and resources, it possesses a certain relative character. On the one hand, this relativity would seem to make policy to combat poverty uncertain and difficult. More importantly, however, it would seem to open policy to many possibilities and diverse creative efforts.

Any policy that seeks to eliminate absolute poverty must necessarily treat relative measures of income, needs, and baskets of commodities, resources, and services. This fact implies that discussions of poverty and development policy must incorporate a certain amount of fluidity, for the very notion of poverty itself as well as its measures are in a state of development. They vary geographically, historically, and culturally.

A PROFILE OF POVERTY AND HUNGER

According to what has become common parlance, the poor are to be found in the "south," that is, largely in Asia, Africa, and Latin America. Where is poverty located within these countries? Statistically, the large majority (from 60–80 percent) of the whole population and of the poor live in rural areas. Those worst off are the landless rural poor who have few resources and only seasonal employment opportunities. A World Bank study estimates that there are more than 80 million small holdings of less than two hectares, small fragments of land that generate income below the absolute poverty level (World Bank 1979). This distinction in the degrees of poverty is best illustrated by an observation of Philip Coombs:

> The most difficult rural circumstances are those in which extensive rural poverty is combined with low levels of mobilizable resources. Countries in this situation include all the South Asian nations, many of the larger African countries such as Ethiopia, Sudan, and Tanzania, and a few Latin American and Caribbean countries like Bolivia and Haiti. At the other end of the scale are countries with pockets of rural poverty, varying in extent and intensity, but with resources adequate to deal with the problem, provided the political commitment is made. [Coombs 1976: 20]

In the World Food Survey published in 1977 (FAO 1977) the Food and Agriculture Organization of the United Nations singled out forty-four countries as Most Seriously Affected (MSA). In Table 1-1, a profile of these countries is presented and some twenty indicators of relative poverty and basic quality of life are reviewed.

I have grouped these indicators around three headings: (1) population and nutrition, (2) health and education, and (3) national income, social expenditures, and energy. Admittedly, these groupings and the indicators chosen are somewhat arbitrary. But they suffice for the purpose of presenting a general sketch, while at the same time a more extensive set of indicators can be found by consulting the sources referred to. At this point, I content myself with a basic descriptive profile of poverty and hunger in the MSA countries. A number of quantitative analytical techniques have been developed in recent years to try to gain a unified interpretation of all such indicators. One of the more interesting has been the construction of a Physical Quality of Life Index (PQLI) (Morris 1978). The PQLI approach aims to provide a unified quantitative estimate of the degree to which basic needs are being met by combining in an index a wide variety of selected indicators (such as the ones presented here). The indices generated are then used to make crosscountry comparisons. Such aggregation may provide some insight. Yet it is not especially helpful in making correlations between different variables in a concrete setting.

One of the problems in analyzing poor countries is that data about them are fragmentary. Nonetheless, some sort of general picture is possible. It may be seen from Section A of Table 1-1 that in these forty-four most seriously affected (MSA) countries, which have a combined population of approximately 1 billion people, present and projected national food supply is precarious. The majority of these forty-four MSA countries are in Africa. In a considerable number of them, population itself (in terms of numbers of consumers versus presently available supplies) seems to be a very serious issue, at least in this relative sense. In 1983 ten years after the MSA list was drawn up, about fifteen countries show better agricultural performance, while thirteen are worse and the rest indeterminate. (For a study of 112 developing countries see Food and Agriculture Organization [1986: 78-82].) In seventeen of these countries, the rate of growth of population is still outpacing the rate of growth in agriculture with the result that domestic food production *per capita* is actually declining. Imports must cover the deficit. This is the case in Kenya and the Ivory Coast even though the agricultural sector growth rate has gradually increased. In twenty MSA countries *per capita* food production has declined, when comparing 1981-83 with

Table 1-1. Poverty Profile of Countries Most Seriously Affected (MSA).[a]

A. Population and Nutrition

Country	(1) Population[b] 1983 (millions)	(2) Population Growth[c] 1973–83 (%)	(3) Population Density[d] to Agricultural Land (persons/square km) (1980) 1 KM² = 100 HA²	(4) Agricultural[e] Production Growth 1965–73/1973–83	(5) Growth of Food Production per Capita[f] in 1981–83 (1974–1976 = 100) and (% population undernourished)[g] 1976	(6) Calories Supply as % of Required[h] 1979/1982	(7) Protein Supply (grams per Capita per Day 1979[i]/1982[j]
Afghanistan	17,2	2,6	209.6	-1,5/–	105 (37)	73/94	56/64
Bangladesh	95,5	2,4	984.2	0,4/3,2	101 (38)	84/83	40/40
Benin	3,8	2,8	199.1	–/2,7	95	103/101	53/48
Burkina Faso	6,5	1,9	319.1	–/–	100	95/79	64/64
Burma	35,5	2,0	335.8	2,8/6,6	121 (22)	113/115	59/62
Burundi	4,5	2,2	–	4,7/2,3	97	96/95	71/60
Cameroon	9,6	3,1	130.8	4,7/1,8	84 (16)	105/91	60/54
Cape Verde	,–	–	–	–/–	–	–	76/–
Central Africa	2,5	2,3	128.4	2,1/2,4	94	94/97	43/42
Chad	4,8	2,1	175.2	–/–	101 (54)	74/68	58/58
Egypt	45,2	2,5	1,441.9	2,6/2,5	92 (8)	117/128	77/81
El Salvador	5,2	3,0	658.3	3,6/0,7	91	99/90	57/56
Ethiopia	40,9	2,7	238.1	2,1/1,2	106 (38)	76/93	57/73
Gambia	,7	–	–	–/–	–	–	55/57
Ghana	12,8	3,1	411.4	4,5/–	65 (20)	88/68	44/41
Guatemala	7,9	3,1	1,744.2	5,8/2,3	102 (38)	73/97	56/58
Guinea	5,8	2,9	379.4	–/2,4	85 (41)	77/86	41/40
Guinea-Bisseau	,8	–	–	–/–	–	–	47/–
Guyana	,8	–	43.2	–/–	–	–	–/58
Haiti	5,3	1,8	569.2	-0,3/0,7	90 (38)	96/84	45/45
Honduras	4,1	3,5	212.1	2,4/3,3	107 (38)	96/95	52/52

India	733,2	2,3	411.6	3,7/2,2	108 (30)	87/93	49/50
Ivory Coast	9,5	4,6	219.9	3,7/4,0	108 (8)	112/115	56/57
Kenya	18,9	4,0	596.9	6,2/3,4	86 (30)	88/88	57/54
Laos	3,7	2,2	369.2	–/–	125	97/90	50/53
Lesotho	1,5	2,5	466.7	–/–	76	107/100	73/73
Madagascar	9,5	2,6	306.6	–/–0,2	90 (17)	109/114	57/57
Mali	7,2	2,5	278.2	0,9/5,0	106 (49)	85/74	55/52
Mauitania	1,6	2,2	–	–2,1/2,6	102 (48)	97/97	70/71
Mozambique	13,1	2,6	389.7	–/–	68 (36)	70/79	33/32
Nepal	15,7	2,6	664.9	1,5/1,0	91 (29)	86/86	46/46
Niger	6,1	3,0	149.9	–2,9/1,6	122 (47)	95/105	67/72
Pakistan	89,7	3,0	420.4	4,2/3,4	105 (26)	106/99	61/56
Rwanda	5,7	3,4	550.9	–/–	114	88/95	56/54
Samoa	,2	–	–	–/–	–	–/–	51/–
Senegal	6,2	2,8	111.5	0,2/0,3	71 (25)	100/101	–/67
Sierra Leone	3,6	2,1	200.0	1,5/2,2	98 (21)	89/85	45/42
Somalia	5,1	2,8	350.3	–/3,5	72 (40)	100/91	72/65
Sri Lanka	15,4	1,7	688.7	2,7/4,1	127	102/107	44/45
Sudan	20,8	3,2	153.2	0,3/3,5	99 (30)	101/96	70/65
Tanzania	20,8	3,3	404.2	3,1/2,6	103 (35)	83/101	48/42
Uganda	13,4	2,8	229.5	3,6/3,0	91	83/78	50/47
Yemen PDR	2,0	2,2	600.6	–/–	84	84/97	–/61
Yemen Arab Rep.	7,6	2,9	267.4	–/2,1	80	76/97	71/77

a. MSA is a classification used by the Food and Agriculture Organization in its *Fourth World Food Survey* (1977).
b. World Bank (1985: Table 1, p. 174).
c. World Bank (1985: Table 19, p. 210).
d. Sivard (1983: 31–35).
e. World Bank (1985: Table 2, p. 176).
f. World Bank (1985: Table 6, p. 184).
g. Food and Agriculture Organization (1977: Appendix M, pp. 127–128).
h. World Bank (1985: Table 24, p. 220); World Bank (1983: Table 24, p. 194).
i. Food and Agriculture Organization (1981: 249).
j. Sivard (1985: 38–43).

Table 1-1. continued

B. Health and Education

Country	(8) People[b] per Physician	(9) Life[c] Expectancy (years)	(10) Infant and Child Mortality per Thousand[d] Infant/Child	(11) Safe[e] Water (%)	(12) Adult[e] Literacy (%)	(13) Schoolgoers in School[f] (%) Primary M/F	Secondary M/F	(14) Teachers (thousands)[g]
Afghanistan	16,730	36	223/29	11	20	56/13	17/4	19
Bangladesh	7,810	50	132/19	40	34	68/51	24/6	258
Benin	16,980	48	148/31	20	26	87/42	26/10	14
Burkina Faso	48,510	44	148/31	14	11	28/16	4/2	5
Burma	4,680	55	93/11	25	70	87/81	20*	134
Burundi	45,020	47	123/25	25	27	41/25	4/2	6
Cameroon	13,990	54	116/19	50	52	99/97	25/13	36
Cape Verde	–	61	–	–	–	–	–	–
Central Africa	26,750	48	142/29	18	33	92/50	20/7	5
Chad	47,840	43	142/29	26	22	34*	2*	6
Egypt	970	58	102/14	76	44	90/65	34/9	252
El Salvador	3,220	64	70/6	57	66	90/65	19/21	19
Ethiopia	69,370	43	168/37	13	12	60/33	16/8	55
Gambia	–	36	–	18	20	–	–	3
Ghana	7,160	59	97/12	45	48	85/66	44/27	85
Guatemala	8,610	60	67/5	53	53	78/67	2*	33
Guinea	17,110	37	158/36	17	24	44/22	23/6	12
Guinea-Bisseau	–	38	–	–	–	68*	–	–
Guyana	–	68	–	81	–	–	–	8
Haiti	8,200	54	107/15	31	30	74/64	13/12	20
Honduras	3,120	60	87/8	70	62	99/98	29/30	21

India	3,690	55	52	93/11	42	93/64	39/20	3394
Ivory Coast	21,040	52	14	121/20	38	92/16	17/9	43
Kenya	7,890	57	25	81/14	50	99/99	23/15	132
Laos	20,060	44	22	159/25	44	99/89	22/14	21
Lesotho	18,640	53	14	109/14	70	95/99	13/20	7
Madagascar	10,200	49	23	66/10	66	99*	14*	35
Mali	20,130	45	6	148/31	15	35/20	9*	12
Mauitania	14,500	46	23	136/16	17	43/23	16/4	3
Mozambique	39,110	46	7	109/16	33	99/72	6*	23
Nepal	30,060	46	15	143/21	20	99/42	21*	47
Niger	38,790	45	32	139/28	10	29/17	–	8
Pakistan	3,480	50	30	119/16	30	57/31	27/7	315
Rwanda	31,340	47	50	125/26	52	72/67	3/1	14
Samoa	–	65	–	–	–	–	–	–
Senegal	13,780	46	43	140/28	23	58/38	16/8	16
Sierra Leone	17,520	38	21	198/54	25	40*	12*	14
Somalia	15,630	45	27	142/30	8	38/21	16/6	10
Sri Lanka	7,170	69	36	37/2	85	99/99	49/54	129
Sudan	8,930	48	42	117/19	26	61/43	20/15	65
Tanzania	17,740	51	15	97/18	70	99/95	4/2	91
Uganda	26,810	49	16	108/21	52	69/51	7/3	51
Yemen PDR	7,120	46	54	137/27	10	99/34	24/11	12
Yemen Arab Rep.	11,670	44	26	152/30	68	99/17	9/2	17

a. MSA is a classification used by the Food and Agriculture Organization in its *Fourth World Food Survey* (1977).
b. World Bank (1985: Table 24, p. 220).
c. World Bank (1985: Table 23, p. 218).
d. World Bank (1985: Table 23, p. 218); "infant" = 0 to 12 months; "child" = 1–4 years.
e. Sivard (1985: 38–43).
f. World Bank (1985: Table 25, p. 222); World Bank (1984: Table 5, p. 158); *denotes estimate for both sexes (a 99% figure estimates full attendance).
g. Sivard (1985: 36–37).

Table 1-1. continued

C. National Income, Social Expenditures, Energy

Country	(15) 1983[b] GNP (million $)	(16) 1983[c] GNP per Capita ($)	(17) % Share of[d] Income, Low 20% (time period)	(18) % Share of[d] Income, Top 20% (time period)	(19) Government Expenditures ($ per capita) Military[e]	Education[e]	Agriculture[f] Investment (1982)	(20) Energy Consumption per Capita kg. of Coal Equiv. 1980	kg. of Oil Equiv. 1982
Afghanistan	–	–	–	–	14	4	3.6*	83	46
Bangladesh	10,690	130	6.2 (76–77)	46.9 (76–77)	2	2	7.6	49	36
Benin	930	290	–	–	7	17	7.6	70	39
Burkina Faso	900	180	–	–	6	6	21.9	16	22
Burma	6,190	180	–	–	6	4	3.4	87	65
Burundi	1,020	240	–	–	12	8	15.1	–	17
Cameroon	7,200	820	–	–	10	21	17.2	154	128
Cape Verde	100*	340*	–	–	–	–	18.1	–	–
Central Africa	600	280	–	–	7	12	13.9	46	35
Chad	320	110*	–	–	3	2	2.2	22	–
Egypt	27,920	700	5.8 (1974)	48.0 (1974)	55	32	3.4	595	530
El Salvador	3,700	710	5.5 (76–77)	47.3 (76–77)	31	28	7.4	357	190
Ethiopia	4,270	120	–	–	13	5	1.8	25	19
Gambia	220*	–	–	–	–	21	35.7	–	–
Ghana	3,720	310	–	–	2	8	2.5	268	111
Guatemala	9,030	1,120	–	–	12	22	2.8	308	197
Guinea	1,910	300	–	–	13	10	1.2	83	54
Guinea-Bisseau	150*	190*	–	–	–	–	20.4	–	–
Guyana	580*	720*	–	–	28	56	167.6*	–	–
Haiti	1,630	300	–	–	5	3	5.9	88	55
Honduras	2,640	670	–	–	15	28	22.9	292	204

India	168,170	260	7.0 (75–76)	49.4 (75–76)	8	8	2.0	210	182
Ivory Coast	7,090	260	–	–	11	48	16.6	248	186
Kenya	4,940	420	2.6 (1974)	60.4 (1974)	18	26	10.4	208	109
Laos	290*	80*	–	–	–	–	1.1	127	76
Lesotho	300	460	–	–	–	20	15.7	–	–
Madagascar	2,850	310	–	–	9	9	7.1	74	59
Mali	980	160	–	–	5	7	24.1	31	22
Mauritania	700	480	–	–	51	22	48.9	199	130
Mozambique	–	–	–	–	13	4	7.3	103	95
Nepal	2,180	160	4.6 (76–77)	59.2 (76–77)	5	4	7.9	13	13
Niger	1,340	240	–	–	–	–	14.4	54	43
Pakistan	25,880	390	–	–	22	7	3.3	224	197
Rwanda	1,560	270	–	–	5	12	9.2	28	35
Samoa	–	–	–	–	–	–	18.8	–	–
Senegal	2,570	440	–	–	10	22	36.9	364	151
Sierra Leone	950	330	5.6 (67–69)	52.5 (67–69)	3	13	7.4	166	102
Somlia	1,540	250	–	–	20	5	6.3	85	84
Sri Lanka	4,770	330	7.5 (69–70)	43.4 (69–70)	5	10	12.8	201	143
Sudan	6,850	400	4.0 (67–68)	49.8 (67–68)	15	21	6.0	101	96
Tanzania	4,550	240	5.8 (1969)	50.4 (1969)	16	24	10.1	69	38
Uganda	3,360	220	–	–	3	4	4.0	34	23
Yemen PDR	850	520	–	–	77	34	16.4	–	934
Yemen Arab Rep.	3,710	550	–	–	96	54	6.6	62	116

a. MSA is a classification used by the Food and Agriculture Organization in its *Fourth World Food Survey* (1977).
b. World Bank (1985: Table 3, p. 178).
c. World Bank (1985: Table 1, p. 174).
d. World Bank (1985: Table 28, p. 228).
e. Sivard (1985: 38–41).
f. Food and Agriculture Organization (1984: Annex Table 12b, pp. 169–171).
g. World Bank (1985: Table 8, p. 188) for 1982; World Bank (1985: Table 8, p. 162) for 1980.

1974-76. The majority (27) of the countries have a deficit aggregate calorie supply. Fifteen of these are worse off in 1982 than in 1974. The FAO estimates of the availability of minimum daily nutiritonal requirements are made in terms of either 1.2BMR (Basal Metabolic Rate) or 1.5BMR (Food and Agriculture Organization 1977: 127-128). A more detailed account of methodology employed is presented in the *Fifth World Food Survey* (FAO 1986: 90-121).

From Columns 4-7, it may be seen that in MSA countries food production trends are either significantly below projected demand or they are actually negative in the *per capita* sense. To the point, only ten MSA countries presently seem to supply enough food in terms of calorie requirements. Aggregate *per capita* protein supply (Column 7) is comparatively low (although desired levels of consumption are not known with certitude).

Another side of the poverty syndrome is glimpsed in the indicators listed in Section B, (Columns 8-14). The rate of literacy and the related levels of education, rates of life expectancy, infant mortality, people per physician, and the number of people with safe water are appalling. The low number of teachers together with low overall secondary school attendance and high illiteracy suggest that the quality of human capital for development will remain low for some time to come. The category of schoolgoers is especially important. In almost every country female children attend school at a sharply lower rate than males. This will only serve to keep women trapped in poverty. These indicators serve to emphasize the fact that hunger is but one aspect of the poverty problem. Furthermore, they suggest that a solution to hunger that would focus upon food supply alone would be ill-conceived. Simply expanding production (or the increase of supply) alone will in no sense automatically solve food and nutrition problems.

Along these lines, very significant data on income and social expenditutures is contained in Section C (Columns 15-20). Many countries seemingly conceal income distribution data. Among thousands of pages of statistics that governments publish, one searches in vain for a hint of this information. Data that are available are not all that reliable and most have been generated in recent years by World Bank estimates. Firm conclusions cannot be drawn from such approximate data. But tentative conclusions at least would call for further research in this area, as perhaps the major issue in poverty studies. Further, while the precise relationship between hunger and income distribution is not known, in a statistical sense, it is clear that hunger and low income seem to go hand in hand. This point has an important implication for policy: Policy cannot simply focus upon increasing production but also must focus upon increasing income and improving distribution for the disadvantaged. In practically all of these countries, GNP *per capita* represents a level of significant poverty. When one considers that those worse off actually receive only the crumbs of this meager pie, it is not difficult to appreciate why life expectancy hovers in the low forties or why infant mortality is high.

Column 19 invites a very interesting comparison regarding comparative budget priorities. In sixteen of the MSA countries military expenditure exceed education and in eighteen military expenditures exceed agricultural investment *per capita*. Most of these countries are beset by civil strife which impedes development. Such aggregate data is in many ways inconclusive, but it does at least suggest a compelling hypothesis about inverted priorities in public expenditures.

These most seriously affected countries reflect diverse arrays of problems in various parts of the world. The nature of the hunger problem tends to be regionally specific. Nonetheless, the FAO study has singled out four groups that are most vulnerable. The first group seriously affected by hunger is the urban unemployed. This is the case not only in poorer countries but also in wealthy countries. They suffer because they lack purchasing power. A second group that is most seriously affected is rural people who are landless. In hard years they remain without any means to care for themselves. They lack both the resources to produce what they need as well as income to purchase it. A third group most affected is composed of pregnant and lactating women. The fourth group is children. Both women and children suffer primarily because they are socially dependent. Women are frequently the object of social discrimination such that they are unlikely to receive a good education or a fair share of resources, even at the family level. Children suffer the most from malnutrition in terms of physical and mental development. For many, the effects of malnutrition during childhood are irreversible and rather than growing to be creative and productive members of society they remain in need of care. These four groups and the households they compose should be the principal target of any food program.

The estimates of how many people are hungry and suffer from malnutrition vary according to definition. In general, the chronically malnourished population in the world is thought to number 70 to 90 million people. Thus the number of people who are "at death's door" because of starvation is somewhat less than 2 percent of the estimated world population. Those with significant, but not completely disabling, deficiency malnutrition are estimated to be about

450 to 500 million people, some 12–15 percent of the world population. As noted, the language of malnutrition often remains fuzzy; one runs across broad estimates of 750 million and even 1–2 billion people suffering from some form of malnutrition. In different studies and proposals, basic definitions, therefore, are of fundamental importance. The numbers and composition of those afflicted by deficiency malnutrition, therefore, depends in practice upon the criteria of the observer (Reutlinger and Selowsky, 1978).

About 40 percent of the forty-four most seriously affected countries surveyed by the FAO in 1974 were better off in 1983. The position of about 35 percent worsened. All have a long way to go.

THE MYTH OF PROGRESS: HOPE FOR A SOLUTION

Whatever "development" means, it promises a way out of the poverty and hunger trap. This promise of liberation is enshrined in the myth of progress. It is worthwhile to examine the guiding vision of development inherent in the myth of progress.

The word myth does not mean false, as many rationalists maintain. Myth is used here to mean a root metaphor of human existence, which presents in both rational and symbolic form the general meaning of human action in terms of human growth and of ultimate reality. As such, a myth provides a paradigm of human growth and development that serves as a guiding vision of all human endeavors and provides them with certain criteria of meaning. Robert Nisbet has argued correctly that a central myth of western civilization, in general, and of the modern world, in particular, is the myth of progress (Nisbet 1979).

The ideal of progress pervades Western civilization. The notion was considerably developed in the modern period and in a special way it sums up the spirit of the Enlightenment and symbolizes the modernization that was to transform political, economic, and cultural systems. It is this more recently fashioned metaphor of progress that sets off the modern from the traditional, the developed from the backwards. In the modern developed world, poverty and hunger have (in principle at least) been vanquished. It is worthwhile to examine this modern ideal of progress in more detail, for it is often unquestionably assumed as the guiding vision of development. As such it constitutes the hidden agenda of planning and policy.

The modern notion of progress clearly affirms the worth of life on earth and the possibility of the continual improvement of human nature. It does not take refuge in an other-wordly spiritualism nor does it stand helpless before the status quo. It does not necessarily reject the past. Rather, the past is seen in an embryonic way, as containing within it the promise of the future. The key to unlocking this future is found in society's faith in the power of reason and science. It is precisely in the rational application of science and technology in areas of economic growth that the development of future potential is to be realized. It is in such growth that people achieve mastery over nature and their destiny. Furthermore, it is assumed that this process is both cumulative and self-correcting; some even maintain that this is "value-free" in a positivist sense.

The dominant philosophies of the Enlightenment articulated a tremendous optimism in the face of the various evils that traditionally plagued the human race. Poverty, ignorance, disease, famines, drought, hunger, and even political economic domination could all be overcome by the application of science and technology and by institutions of democratic freedom guided by the light of reason in the pursuit of self-interest.

The notion of progress as it has developed in the modern period implicitly asserts the superiority of European culture and of western civilization and institutions. In this way the "development" that it spawned does not propose some sort of neutral technological advance but western social ideals of political economic organization. These ideals are grasped in the two dominant paradigms of the "modern" world: socialism and capitalism. In what follows, I comment briefly on each paradigm in terms of their visions of politics and economic life.

Both socialism and capitalism espouse a secular approach to political economic affairs. Socialism does so because it is (in its Marxist form) atheistic and considers religion to be false consciousness, an opiate of the people. In a different way nonatheistic forms of socialism as well as most forms of capitalism are nonetheless secular. First of all, they emphasize the value of this life on earth as opposed to an other-worldly spiritualism that tends to trivialize it. Secondly, in their interpretations of social reality, they subtly remove whatever religion there is from the realm of political economy to the private, inaccessible sphere of inner worldly consciousness. The legitimacy of institutions is based upon human reason and (democratic) assent, not religious authority. In much (but not all) modern liberal thought, religion has become privatized. The result is curiously the same as the atheist denial of religion, for in no case should religious values be mixed with either politics or business. Thus in prevailing "modern" thought, politics and economics are not seen in religious terms either because there is no authentic religion or because religion is generally privatized. In the same vein, politics and economics are often held to be value-free. Political and economic sciences are assumed to represent rational, objective, and value-free laws of behavior. Whether in scientific socialism or laws of supply and demand economics is insulated from ultimate reality and values.

In both the paradigms of socialism and of capitalism, the idea of progress also connotes a democratic polity where people are ruled by reason and where authority is based upon consensus and derived from the consent of the governed. Democracy has taken very different paths under democratic liberalism and socialist collectivism mainly because each paradigm expounds a fundamentally different view of the human person and of society. Liberalism focuses upon the importance of the individual. It accords primary importance to individual liberty and accepts as valid the principles of self-interest and mutual self-interest (the social contract entered into freely). Collectivism primarily understands human liberty in terms of some group—e.g., workers and peasants. It is inseparable from solidarity (entailing the subordination of the individual to the group) and the creation, through absolute power if necessary, of a new type of human being (e.g., socialist persons). The transition from present reality to future ideal is effected through the leadership of a vanguard party, which theoretically is both enlightened and benevolent. Thus, of the two fundamentally different visions of society and development in the modern world, one sees progress in terms of freedom from any kind of oppression of the individual, and the other sees progress in terms of power that enfranchises the chosen group (for example, the proletariat) and creates the new person and the new society.

It is no surprise that these two paradigms diverge also on their vision of the economy. Both attempt to be scientific as well as rational. Liberal democracy does so in terms of the market that accords maximum scope to private initiative and individual liberty. There are, of course, conditions for fair market practices; in fact, the maintenance of such fair conditions is a primary role of government. In the scenario of market rationalism, it is supposed that both individual development and the development of society will occur if the fair conditions of individual liberty and the social contract are maintained. Supply and demand will equalize themselves in the free play of market forces and optimal resource use will be assured.

Collectivists do not believe this scenario and the reason is found in power abuses and exploitation by dominant classes (for example, they cite an oppressive coalition of property owners, military rulers, and clergy). The scenario they propose is, first, taking control of society, through an absolute exercise of power if necessary, and then

administering the economy through a system of rationally based
national planning that will both take account of all needs (demand)
and manage resource use so as to guarantee desired supply. They
intend to be plan-rational rather than market-rational. Compliance
with the plan should be elicited by its very reasonableness. Once the
old guard is ousted, the impeccable motivation and efficiency of all
remaining participants is assumed. Nonetheless, there remains the
civil power of sanctions and coercion to deal with contradictions, as
they are called.

TOWARD EFFECTIVE POLICY: REAPPRAISING
PROGRESS AND DEVELOPMENT

Discussions of international economics and development today are
dominated by the modern ideal of progress and these two paradigms
of the modern age. This may seem curious, but upon reflection it is
not surprising. For each paradigm, in its ideal interpretation of progress (once all the relevant presuppositions about the human person
and ultimate reality are granted), possesses an inner logical coherence
with seemingly total explanatory power in the political economic
field. Furthermore, when things do not work as they should according to the ideal scheme of things, there are explanations. Failures are
described to social dysfunctions (e.g., "market imperfections" and
"class enemies") rather than to any fundamental flaw of the paradigm. Such explanations have not proven to be convincing, however,
and development policy remains beset with three problems: overall
legitimacy, the lack of resources, and inefficiencies in organization
and management.

The legitimacy crisis is the most complex. It touches three tightly
connected phenomena: growing poverty amid growth, the "western-
izing bias" of development models, and the ethical values that underlie analysis and policy choices. Critics maintain that the fact that
development does not reach the poor is not a random technical or
organizational dysfunction; rather, it is inherent to the system. To
put it starkly, the claim is that the system produces poverty. Therefore, it is not legitimate. Secondly, while the economic success of the
western world is widely recognized, it is increasingly questioned
whether economic modernization necessarily means westernization.
As a result there is an increasing emphasis in development circles on
finding an "African way," a "Chinese way," or an "Indian way."
Such discourse questions the western underpinnings of the ideal of
progress. Finally, both of these points are linked to the question of
values and paradigms of overall human development that should

guide economic development (Goulet 1983; Gritti and Masini 1981). Those formulating economic policy therefore enter a far broader universe of discourse rooted in values and culture. I return to these matters in Chapter 6. Suffice it to note here that the adequacy of development policy will be measured against larger issues of human development as well as against technical results.

The legitimacy crisis is linked to two other problems. One is in the area of resources and the other is in the area of management and organization. These problems are more practical than normative in character. They focus upon what is actually being done, how and for whom.

The resources crisis touches both human and nonhuman resources. Human resource questions have to do with population numbers, rights to migration, and the development of human capacities. These issues directly relate to programs designed to meet basic needs and to foster human rights. Nonhuman resources comprise both renewable and nonrenewable categories. The main issues are the accumulation and distribution of scarce economic production factors (especially capital) as well as measures to protect the environment and avoid the waste of scarce resources (especially energy) through either careless or frivolous use.

The management and organization crisis includes planning and administrative skills, but is chiefly concerned with the organizational politics of large complex bureaucracies, intergovernmental pacts touching the terms of trade, transfers of credit, and so forth. The question is: Are the large complex organizations that dominate public life today capable of assessing and reacting effectively to social problems such as persistent poverty?

The above crises of legitimacy, resources, and social organization and management have provoked a reexamination of the meaning and adequacy of contemporary models and approaches to development. The debate has shifted over the terrain of narrow economic growth models, to redistribution with growth, to strategies of basic needs and popular participation in development. The ferment ranges from resource management and the diffusion of technology to social power and structure and the very philosophical basis of progress and development.

What sort of development policy is needed? Poverty represents both a global and local problem. It is global in the sense that it derives from international conditions, especially those surrounding political elites, migration, trade agreements, and finance. Yet as a social reality it is also decidedly local, such that the causes of poverty in Bangladesh will differ from the causes in Haiti or Zaire. Although the same variables may be discussed, they will not necessarily hold the same importance everywhere.

Different constellations of causes clearly will call for different solutions. From what I have said above, a general structure of the poverty/development problem emerges. Following Martin Rein (1976), social analysis and policy proposals must strive to fulfill the following conditions, that they be:

- empirically comprehensive, taking care that neither relevant data or questions are omitted
- technologically feasible, assuring that the requisite resources and know-how are available
- value-critical, taking account of cultural influences and the over-all guiding norms of human development (e.g., the ideal of "progress")
- systems-manageable, being capable of being implemented in the face of elite groups, bureaucracies, and interest groups

If the structure of the policy problem is basically represented by the above four conditions, as I think it is, then it is worthwhile asking just how those conditions may be met. I devote myself to that question in the following chapter, where I present the elements of diagnostic method.

REFERENCES

Altimir, Oscar. 1982. *The Extent of Poverty in Latin America.* Staff Working Paper No. 522. Washington, D.C.: World Bank.

Chambers, Robert F., R. Longhurst, and A. Pacey, eds. 1981. *Seasonal Dimensions to Rural Poverty.* Totowa, N.J.: Allanheld, Osmum Co.

Coombs, Philip. 1976. *The Assault on World Poverty.* Baltimore: Johns Hopkins University Press.

Elliott, Charles. 1975. *Patterns of Poverty in the Third World.* New York: Praeger.

Food and Agriculture Organization (FAO). 1977. *The Fourth World Food Survey.* Rome, Italy: Food and Agriculture Organization.

_____. 1981. *Production Yearbook.* Rome, Italy: Food and Agriculture Organization.

_____. 1986. *The Fifth World Food Survey.* Rome, Italy: Food and Agriculture Organization.

Goulet, Denis. 1983. "Obstacles to World Development: An Ethical Reflection." *World Development* 11, no. 7: 609–24.

Gritti, Roberto, and Eleanora Masini, eds. 1981. *Societa e Futuro.* Rome, Italy: Citta Nuova.

Maslow, Abraham. 1963. *Toward a Psychology of Being.* Princeton, N.J.: Van Nostrand.

McNamara, Robert. 1977. "Address to the Board of Governors." Speech given at the World Bank, Washington, D.C.

Morris, David. 1978. *Measuring the Condition of the World's Poor, The Physical Quality of Life Index.* New York: Pergamon Press.

Nisbet, Robert. 1979. *History of the Idea of Progress.* New York: Basic Books.

Nutrition Foundation. 1976. *Present Knowledge in Nutrition.* 4th ed. New York: Nutrition Foundation.

Rein, Martin. 1976. *Public Policy.* New York: Penguin.

Reutlinger, Schlomo, and Marcelo Selowsky. 1978. *Malnutrition and Poverty, Magnitude and Policy Options.* World Bank Staff Occasional Paper, no. 23. Baltimore and London: The Johns Hopkins University Press.

Sen, Amartya. 1983. "Poor, Relatively Speaking." *Oxford Economic Papers* 35, no. 2: 153–69.

Townsend, Peter. 1979. *Poverty in the United Kingdom.* London: Penguin.

U.S. Government, Department of Health, Education, and Welfare. 1976. "Study of the Measure of Poverty." *Social Security Bulletin* 39: 34–37.

World Bank. 1979. "Growth and Poverty in Developing Countries." Staff Working Paper No. 309 (Revised). Washington, D.C.: World Bank.

_____. 1983. *World Development Report.* Washington, D.C.: World Bank.

_____. 1984. *Population Change and Economic Development.* Washington, D.C.: World Bank.

_____. 1985. *World Development Report.* Washington, D.C.: World Bank.

_____. 1986. *Poverty and Hunger.* Washington, D.C.: World Bank.

2 ELEMENTS OF DIAGNOSTIC METHOD

The structure of the problem presented in the preceding chapter poses special difficulties, for one must do several tasks at once. Development policy must rest on a basc that is empirically comprehensive and, at the same time, must be assessed on levels of technological feasibility, systems manageability, and values. I term my method diagnostic because it entails running through a number of different but related steps that are geared to satisfying the above criteria before arriving at a conclusion.

THE PROBLEM OF AN ADEQUATE ANALYTICAL FRAMEWORK

How should the problem of poverty and hunger be approached? The question is not easy for the so-called facts have meaning only within an analytical interpretative framework (the scientific paradigms of the researchers). Historically, the poverty debate has been primarily framed by Malthus and Marx. The important point that the two thinkers have in common is that for them poverty is not a random occurrence or the inexplicable result of some cruel fate. It grows out of social systems and proceeds primarily from human responsibility. From that point, Marxists and Malthusians part company. Discussions have lasted well over a century. Yet social scientists have not succeeded in developing an adequate analytical framework.

Dissatisfaction with both development theory and practice is not new. For many years, leading treatises in development have tended

25

to be classified as either "sociology of development" (studying social class, institutions, and structures) or as "economics of development" (studying technological changes, prices, incentives, and growth).

Socialists have dominated much of the sociological literature. They have attempted to engineer a "new order" and have tended to advocate specific patterns of wide ranging structural change. For decades, those of a Marxist persuasion have criticized economists of development for their allegedly narrow concentration upon growth and technical inputs (the production forces) while neglecting the role of social classes and institutions (production relations).

The economics literature has been dominated by market-oriented technocrats. It has often prided itself upon being value-free and scientifically rigorous (i.e., quantitative) and has contented itself with fine-tuning existing social processes and structures.

Historically, each school has made significant contributions; however, they frequently failed to communicate with each other. More recently each has come to be narrow and rigid. The result is that the field of development is a beached whale. It cannot live in the dogmatic atmosphere of bureaucratic socialism and is so weighed down by the presuppositions and rigor of North Atlantic quantitative models that it cannot turn itself around.

Contemporary problems of poverty are rooted in a deeper crisis in the social sciences themselves. This crisis is evident in three areas: (1) determining the components of a "social fact," (2) assessing what is required to achieve comprehensive social analysis, and (3) presuppositions regarding social change. These points will be discussed throughout the remainder of this chapter as I set forth the prerequisites of an adequate method and clarify the characteristics of an approach to development based on diagnostic method.

WHAT IS A FACT?

Both market technocrats and socialist planners continually appeal to facts. But what is a fact? On the one hand, western neo-classical thinkers advocate quantitative "rigor." The rigor mortis that has overtaken North Atlantic social science is perhaps nowhere better illustrated than by the canned programs that are marketed for statistical packages. These programs have come to impose a technological dogmatism over development discourse. They assume an easy ismorphism between quantitative techniques and human behavior and, accordingly, frequently fail to distinguish narrowly defined statistical significance from political, economic, or overall social relevance. On the other hand, the procrustean ideological frameworks of bureaucratic and dogmatic vanguard parties have all the freshness about them of Lenin's mausoleum and are even less appealing. Insofar as these two schools of development represent the dominant paradigms in the social sciences today, it is helpful to begin by reexamining their historical antecedents: Malthus and Marx.

Both Malthus and Marx were acutely aware of poverty and hunger. If it might be presupposed, for the convenience of argument, that the two could have more or less agreed upon the empirical description of poverty (that is, on the descriptive observations of the phenomenon), then why is it that they do not understand it the same way? The point is this: What is taken as a "fact" in social science analysis combines a level of empirical observation with a framework of interpretation (Bernstein 1978: 21–66, Blaug 1980: chs. 1, 2, 15; Galtung 1980; Katouzian 1980: ch. 6). This framework of interpretation is tied into (1) criteria regarding valid methods of reasoning and (2) a general worldview. If empirical observation, methods of reasoning, and worldview all go into what is meant by a fact, then one can say that on all three levels scientific assessment of reality is threatened by bias on the part of observers. Such bias may be collective or individual, conscious, or latent (Lonergan 1957: ch. 6; Kuhn 1967). See Figure 2–1.

Given the complexity of processes of observation and interpretation, it is not surprising to see differences of opinion. Malthus understood the phenomenon of poverty and hunger, in the economic sense, as a problem of excess demand in the face of irremediable scarcity. Marx gave little attention to this side of the question and, instead, understood the phenomenon in terms of the supply side of the equation and, in particular, in terms of the control of the means of production by a certain social class. Leaving aside the possibility that both Marx and Malthus may have misevaluated the dynamic nature of science and technology, one can see that according to Marx's facts there can be no real development without structural change (resulting from class struggle). According to Malthusian facts the primary problem is located in controlling population growth and distribution. With the benefit of historical hindsight one may appreciate that both the Marxist and Malthusian typologies of development are too reductive, with respect to the level of empirical observation as well as with regard to canons of reasoning. Neither emerges with an adequate analysis of poverty. This historical problem of interpretation is very alive in development circles today and provides a challenge to reexamine scientific method and bias.

Scientific method involves three distinct stages in assessing reality: empirical observation, questioning, and the formulation of a hypo-

Figure 2-1.   Elements of Comprehensive and Integrated Analysis.

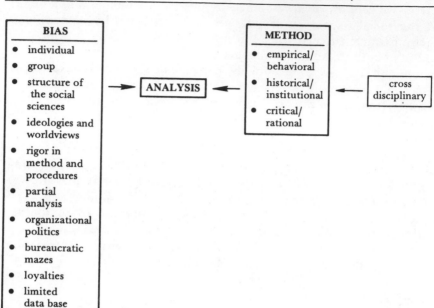

thetical model or paradigm to "explain" correlations if not causes among data ("what is it?") and, then, a further set of questions that test the hypotheses of the model as to their probability and acceptability ("is it so?"). Bias can invade all levels. Observers may selectively focus on certain phenomena and filter out others. Certain conditions may be incorrectly assumed to be irrelevant or held constant. Further questions may be suppressed. Facts become distorted when the level of empirical experience is too limited, assumptions are unwarranted, or pertinent questions are suppressed. The result is that understanding becomes biased and judgment clouded (Lonergan 1957: chs. 6, 7).

It is clear that some might despair at ever arriving at the facts or even a probable approximation of them. For just the bare bones of empirical observation, hypothetical understanding, and judgment of validity pose formidable methodological problems. Indeed, when one consciously attempts to address further analytical dimensions that derive from the sociology of knowledge, the psychological drives of researchers and other predispositions deriving from their worldviews, the matter becomes almost intractable.

A thorough examination of economic methodology is beyond the scope of this work. At the same time, a number of recent thoughtful works provide a backdrop for my own opinion (Bell and Kristol 1981; Blaug 1980; Buchanan 1979; and Mishan 1982). There are many facets of the problem. I restrict myself to commenting upon thee of them.

The first problem is that *social* problems are approached in an isolated way. In the Marxist and Neo-Malthusian typologies, one of the main problems of each paradigm is found in the very isolation of some facts from others, where one finding tends to become interpreted in isolation from other results. Adequate social science method must move from isolated facts to integrated facts, where all findings are interrelated and interpreted in terms of each other. On this point, a severe methodological problem stems from the vastly expanding division of labor in the social sciences and the compartmentalization that derives from such structural changes in scientific organization. The result is that partial facts become more and more isolated and that integrated and comprehensive analysis becomes more and more elusive.

It is commonplace in many North Atlantic universities (and far more so in North America than in Europe) that anthropology, sociology, political science, economics, demography, and operations research would all be separate departments and that students of one would have little or no contact with the other, not even to mention historical and philosophical analysis. There are definite gains to be garnered from increased specialization. But unless reform in the curriculum for training social scientists takes place, analysis of development will increasingly produce partial and isolated rather than integrated analysis of social facts. Such analysis will lead to fragmented rather than comprehensive policies. Indeed, it is not difficult to find many contemporary development models that exemplify overly reductive analysis and fragmented planning in such places as Brazil, Iran, Zaire, China, Tanzania, and Mexico. If the above problems are actual issues that characterize the analysis of development today, social science method must explicitly anticipate them in order to avoid or at least to minimize the related negative consequences.

A second problem is the bias of social scientists. The best way to overcome bias is perhaps to ask not what confirms one's hypotheses but rather what disproves them. In practice this is hard to do; for, at least to the committed scientist, bias tends to appear as reasonable. It is often undetected and therefore unquestioned. The more probable way of overcoming bias would be to speak with one's "intellectual adversaries." In that way, data overlooked or questions skipped over would be more likely to surface. To overcome bias, the psychological proclivities and philosophical presuppositions of observers must be scrutinized. In addition, many institutionalized problems (structural biases) in social science organizations must be overcome.

For example, research institutes, university faculties, and social science periodicals are commonly in the hands of a particular school of thought primarily talking to itself. The institutional character of the social sciences as a knowledge system is by no means neutral. The very organization of the sciences themselves provides evidence of hegemony of certain "in" groups that have disproportionate voice regarding the direction of funding, the content of journals, promotions, and honors. I am not saying that there is nothing but collective bias. Rather, collective bias is always a distinct possibility and it cannot remain unexamined.

This point has been set forth in a comprehensive way by the Frankfurt School. Jurgen Habermas highlighted the problem in his analysis of the interrelation between knowledge and interests and preferences, whether they be individual or collective (Habermas 1973). There is clear evidence of such possibilities of bias, even among scholars who conscientiously try to be unbiased. An interesting example is furnished by Martin Upton's analysis of the "unproductive production function" (1979). He points out that the statistical analysis involved in production functions is often so circumscribed by unrealistic presuppositions that the results of such analysis possess little socioeconomic relevance, although they may be statistically significant. Such narrow studies serve more academic career and professional advancement than knowledge about development. Also important is the fact that researchers focusing on such narrow concerns end up giving little time or attention to more substantive historical issues, such as power (Mokken 1981). In addition to the above, development research is often further circumscribed by what Robert Chambers has called academic tourism (Chambers 1981) coupled with bias towards macro/urban questions as opposed to micro/rural research. In such cases, the structure and design of field research itself is biased toward lack of perception.

A third methodological problem involved in assessing the facts stems from the accepted criteria of analysis: What are adequate criteria and what represents adequate data to meet those criteria? There is a tremendous controversy these days in the social sciences over the tools of the trade. There is an almost unbreachable gap between those who favor quantitative statistical rigor versus those who primarily employ historical/institutional analysis. In my view, some sort of diagnostic method is required that submits the data in question to both frameworks. The only valid reason for excluding one analysis or the other would be to show that the methodology in question yields no valid insights. No set of questions should be excluded *a priori*, particularly in the analysis of a phenomenon such as poverty. There is a tendency in many parts of the North Atlantic to substitute qualitative value judgments with quantitative indices. The pretense that the subsequent analysis is value-free because one generates numbers in a specific way leaves one's analysis of poverty in a confused state. It would be far more fruitful to specify as clearly as possible one's value assumptions and to be explicitly value-critical. Such a specification would actually facilitate the task of keeping value statements distinct from more positivist statements which purport to be value-free.

As Bernstein (1978) has so well shown, North American social science is shot through with positivist fundamentalism. In its origins, positivism was in many ways fruitful and refreshing. But as the history of thought so copiously attests, liberating ideas are often transformed into ideological straightjackets. This has happened in the field of development. Sterile enslavement to positivism in the name of rigor suggests a comparison between the contemporary state of North American economic analysis and the nadir of scholasticism in philosophy, when intellectual dynamism gave way to empty formal procedures. The canons of narrow empiricism (increasingly based upon unrealistic assumptions), the formalism of mathematical logic, and the assumptions of isomorphism between certain types of quantitative method and human behavior have rendered much of economic analysis a nonsocial science.

The lamentable lack of historical and institutional analysis has meant that there is no significant understanding of human intentionality as embodied in history, narrative, and symbol. Humans are, after all, self-interpreting as well as self-constituting creatures. Their economic activity is grounded in root metaphors and paradigms of "progress" and "frontiers," "homelands," "manifest destiny," and "free markets." The neglect of historical and institutional analysis trivializes the social sciences in general and economics in particular. For all that, I do not propose banishing neoclassical or neo-positivist analysis. Rather, I argue for a certain priority of political economy over narrow neoclassicism as a basic integrative framework of economic thought. Along this line, I find the most sophisticated methodology today not in economics departments, but in business decisionmaking as undertaken by modern corporations. Modern corporate management is generally far more aware of socio-cultural and historical factors. This is not to deny that there is a certain logic to neoclassical theory that can provide a fruitful organizational and heuristic orientation in research. Rather the fruits of such inquiry must be intelligently integrated with the broader findings of historical and institutional analysis.

The above three points obviously overlap and, insofar as they are found in actual social scientists themselves, represent the possibility of bias that may result not merely from individual shortcomings but from the collective structuring and accepted methods of the social sciences themselves.

The area of development is in serious need of a diagnostic analysis that would approach the observed phenomena from a number of different standpoints simultaneously. Such a diagnostic analysis would seem to be fundamental for arriving at a set of policies that would prove comprehensive. Determining the facts is complex. In what follows I take a probative look at the concrete case of poverty in order to establish the elements of comprehensive analysis, which serve as the basis for the rest of the book.

ELEMENTS OF COMPREHENSIVE
AND INTEGRATED ANALYSIS

One of the key tasks in social analysis is to be empirically comprehensive. This calls for carrying out and integrating a number of different procedures. Such analysis of development aims to overcome the methodological problem of isolated empirical facts and fragmentary policies by attempting to understand social facts as parts of social systems and as parts of an organic whole. It does not preclude specialized studies of minutiae, rather it sets down as a prerequisite that reintegration of all such aspects be an indispensable part of research and not be left to happenstance. Thus, in development literature, it is appropriate to study hunger as a "malnutrition fact" stemming from protein-calorie deficiency or to study farmers as profit maximizers. But this information must be integrated with other knowledge so as to arrive at a knowledge of hunger or of farmer decisionmaking as *social facts*. To achieve this, historical, institutional, and cultural analysis is necessary.

In Chapter 1, a descriptive profile of poverty was presented. At issue here are the means by which one may begin to understand and overcome poverty. I maintain that to achieve comprehensive and integrated analysis of poverty four distinct points must be examined:

scarcity, technological transformation, power, and socio-cultural values. The reason these points are important is that each suggests a line of investigation that is of vital importance in order to understand poverty. In this chapter, I briefly clarify the significance and analytical necessity of each of these points by taking the example of hunger. In Chapters 3–6 I carry out a more detailed analysis.

The scarcity aspect of hunger is well known and is presented in both the general literature on demographic policy as well as in ecological and environmental studies. A potential cause of poverty is found in the very physical location and geographical characteristics of the milieu where the poor are found. For example, along the large northern strip of Africa, the indigenous peoples have to contend with sporadic and insufficient rainfall. In many parts of Asia the success of agriculture is critically dependent upon the monsoon. In addition to climate causes of poverty are to be found in the lack of availability of good land and other resources. All these natural forces combined may present an ambience too arduous to make it possible to accumulate a surplus upon which a more developed economy might be based. Without a doubt, there are certain parts of the world where the population/environment balance can be said to be somewhat acute; namely, in South and East Asia (Borgstrom 1965; Paddock 1978; Tuve 1976). Critics accuse third-world countries of overpopulating their lands beyond their "carrying capacity." But this scarcity hypothesis explains considerably less data in Africa and Latin America.

To what extent is today's population pressure at the root of hunger? How much data does it explain? The "carrying capacity" model of poverty does possess explanatory power. But it is regionally diverse. It also fails to account for actual patterns of distribution of both resources as well as goods and services.

Although few would agree with the old-line Marxist position that no population control is necessary, one cannot deny that restrictive international migration policy, spending for armaments rather than to develop agriculture, and the lack of attention to human resources are part of the problem. As a result, neo-Malthusian analysis remains an integral part of comprehensive analysis but cannot adequately represent the whole. In Chapter 3, I discuss the scarcity hypothesis in more detail. My point here is to show that it is a necessary element in the understanding of poverty and hunger. There are others as well.

To begin, what is the potential of technology? The point is to transform traditional agriculture into efficient science-based agriculture (Chou 1977; Duncan 1976; Schaller 1976; U.S. Department of Agriculture 1974; Wortman and Cummings 1978). Considerable work has been done on how to transform agriculture and elicit the participation of small farmers in rural development. If per capita food availability is to be increased 1 percent a year, then agriculture in Less Developed Countries (LDCs) must grow at an average of 3–4 percent a year over the next twenty-five years. Perhaps the most crucial issue is the supply and distribution of the factors of production. Agricultural development includes, among other things, improving the quality of land as well as the skills of farmers.

Following a report by the National Academy of Sciences, long-run efforts must be devoted to (1) development of productive capacity and improvement of technology (understanding weather, pest management, and so forth), (2) improving markets, particularly storage and processing capacity, (3) changing patterns of consumption, and (4) improvement of infrastructure (National Academy of Sciences 1977a, 1977b).

These first two points of comprehensive analysis (scarcity and technology) are generally given ample attention in North Atlantic studies of poverty. They both possess considerable explanatory power. Yet large portions of poverty data are not adequately explained by them. For example, why do so many people lack resources and technology? Structural questions must be raised, such as access to resources and liberty to participate in social systems.

Power is for the most part little mentioned by first-world experts, although it receives the primary emphasis from Marxists. Indeed, there is a great deal to be considered here, whether or not one accepts the dialectic of class warfare (George 1977; Lappe and Collins 1977, 1979; Power 1977; Sinha 1976; Tudge 1977; Ward 1968). One of the main discoveries about poverty is that it is not only influenced by demographic considerations and the technological base. More importantly, it represents the state of powerlessness and disenfranchisement.

The structures and institutions of power that characterize a particular society can cause poverty. These structures include cultural, political, and economic forces—in short, the social, political, and economic institutions, organizations, or systems that influence or govern the lives of people. For now, I concentrate on political economic structures. Institutions and structures are, of course, made up of people. But, somehow, they seem to take on their own life and will. Especially for the poor, institutions and structures become an alien "they." They exert influence over people, taking on more authority and power, until people come to be regarded as helpless. There are many structures that affect people's lives adversely and restrict opportunity. There are totalitarian political structures that enslave people, economic structures that deprive the poor of productive resources and income, and economic structures that erect barriers for people who would enter the market. Further, there are broader social structures that underlie the political economy and stratify people into rigid classes and roles. In this sense, social structures serve but one end: satisfaction of the wants of the dominant groups, with the good of the masses considered secondarily, if at all. Charles Elliott has stated the case:

> The privileged owe their privilege to their ability to secure superior access to productive assets—land, credit, education, and employment (which is dependent upon) the interplay of political, social, and economic forces that combine not only to give specific groups preferential opportunities but also to reinforce that pattern and, all things being equal, make it increasingly open and malleable. [Elliott 1975: 18]

Linked to the question of power is that of the legitimation of social structures and patterns of power. This brings up a fourth issue: the relation of poverty to culture and values (Eisenstadt 1973; Freudenberger and Minus 1977). The Marxists and the Freudians have long noted the negative effects of cultural systems and, especially, of religion on human development. The general hermeneutic has emphasized the legitimating functions culture and religion play in erecting unjust power structures. For the most part these critics do not admit a possible prophetic function (as with liberation theology in Latin America, the Islamic renewal, or the countering of the dominance of the totalitarian regimes in many countries primarily by cultural and religious groups). For example, it must be acknowledged that it is very difficult to grasp the meaning of hunger in Latin America without analyzing the function of a certain type of Catholic christianity. Along the same lines, Hinduism plays a role in sustaining poverty in India as do animist and folk religions in parts of Africa and Asia. This area of contemporary development literature is perhaps the weakest of all, whether in acknowledging the role of cultural and religious institutions in causing poverty or in designing development models that can be adapted successfully to cultural values and priorities. Perhaps the best example of the importance of culture to development in recent years is that of Japan and its two former colonies of Taiwan and South Korea. Their philosophic and religious cultural backgrounds seem to have been more successfully integrated with development policies.

In my opinion each of the above four elements yields different but complementary insights and each is germane to a correct understanding of development. Further, they seem to be always important although, comparatively speaking, one element such as population may be more important in one place such as India rather than in another such as Argentina. These four points do not yield a general model of development—indeed, they suggest that there can be no universally valid model—but they do yield general categories of consideration. These categories are not idealistic in origin but have been established as relevant by the volumes of research carried out in recent times, especially in the period following upon de-colonialization. Thus, they represent principles of investigation that are revisable upon the basis of future research.

To conclude this section, the above four diagnostic points must be considered simultaneously if poverty and development are to be correctly understood. They represent a comprehensive and integrated approach to poverty because they combine empirical-quantitative and technical analysis with historical-institutional analysis. Only if all of these points are attended to simultaneously can poverty be understood as a *social fact* and appropriate development strategies shaped.

FROM ANALYSIS TO POLICY: ASSUMPTIONS REGARDING SOCIAL CHANGE

The goal set by the World Food Conference of 1974 is significant primarily because it wove hundreds of different threads of opinion and philosophical orientation into one strand, which, in potential at least, possessed the strength for people to pull themselves out of misery. It is instructive to review part of the final declaration (U.N. World Food Conference 1974):

> All governments should accept the removal of the scourge of hunger and malnutrition, which at the present afflicts many millions of human beings, as the objective of the international community as a whole, and should accept the goal that within a decade no child will go to bed hungry, that no family will fear for its next day's bread, and that no human being's future and capacity will be stunted by malnutrition.

To be sure, motivations for subscribing to the statement vary. Some people were moved primarily by compassion, others by the potential market that well-fed people would constitute as customers; others still by the fact that hunger is a destabilizing element in the present world order. Yet, at the time of the Conference, a unifying consensus underscored the potential for the human community to pull itself out of its malaise. Most observers would agree, however, that in the twelve years that have elapsed since the Conference little has happened in terms of positive social change. In fact, in many places the problem has actually gotten worse.

When people humanistically concerned become befuddled by technical as well as political complexities, they may be tempted to highlight a single issue and seek a "single-factor solution." Such is often the case with the world economic system, where for some the problem is simply overpopulation or capitalist corporations or environmental limits or political manipulation. But the world economic system is, after all, extremely complex, itself containing many subsystems. The phenomenon of poverty in one place is rarely the same either in scope or in cause as poverty in another place. There is not one economic problem but a multiplicity of economic problems. While single factor analysis is important, the various bits of the poverty mosaic must, in the end, be set in relation to each other so as to depict the design and constitution of the whole system.

The list of the causes of poverty is long and includes natural resource endowment, colonial heritage, peripheral economic status, sociocultural values and levels of achievement, the nature of the political authority systems and related institutions as well as the conditions of international capital, and technology transfer. The search for good policy must be based upon sound analysis of social systems. For instance, there is not one integrated food system but many systems with different and often conflicting social goals, priorities, and constraints. A policy articulated in terms of problemsolving rather than systems transformation has little hope of success. It is not that certain proposals may not be logically coherent but that their implementation has little likelihood in light of the operational dynamics of the systems in question. It would be useful to take some examples culled from current literature.

Solving the problem of population growth is important, but as a solution to the hunger problem it is facile. There are an estimated 450–750 million people (depending on criteria) suffering from serious hunger malnutrition. Scarcity? There are over 320 million metric tons of food and feed grains on reserve in the world's granaries (Table 3-3). Indeed both the United States and the European Economic Community (EEC) spend a large portion of their budgets managing excess reserves. The arithmetic has been done so often it is tedious. In an aggregate sense the hungry can be easily fed. Perhaps there is a relative hunger program in terms of local production? Plausibly, yet even "poor" India (in 1985) had nearly twenty-nine million tons of wheat and rice in stock and was projected to sell more than 2 million tons on the world market (U.S. Department of Agriculture 1985: 16). In countries "most seriously affected," the evidence is overwhelming that the hungry are those who are indigent, that is, without either the resources to produce food nor the income to purchase it; they are hungry not primarily because of scarcity but because they have no access to the system. Lowering population growth by itself does not solve the distribution problem.

It has been pointed out that more than 60 percent of grains in the developed countries (both North Atlantic and Eastern Europe and the USSR) are used as feed for animals (Figure 3-1). Would not a simpler diet of less meat be helpful? Clearly not immediately. In itself, this would simply add to the already existing surplusses.

It is estimated that in poor countries nearly 20-35 percent of food (especially fruits and vegetables) is wasted due to pests, lack of processing, and other storage problems. For most countries, control of wastes would eliminate their food deficit. This is a plausible solution, but to set up food processing, transportation, and marketing calls for capital, management skill, and technology, all of which are scarce in poor countries. So the probability of such a solution is slight.

Why not cut down on export crops (coffee, tea, cocoa, rubber, and tropical fruits) and plant food crops? To change allocation priorities is again sensible if the local elites can be displaced. But there is a further problem that a change in this policy would directly affect the accumulation of capital and foreign exchange. It would also impede whatever benefits the presence of transnational corporations might possibly confer in the area of developing a food industry (to eliminate waste, for example).

Land reform is widely thought to be necessary to put productive means in the hands of the poor. Indeed in Latin America and Africa, by a conservative estimate, hardly 30 percent of potential agricultural land is used. But land reform, should it be politically possible to implement it, is useless without a complementary program for inputs (especially credit and extension) and channels of marketing.

The list could easily be extended: green revolution, research in tropical agriculture, credit and marketing cooperatives for small farmers, appropriate technology that complements rather than displaces labor, irrigation schemes and ecological resource management, an international food reserve, nutritional education, food stamps, price controls, breast feeding and infant formulas, climate control, elimination of dangerous chemicals, changing the social position of women, new patterns of industrialization and urbanization, energy use in agriculture, and the production of energy from biomass agriculture.

However one schematizes the above issues, or however much any single one of them may be built up into a *cause célèbre*, it is clear that a problem-solving approach will only have a cosmetic effect upon world hunger for each of the above variables is related to all of the others and nothing short of a systems-approach is sensible.

It is also exceedingly difficult. *A priori* one might say that there does not seem to be a reason for saying there could not be a number, even a large number, of feasible solutions. That is, there are several possible policy mixes (with differing goals, priorities, and constraints). The task of policymakers is to find one that might work and indeed be better than the status quo if not the elusive best. While many policy mixes might theoretically work, it is important to find at least one that has some chance of succeeding in the real world of the military arms of COMECON and NATO, the machinations of the transnationals, and the intrigues of bureaucrats. In conclusion, an adequate policy framework can only be one that is based on systems analysis, integrating in some manner (which seemingly would have to be largely experimental) the cultural base, the power structure base, the technological base, and the demographic-ecological base of hunger. A reductive problemsolving approach analytically produces more heat than light and, in terms of policy, substitutes good will and concern for significant action.

It is therefore necessary to reexamine the notion of social change that underlines development policy. Single factor solutions may pinpoint indispensable issues but in and of themselves they are insufficient. The single most important question in development today is how to effectively bring about positive social change (see Figure 2-2).

To gain a perspective on social change it is helpful to take a look at the elements of social experience. Social experience is much more than an aggregate of individual actions—society is not a pile of sand. It is truly collective in nature, and, thus, social relations are clearly distinct from either interpersonal relations or individual actions, although both of the latter may have clear social implications.

The first point to note in social experience is that it possesses an element of pattern and routine. There are rules of the game to be followed. For example, there are rules for registering in a school, traffic, etiquette, obtaining food in markets, land tenure, and for profits. Every society has its customs and laws, and these are found in political, economic, and cultural spheres.

Not only are there rules of the game in any social experience but one finds that different people operate on various levels or strata of the social system and play different social roles. There is always a division of labor and of responsibilities. Different jobs and offices

Figure 2–2. Elements of Social Change.

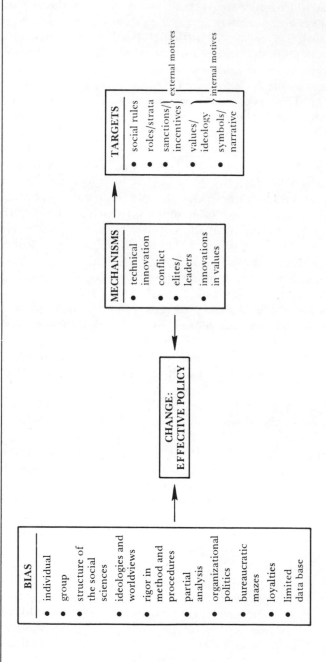

carry different levels of power and prestige. In the food system, there are countless different types of participants, with different roles and degrees of power.

How to get people to participate and keep the rules? In every social system, there are a series of incentives and rewards for those who distinguish themselves in playing by the rules of the game. And there are sanctions and punishments for those who do not. These positive and negative stimuli serve to keep people in line. Even though people may not have internalized the rules of the game, (i.e., follow them out of conviction), they still will follow them out of perceived self-interest. But pattern maintenance is most assured when people internalize the rules and become convinced that the system is fair and efficient.

Why do people internalize the rules? The answer to this question is found on the levels of values and ideology. Ideology in this case means an all-embracing view of ultimate meaning and reality, a world view (such as the ideal of progress) that confers inner meaning upon the rules. Ideology grounds personal and social values and explains why the rules of the game are sensible and good and are conducive to overall human development. It is on the basis of values and ideology that people internalize the rules and accept them as their own.

Values and ideology tend to be rational and philosophical. Rules and values also are found in a presentational mode of narrative and symbol (for example, the self-made person, the white man's burden, the long march, and the frontier). This point has far-reaching implications for social psychology and behavior. Every social group narrates the glorious stories of its past and recounts the great deeds of its saints and heroes. It also has stories of enemies, devils, and demons. The symbolic presentation of the rules and values in terms of great people and great deeds takes the rules and values out of the abstract and makes them living and tangible models to be imitated. If the market system expresses the rules of the game, and the underlying ideology and values are those of private enterprise and individual freedom, it is the self-made person, with the virtues of hard work and thrift, who symbolizes the whole system and who functions as a concrete model for others to imitate.

In the simplest sense, social change implies altering any of the principal elements of the social experience that I have outlined above: rules, roles and social strata, incentives and sanctions, values and ideologies, and symbol systems. In day-to-day life, they are so completely intertwined that a change in any one element leads to a change in all of the others. To give a brief example, if one takes the historical case of the abolition of slavery, it is immediately evident that changes in all of the above elements were involved. The pivotal change is always in the internally legitimating elements—values and ideology and symbol systems—for these provide the rules of the game, social roles and strata, as well as sanctions with their underpinnings.

Social change calls for reform in either one of two ways. The first is to reform behavior positively so as to better attain the social objectives or ideals that the people themselves commonly accept. This represents the case of those who attempt to fine tune the market system in development today. They accept the values and ideology of progress together with its entrepreneurial and working-class saints and heroes. Another approach, though, is to seek a radical revision of social rules and ideologies that are perceived as damaging to the human community, as was the case with the rules of slavery. This is the focus of liberation movements when people speak of revolution and liberation from dependence. One's notion of social change is inextricably bound up with one's view of history and theory of historical processes. To recall but a few examples, Marxist notions of social change are inspired by what they see as the culmination of inevitable social forces of class conflict. On the other hand, much of western Europe and North American social theory seems to base itself upon scientism and its component belief of inevitable evolution and progress.

The process of social change is very difficult to analyze or to categorize in terms of velocity, complexity, continuity, extensiveness, or cumulativeness. Social change may proceed from either primarily cognitive or noncognitive bases and may manifest itself on both micro-social or macro-social levels (Lauer 1982). While I would contend that there may be certain analytical elements that are recurrently important in the analysis of social change (that is, there is a theory of social change), there is not a set process or strategy of social change (that is, there are no universal laws of social change or of history).

What are the recurrent elements in a process of social change? These are the elements that provide us with the focus for development policy. I have identified them as the prevailing social rules, dominant ideologies, sanctions, symbolic media, and nature of social stratification and concomitant roles that determine the degree to which various people participate in power.

What are the dynamics leading to change in these basic elements? It is difficult and perhaps impossible to pinpoint all of them. But the principal ones can be grouped under four categories. First of all, innovations in material culture (as seen in the diffusion of technology). Technical innovations may take various forms such as changes in the physical ambience when water is made available to formerly desert areas, or changes in education. Perhaps the most powerful changes in recent years have been those in the scientific infrastructure of society, spanning gunpowder and the printing press to mathematics, the physical sciences, biological and genetic engineering, and electronic technology. Without a doubt, the scientific infrastructure of society is of pivotal importance in assessing the scope for social change in a certain social setting; it provides a fundamentally new set of possibilities.

A second source of change arises from values and worldview. The current Islamic revival provides a case in point. Islamic leaders are calling for development policies that are in accord with Islamic values. In the area of banking this means new rules of the game for capital accumulation and interest. In much of the third world today, development is spurred on by values of human dignity and opposition to the social injustice that poverty represents.

Thirdly, conflict is a source of change. Examples are provided by the American, French, Russian, and Chinese revolutions. Social conflict, however, need not necessarily be violent. Gandhi's strategy in India was one of active confrontation based essentially on nonviolence.

Lastly, the innovations of social elites or leaders stimulate change. These elites may correspond to government elites, as in the case of Meiji Japan where some 100 leading families pioneered the modernization of Japan, in youth who are not tied down by the past or by traditions, or in great personalities or charismatic leaders such as Gandhi. These are all potential carriers of social innovations, which, once introduced, function as mechanisms of social change and lead to new rules of the game that eventually become routine.

There are of course many other theories that come into play that cannot be adequately considered here. For example, is history cyclic or linear? If linear, does it follow an evolutionary pattern? Are there necessary stages to development or laws of history? To my mind there is no one theory of social change that establishes a general and recurrent pattern of change; thus I do not think that there are scientific laws of history (or of development). Nonetheless, I do think that there are recurrent dynamics that generally focus upon the five elements I have outlined and are stimulated by the four mechanisms I have indicated above.

If, however, one compares historical examples—the abolition of slavery, the American, Chinese, French, and Russian Revolutions, the Industrial Revolution, and the recent Islamic Revolution—one finds very different patterns and processes. Events such as the French and Chinese Revolutions as well as the Industrial Revolution exhibit all of the characteristics of which I have spoken. Indeed, key elements of the process of social change may be identifiable in those historical circumstances. Yet it is not clear that there is a general, comprehensive theory of social change or that there are "laws of history." Although it would appear that certain analytical elements may be identifiable as recurring, the interrelations of these elements among themselves or even their relative importance cannot be established for all places at all times. While Marx may have shown, with some deal of success, that ownership of the means of production is always important, he did not succeed in framing an absolute theory of its importance.

THE DYNAMICS OF DEVELOPMENT POLICY: STRUCTURES, PROCESSES, AND PARTICIPANTS

Development policy attempts to effect social change. Yet there is no unique model of such change. Normally in the analysis of development the focus falls upon the nation-state. This is more than a convenience. It connotes that the state is the key actor on the scene and that both the causes as well as the solutions to development are to be sought primarily on the level of intrastate and interstate political and economic policies. The nation-states throughout the world exhibit a wide variety of characteristics. Accordingly they are grouped in various ways. The democratic market-oriented economies, which comprise the Organization for Economic Cooperation and Development (OECD), are often referred to as the first world. The second world is comprised of the USSR and the developed centrally planned economies that make up the Council for Mutual Economic Assistance (CMEA or COMECON). These first two groupings together make up the developed countries and are also referred to as the North.

The rest of the countries of the world together constitute the developing countries, also referred to as the third world or the South. Such an aggregate grouping is generally recognized as inadequate, however, for these countries are quite heterogenous. It must be pointed out that the terminology employed by various authors is not altogether standard. But frequently enough one finds that the OPEC countries, who (until recently) had ready amounts of capital, are referred to as the "middle-income oil exporters." Other "middle-income" countries are referred to as newly industrialized countries (NICs) and sometimes as the fourth world; finally, the resource-poor "low-income" countries are said to comprise the "hard-core poor" or the fifth world. The main point is that the various developing countries face different prospects in terms of economic resources. It may be useful to speak generally in terms of North/South, but at the same time individual developing countries must be analyzed according to their social, political, and economic structures and conditions. In this context, particular attention must be paid to planning and market policies as well as to the conditions of various economic sectors and social classes.

Most analysts agree with the conclusion reached by the National Academy of Sciences in 1977 that the persistence of poverty and hunger in the world today is due to the lack of political will. In this sense there is a paralysis in the body politic. But for all that, no one has come up with a clearly workable model of social change or of development. It is easy to describe the mess. The question is how to get out of it. The formula of prophetic denunciations plus slogans has little currency. While prophetic denunciation is necessary, it must be accompanied by a long and patient search for alternatives that will work, not simply on paper but in the limited context of actual systems.

To clarify the issue it is worth examining the general structure of society, in terms of types of participants in policymaking and types of roles these participants might play. For a comprehensive scheme, see Figure 2-3.

There are three basic types of participants involved in the formulation of public policy. These are authority systems, exchange systems, and persuasion systems; all play a vital role in terms of world poverty (Lindblom 1977).

Within a certain defined public group, such as India, the authority system is the government at its various levels, together with its powers over certain aspects of social life and its enforcers, such as judges and police force. The United Nations is not a union of peoples; rather it is a union of representatives of authority systems ("legitimate" or not). This is important, for all the rhetoric about national sovereignty often functions as a new opiate of the people. The sacred cow of nationalism has spawned the national security state ideology. From Somosa to Pol Pot more than one wolf has dressed himself in this sheep's clothing and wielded abusive power in the guise of national sovereignty. The record shows that the primary cause of indigence and hunger is frequently to be laid at the door of the authority system. What is so annoying about the most of the documents of the UN, FAO, World Bank, OECD, ASEAN, and OAU is that they so easily omit any meaningful critique of prevailing authority systems either in a national or international context. As should be obvi-

Figure 2–3. Flow Chart: Dynamics of Method and Policy Analysis.

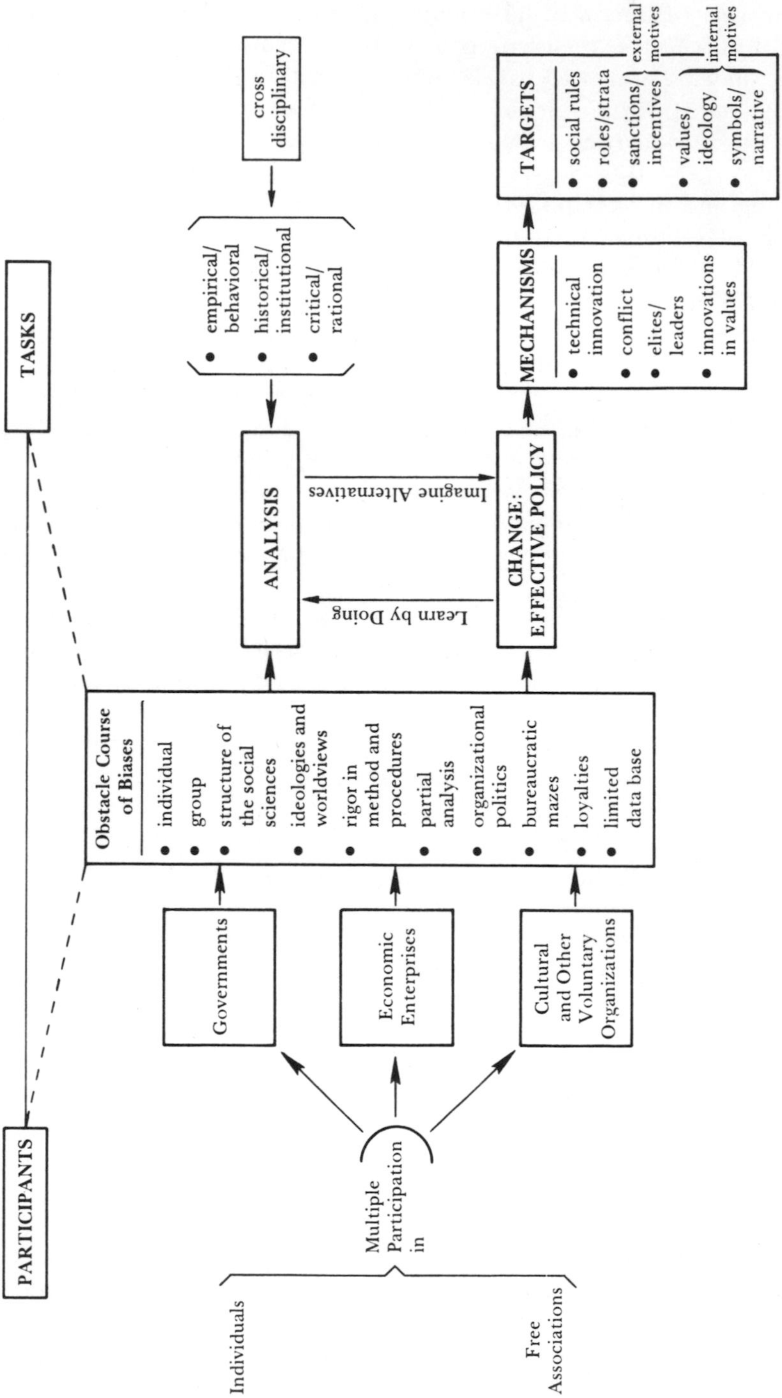

ous, no systems-analysis approach can afford to neglect this point (problemsolving approaches can be a convenient form of anesthesia).

The second most important type of system in the area of food policy are the participants in the exchange systems, the participants in markets. This includes everyone involved in production, distribution, and consumption of goods and services, from households, artisans, and small shopkeepers to large corporations. For anyone involved in the market, whether ostensibly public or private enterprise, is involved in allocating scarce resources. The way production and market participants respond to the questions of what to produce, how to do it, and for whom is a matter of social power and concern. Especially in the case of modern markets, which are highly oligopolistic if not monopolistic, social priorities and goals are often perverted. It should be clear that when the elite of the authority system strike a deal with the elite of the exchange system, whether on a national or transnational level, the plight of the indigent and hungry is a matter of little concern. A case in point: If the Mobutu family and the Marcoses have been able to carve up the wealth of Zaire and the Philippine Islands, it is only possible because of the Swiss Banking system and corporate/government contacts in France, Belgium, the United States, and elsewhere. One hand cannot clap.

Persuasion groups are represented by universities, churches, voluntary organizations stemming from labor and ecology. They neither have the power of civil authority nor do they control the market exchange processes. But they have relations with both. Marx noted how religions lull the masses into an opiated passivity. Latin American liberation theology and the Ayotollah Khomeini have shown, however, the persuasive prophetic power of religion. Indeed the *legitimating* as well as the *prophetic* functions of religion can be easily documented. There is a socio-cultural base to hunger. Hunger in India will have reference to Hinduism, in Egypt to Islam, in Brazil to Catholicism, in Thailand to Buddhism. Religious opinion, student and university opinion, and worker opinion cannot be ignored. Such opinion plays a fundamental role in defining social priorities and in galvanizing political will.

How to motivate all of the above participants? The chief obstacle to overcoming poverty in the world today is neither scarcity of resources due to demographic growth nor the lack of the technical capacity but the absence of the political will. Political will primarily touches culture and social power. Motives for concern vary: some are moved by moral concern and social justice; others by the political economic instability that empty stomachs provoke; others still by the costs of managing embarrassing food surplusses and the opportu-

nity costs of profits foregone because the indigent represent no effective market.

The fundamental practical issue is what might motivate people,
individually and collectively, to galvanize the political will to overcome poverty. Underlying this question are very deep issues of ontol-
ogy and philosophical anthropology that cannot be addressed in this
work. Suffice it to say that in contemporary discourse there are both
the Coriolanus' and those who want vast social reform. The latter
seem to divide roughly into two principal groups: those tribunes of
the people who speak of human dignity, solidarity, and justice and
who essentially provide moral motivation, and those who speak, as
Menenius, of mutual self-interest (not so much because they eschew
justice, although they may, but because they wish to deal with the
"real world").

Those advocating justice are accused of being utopian; moreover
they do not seem to agree among themselves as to what constitutes
proper justice. Yet this level of discourse is highly important in overcoming hunger for it alone attacks the sociocultural base of hunger,
that is, the dominant social values and ideologies that underpin the
persistence of hunger. To see that this approach is important one
need only to look at events in Central America and southern Africa,
at Mao, Gandhi, Martin Luther King, and the Ayotollah Khomeini.
While the reexamination of values and the cultural base of hunger is
a necessary condition, it is not sufficient to overcome hunger.

The "realists," who basically accept the existing structures of
power, are shortsighted in their neglect of the cultural base of hunger. Yet the motivational impact of their approach is most significant
and worth noting. It does not appeal to the dispossessed but to those
in power.

The short-term capitalists, whose strategy seems to be to grab
what they can and run, are widely criticized by the long-term capitalists, as seen in the Brandt Commission Report, World Bank statements, and the influential *The Economist* magazine. Their argument
toward the Mobutus and Marcoses of the world is straightforward:
By taking it all now you run the risk of political instability and losing
it in the future. The long-term capitalists were only to play Cassan-
dra to Somoza and the Shah. The "realists" also propose a second
argument that is more telling: if you integrate the poor into the system and so plan things that all meet their basic needs and have some
income, not only will there be political stability but vast new markets. The enlightened first-world capitalists have bought this long-
term logic of mutual self-interest and are rushing to talk of opening

up markets, transferring capital and technology, and "managing interdependence" in the global village.

The gambit turns upon persuasion; and here it is clear the persuasion among the dispossessed turns upon justice and the persuasion among the principalities and powers turns upon self-interest. An authentic realist grasps both of these points. Furthermore, if the ends sought are different across various groups of participants, so too are the means available. What is viable in one region is not practical in another because of the shifting nature of resource endowment as well as of institutions and social processes.

The poverty problem is complicated, but it can be solved. The preceding discussion serves to underline the fact that development theory has a two-fold task: (1) to provide an integrated social analysis of what is happening as well as (2) models of policy that in the concrete embody the organizational means to arrive at social change that would be both more technically efficient and morally just. Both tasks involve the complex process of division of labor and organizational politics between all the various participants mentioned above.

My point is firstly, that a diagnostic method is necessary to achieve adequate analysis of the problem of poverty. Secondly, development policy must be explicitly cast in terms of social change. Thirdly, all of this must be "systems manageable" in terms of actual social structures, processes, and participants.

REFERENCES

Bell, Daniel, and Irving Kristol, eds. 1981. *The Crisis in Economic Theory.* New York: Basic Books.

Bernstein, Richard J. 1978. *The Restructuring of Social and Political Theory.* Philadelphia: University of Pennsylvania Press.

Blaug, Mark. 1980. *The Methodology of Economics.* New York: Cambridge University Press.

Borgstrom, George. 1965. *The Hungry Planet.* New York: Macmillan.

Buchanan, James M. 1979. *What Should Economists Do?* Indianapolis: Liberty Press.

Chambers, Robert. 1981. "Rural Poverty Unperceived: Problems and Remedies." *World Development*, January, 3–11.

Chou, Marilyn, ed. 1977. *World Food Prospects and Agricultural Potential.* New York: Praeger.

Duncan, E. R., ed. 1976. *Dimensions of World Food Problems.* Ames: Iowa State University Press.

Eisenstadt, Samuel N. 1973. *Tradition, Change, and Modernity.* New York: John Wiley and Sons.

Elliott, Charles. 1975. *Patterns of Poverty in the Third World.* New York: Praeger.

Freudenberger, Dean, and P. M. Minus, Jr. 1977. *Christian Responsibility in a Hungry World.* Nashville: Abingden.

Galtung, Johannes. 1980. "Interdisciplinare Forschung Zugunsten des Menschseins." *Orientierung,* September, 91–94.

George, Susan. 1977. *How the Other Half Dies.* Montclair, N.J.: Allenheld, Osmun Co.

Habermas, Jurgen. 1973. *Erkenntnis und Interresse.* Frankfurt, Germany: Suhrkamp.

Katouzian, Homa. 1980. *Ideology and Method in Economics.* New York: New York University Press.

Kuhn, Thomas. 1967. *The Structure of Scientific Revolutions.* Chicago: University of Chicago Press.

Lauer, Robert T. 1982. *Perspectives on Social Change.* 3rd ed. Boston: Allyn and Bacon.

Lappe, Frances Moore, and J. Collins. 1977. *Food First.* Boston: Houghton, Mifflin and Co.

_____. 1979. *World Hunger: Ten Myths.* San Francisco: Institute for Food Policy and Development.

Lindblom, Charles. 1977. *Politics and Markets.* New York: Basic Books.

Lonergan, Bernard. 1957. *Insight.* New York: Philosophical Library.

Mishan, E. J. 1982. *What Political Economy Is All About.* New York: Cambridge University Press.

Mokken, Robert J. 1981. "Political Aspects of Economic Power: A Critique of the Market Concept." In *Politics As Rational Action,* ed. Leif Lewin and Evert Vedung, 61–81. New York: D. Reidel Publishing Co.

National Academy of Sciences. 1977a. *Supporting Papers: World Food and Nutrition Study.* Washington, D.C.: National Academy of Sciences.

_____. 1977b. *World Food and Nutrition Study.* Washington, D.C.: National Academy of Sciences.

Paddock, Paul, and William Paddock. 1978. *Times of Famine.* Boston: Little, Brown and Co.

Power, Jonathan. 1977. *World of Hunger.* New York: Macmillan.

Schaller, Frank W., ed. 1976. *Proceedings of the World Food Conference of 1976.* Ames: Iowa State University Press.

Sinha, Radha. 1976. *Food and Poverty.* London: Croom Helm.

Tudge, Calvin. 1977. *The Famine Business.* London: Penguin.

Tuve, George L. 1976. *Energy, Environment, Population and Food.* New York: John Wiley and Sons.

United Nations. 1974. *General Report of Proceedings of the World Food Conference.* New York: United Nations.

Upton, Martin. 1979. "The Unproductive Production Function in Agricultural Economics." *Agricultural Economics* 30, no. 2: 34–49.

U.S. Department of Agriculture (USDA). 1974. *The World Food Situation and Its Prospects to 1985.* Economic Research Service Foreign Agriculture Economic Report No. 98. Washington, D.C.: Government Printing Office.

_____. 1985. *South Asia: Outlook and Situation Report.* Washington, D.C.:
. Government Printing Office.
Ward, Barbara. 1968. *The Lopsided World.* New York: W. W. Norton and Company, Inc.
Wortman, Sterling, and R. W. Cummings, Jr. 1978. *To Feed This World.* Baltimore: The Johns Hopkins University Press.

SOCIAL ANALYSIS
OF DEVELOPMENT

3 POPULATION, RESOURCES, AND SCARCITY

The most startling demographic development in recent years has been the dramatic increase in life expectancy in almost all regions of the world. The death rate has decreased sharply, especially in the category of infant mortality. As health care has improved and as levels of nutrition have been raised in most countries, the population problem has seemingly compounded itself. With the majority of the global population under the age of twenty-five, the world faces a record number of potential parents. There is, therefore, a built-in dynamic in the structure of the population that makes zero population growth a goal that is not immediately realizable (if ever).

Nonetheless, a turnaround in the population-resources race has already taken place in many parts of the world, generally in the "first world" of the OECD (Organization for Economic Cooperation and Development) countries and the "second world" of the USSR and the COMECON countries of eastern Europe. There is broad discussion as to why population has stabilized in these areas and, indeed, whether the demographic controls and motivating factors operative there can be transferred to other areas of the world where the so-called population time bomb continues to tick away. While the developed countries, with a growth rate of about 0.5 percent are approaching zero population growth, the less developed countries have an average growth rate ranging from 2.0 to 2.3 percent (depending upon assumptions) (Table 3-1). Although Latin America (2.7%) and Africa (3.4-4.0%) are projected to have high growth rates, their

55

Table 3-1. Population Size and Rate of Increase for the Major Regions and Areas, Medium Variant, 1960–2025 (as assessed in 1980).

	Population (millions)								Average Annual Rate of Growth (percentage)							
	1960	1970	1975	1980	1985	1990	2000	2025	1960-1965	1970-1975	1975-1980	1980-1985	1985-1990	1990-1995	1995-2000	2020-2025
World Total	3,037	3,695	4,066	4,432	4,826	5,242	6,119	8,195	1.99	1.91	1.72	1.70	1.65	1.60	1.50	0.96
More developed regions	945	1,047	1,092	1,131	1,170	1,206	1,272	1,377	1.19	0.84	0.71	0.68	0.61	0.58	0.48	0.24
Less developed regions	2,092	2,648	2,974	3,301	3,656	4,036	4,847	6,818	2.33	2.32	2.08	2.04	1.98	1.89	1.77	1.10
Africa	275	355	407	470	546	635	853	1,542	2.48	2.73	2.90	3.00	3.02	2.99	2.90	1.91
Latin America	216	283	322	364	410	459	568	865	2.80	2.54	2.45	2.38	2.28	2.15	2.02	1.48
Northern America	199	226	236	248	261	274	299	343	1.49	0.86	0.95	1.04	0.95	1.05	0.70	0.42
East Asia	816	991	1,096	1,175	1,250	1,327	1,475	1,712	1.94	1.96	1.38	1.24	1.20	1.09	1.02	0.38
South Asia	877	1,116	1,257	1,404	1,565	1,731	2,075	2,819	2.40	2.36	2.22	2.17	2.02	1.90	1.72	0.95
Europe	425	459	474	484	492	499	512	522	0.91	0.63	0.40	0.34	0.30	0.27	0.24	0.03
Oceania	16	19	21	23	25	26	30	36	2.08	1.85	1.47	1.44	1.36	1.29	1.19	0.61
USSR	214	242	253	265	278	290	310	355	1.49	0.95	0.93	0.93	0.84	0.70	0.64	0.50

Source: United Nations (1981).

situation is not alarming on the basis of natural resource considerations. However, on the basis of economic conditions (especially the job picture), the situation appears far more grave. Turning to Asia, which contains nearly 60 percent of the world population, future available natural resources are severely limited and, leaving migration policy aside, the necessity to bring the birth rate under control is clearly more critical. The employment situation also is critical.

The developed countries have been arguing that the failure to act swiftly to limit population growth would threaten the survival of the world or at least its peace. Observers such as Julian Simon have argued just the opposite (Simon 1981). Poor countries have generally countered doomsday scenarios with calls for more equitable distribution of resources. Some elements of this debate will be taken up later in this chapter when demographic planning is discussed. First, I review projections of when world population will taper off and at what level.

Most UN and international organizations, as well as many national universities, research institutes, and government departments make population projections. Here it is not possible to discuss the rationale of the various models used or to explain why different assumptions are made (e.g., of the present population base of China and related growth rates—where differences in the base of more than 50 million have been found). Depending upon the set of assumptions, profoundly different projections may emerge. Recently, UN specialists have asserted that the world population growth rate has dropped below 2 percent for the first time, and that population in the next century will level off at 5 to 8 billion; only a few years ago the UN projections stood at 12 billion, while others exceeded 20 billion (Brown 1976; United Nations 1981; World Bank 1984).

Along with the population projections there is considerable activity in the field of projecting the technical productivity of the world's agricultural sector and estimating its future "carrying capacity." Here, too, considerable differences exist between doomsday models and those that are more positive. To clarify the question it is important to grasp what, in fact, are the effects of increased population on the food sector and on the environment.

The increased demand for food obviously comes from people. But it has two components. The first is quantitative and simply reflects the fact that increased numbers of people in the world cumulatively increase the demand for foodstuffs to maintain at least basic levels of nutrition. But the second factor is qualitative and reflects people's demand for a higher quality of life that entails more affluent types of diets (basically ones that consume more meat).

Table 3-2. Projections and Extrapolations to 1985 of Food Demand and Production in Developing Countries and Comparison with Actual Trends of Food Production and Population, 1974-1984.

	Food Demand Growth 1974[a]	Population		Food Production			
		Extrapolation to 1985	Actual Trend 1974-84	Extrapolation to 1985	Actual Trend 1974-84	1982 to 1983	1983 to 1984
Developing Market Economies	3.6%	2.7%	2.5%	2.6%	3.0%	2.5%	2.4%
Africa	3.8	2.9	3.1	2.5	1.9	-3.7	3.6
Far East	3.4	2.6	2.3	2.4	3.6	8.2	1.7
Latin America	3.6	2.8	2.4	2.9	3.0	-0.9	3.1
Near East	4.0	2.9	2.7	3.1	2.6	0.2	1.7
ACPE[b]	3.1	1.6	1.4	2.6	4.1	6.5	3.1
All Developing Countries	3.4	2.4	2.1	2.6	3.3	3.6	2.6

a. World Food Conference projections, 1974.
b. ACPE = Asian Centrally Planned Economies.
Source: Food and Agriculture Organization (1985: 8, 49).

At present, it is estimated that roughly 80 percent of the new annual demand for foodstuffs derives from increased numbers of people on the globe. In poor countries the quantitative component is, of course, much higher. Table 3-2 presents data on general food production with relation to population growth over the 1974-84 period with extrapolations for 1985. Africa's population outpaced food production by 1.2 percent. Few observers think that this situation will change quickly. South Asia and Latin America have only kept slightly ahead of population.

The affluence component of food demand has been growing, however, even in poor countries where there is a shift from coarse grains to wheat and rice. Also, the use of grains as agricultural feeds for livestock, poultry, and fish continues to increase. In first- and second-world countries, the majority of new demand actually stems from affluence and the primary nutrition problem is fast becoming that of obesity and diets that are unbalanced because of nutritional ignorance rather than through lack of availability of products. In these rich countries there are, however, people who suffer from malnutrition that derives from lack of food. They are those who are poor, unemployed, or otherwise marginal in the social structure.

At this point, however, the focus is on those countries where hunger is endemic. A study of the U.S. National Academy of Sciences reached the conclusion that the primary hunger problem today is not simply actual or projected population in terms of numbers to be fed with scarce resources but rather the distribution of both food and the means of production necessary to produce food (National Academy of Sciences 1977).

THE FUTURE POPULATION-FOOD PROBLEM

The real dilemma is the future population problem. According to Arthur Dyck, in this debate one finds three principal orientations: the crisis environmentalists, the family planners, and the developmental distributivists (Dyck 1976). Before discussing policy and planning, I review these positions.

The crisis environmentalists take a view of population that is predicated upon the carrying capacity of the ecosystem. They see clear limits to the environment both in terms of water and land as well as in terms of available energy; when population pressures upon the land are too great, the ecosystem suffers stress and begins to deteriorate. Foremost among thinkers in this area are Garrett Hardin (1973), Paul Ehrlich (1976), and the Paddocks (1978). Examples abound of ecological catastrophies, and these authors make very important contributions in calling attention to the eutrophication of lakes and rivers (as is the danger with the Great Lakes), the advancing desert (as in the Sahel desert in Africa), poor water management (as in the Ganges Plain), and soil mismanagement (as in the Brazilean selva and Amazon settlements).

In terms of population, there are two types of argumentation that are advanced. The first is a global argument and states that the carrying capacity of the earth is so limited and fragile that it cannot sustain continued increases of population. The present situation is interpreted in crisis proportions. In caring for the ecosystem it is argued that it is imperative to bring birth rates down immediately and strive for zero population growth. The second argument is more regional: population pressures are causing local environmental stress. For example, both in the Sahel as well as in Java one can make the case there are too many people for the region.

The metaphors frequently employed in this line of argument are those of "triage" or of a "lifeboat" (Aiken and LaFollette 1977). In each case what is assumed is a severely limited set of resources, and an increasing population laying claim to these resources. The conclusion is that, as unfortunate as it may be, some may have to do without. The ethical principle here is utilitarian and claims that a "lifeboat policy" represents the lesser of two evils and that the real moral imperative is to limit births and to prevent future increasing population pressures. Embedded in these metaphors of "lifeboat" and "triage" is also an argument for a certain quality of life, such as that enjoyed in OECD countries.

But does the "lifeboat" situation simply derive from too many people? It can also arise from the demand of affluence: present U.S. energy and consumption patterns, for example, simply cannot be extended to the world population. In fact, the burgeoning third-world populations, which are beginning to make an ever bigger claim on the world's scarce space and resources, are primarily perceived as a threat to the U.S. lifestyle. The crisis environmentalists do not seem too inclined to talk of a radically different international economic order, with different patterns of resource distribution.

The family planners group seems to argue that population is really the main problem with hunger. The poorest and the most hungry continue to have the most children (Simmons 1979). Since the quality of life of the poor is apparently so miserable (the evidence being that they are asking for aid), it would seem that many of their children are unwanted in the sense that they were conceived either through ignorance (the lack of information and education) or the lack of means with which to limit births.

The positive contribution of family planners is that people should not have children that they do not want or would not be able to care for and raise in a healthy way. In fact, proponents claim that to do so is irresponsible behavior. Furthermore, it is irresponsible with reference to society, which often ends up with the social burden of meeting the needs of the children as well as taking care of them when they are adults. It causes even more pressures on already scarce social resources. The planned parenthood argument emphasizes liberty of choice over mere utilitarian concerns. It is an argument not based simply on the limits of the ecosphere but rather on (1) the existential limits a family may face, for whatever reason, (2) the problem of improving the quality of life for all, and (3) the right to free choice in doing so.

Again, with this group primary attention is not placed on the international political economic order and structures but on individual liberty and, hence, individual responsibility toward one's prospective children and toward society. This approach seems logical enough and has represented the common wisdom of the majority of first-world countries that have given primary emphasis in both their own and international budgets to family planning programs. While these programs have taken hold in the developing countries, they have failed to have the desired effects in poor countries (although they have had some effect). This fact has forced people to reexamine what, after all, are population control variables.

At this point two observations are in order for they form the basis of the third position, that of the developmental distributivists. The first observation concerns the use of grains (Figure 3-1) and the second concerns world stocks of agricultural products (Table 3-3).

The world uses nearly 45 percent of grain produced for animal feed. Another 3-4 percent is wasted. The United States uses well over 70 percent of grains produced for feed. Japan and the rest of the first world is similarly high in this regard. Brazil is over 55 percent and the rest of Latin America is moving in this direction. By contrast, India and East Africa use nearly all cereals for human and industrial use (producing oils and sweetners for example). At issue is the affluence of diets in rich countries and the competition in the world of food versus feed. Clearly a reallocation of grains for food rather than feed would yield sufficient amounts to satisfy the needs of all.

Some patterns of cereal usage, however, are misleading. Table 3-3 provides evidence that on a macro level the world is engulfed in tremendous food surpluses. In 1983 there were over 160 million metric tons of wheat and rice and another 160 million tons of coarse grains.

Figure 3–1. Average Grain Use, Selected Regions, 1977–1985 (by percent of total).

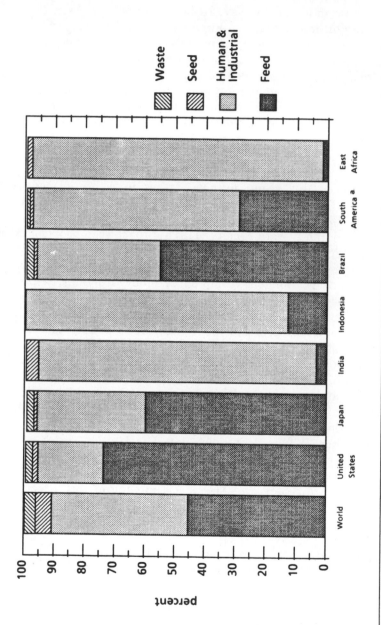

a. Except Brazil, Venezuela, and Argentina.
Source: Derived from Winrock International (1981: 73) and Food and Agriculture Organization (1986: 78–82).

Table 3–3.   Carry-over Stocks of Selected Agricultural Products, 1978–1985.

	Date	1978	1979	1980	1981	1982	1983	1984[a]	1985[b]
		\multicolumn{8}{c}{*Crop Year Ending in*}							
		\multicolumn{8}{c}{*million tons*}							
CEREALS									
Developed Countries		147.6	178.1	157.6	135.9	178.7	217.3	145.1	169.6
Canada		20.6	23.2	15.4	14.0	16.3	18.7	13.5	12.6
United States		74.2	72.6	78.1	62.2	101.8	141.0	71.2	87.8
Australia		1.6	5.8	5.0	2.7	5.4	2.6	9.0	8.4
EEC		13.6	17.6	15.7	15.8	13.7	18.4	12.9	26.1
Japan		8.8	9.9	10.7	8.8	7.1	5.1	4.5	5.1
USSR		10.0	30.0	16.0	14.0	14.0	14.0	19.0	14.0
Developing Countries		95.1	99.6	101.6	101.2	105.7	105.1	120.8	128.5
Far East		73.8	81.8	82.3	76.5	77.8	79.0	95.8	102.0
Bangladesh		0.6	0.2	0.8	1.3	0.7	0.5	0.8	0.8
China		40.6	47.7	54.6	47.9	45.6	50.6	57.0	60.4
India		14.7	14.9	10.9	7.1	7.7	7.6	12.8	15.6
Pakistan		0.6	0.7	1.0	1.5	2.4	2.7	2.5	1.3
Near East		8.8	6.7	8.8	9.8	12.3	11.4	13.4	13.9
Turkey		3.5	1.4	0.8	0.5	1.1	0.9	0.3	0.3
Africa		4.7	3.8	2.7	3.5	4.4	4.4	3.1	3.2
Latin America		7.7	7.4	7.7	11.4	11.2	10.3	8.5	9.4
Argentina		1.7	2.3	1.5	1.0	1.6	2.3	1.3	1.5
Brazil		1.8	0.7	2.0	2.8	2.0	2.4	1.7	2.0
World Total		242.8	277.7	259.2	237.1	284.5	322.5	265.9	298.0
Wheat		98.3	118.0	104.7	97.7	106.0	120.0	130.8	143.3
Rice (milled basis)		40.8	45.0	44.3	43.1	44.9	42.2	45.3	50.5
Coarse grains		103.8	114.7	110.2	96.3	133.6	160.3	89.9	104.2
SUGAR (raw value)									
World total	1 Sept.	30.5	31.5	25.4	24.8	33.0	38.7	39.5	39.3
COFFEE									
Exporting countries[c]		1.92	2.08	1.99	1.86	2.60	3.05	3.35	3.40
DRIED SKIM MILK		\multicolumn{8}{c}{*thousand tons*}							
United States	31 Dec.	265	220	266	404	582	633	590	468
EEC	31 Dec.	840	316	303	387	670	1000	800	550
Total		1105	536	569	791	1252	1660	1391	1018

a. Estimate.
b. Forecast.
c. Gross opening stocks at the commencing of the coffee years.
Source: Food and Agriculture Organization (1985: 175).

Dried skim milk was over 1 million tons. For the present, there is no shortage of food in the world. Nor is there projected to be in the future.

There are, however, local shortages, both regionally (especially Africa) and within nations (the landless, the unemployed, and dependent women and children). Thus, the issue of distribution comes to the fore.

The developmental distributivists consider that the family planners and the crisis environmentalists have their priorities wrong. The Marxist antagonism to Malthus is well known. But at the 1974 Bucharest Conference an unlikely coalition of socialists, third-world countries, and religious groups was not only arguing for development and better distribution in today's world as a matter of justice but also as a means to control population (Teitelbaum 1974). Development and fair income distribution are seen as the necessary demographic preconditions to provide a milieu in which balance with the ecosystem might be achieved and measures of family planning might successfully be adopted in practice. Furthermore, the lifeboat scenario is rejected as an inadequate metaphor of the situation and a call has been made for a new international economic order. The over-consumption deriving from the affluence of the first and second worlds is seen as a greater injustice, and also a greater threat to the environment and food supplies, than the simple increase of population in poorer countries.

In the area of how population relates to development, it is clear that each of the orientations mentioned above analyzes the problem in a different way and has arrived at different sets of priorities. If they were involved in allocating a country's development budget, each would do so in quite different ways.

Nonetheless, each group would do something about population. Before getting down to details, I think it useful to review the types of policies that are generally available. Two types of policies emerge: policies that are population influencing and those that are population response (Dyck 1976).

POPULATION INFLUENCING AND POPULATION RESPONSIVE POLICIES

Population-influencing policies are all those measures that aim to bring down the birth rate (as well as lower the death rate in an attempt to improve the quality of life). Foremost among the means used are a variety of methods of preventing conception; the variety stems from the pace of technology, the search to achieve greater efficiency and to avoid negative medical side effects as well as from judgments of conscience regarding what means are morally permissible.

Population-responsive policies are measures adopted to deal with an increasing or decreasing population. The set of social services that a government decides upon, policies on migration or human resource development all reflect decisions responsive to population conditions.

The need for some sort of population control is widely accepted. At the same time considerable controversy persists over what should be the goals of population planning in a more specific sense, and what means (e.g., incentives) are both effective and acceptable to attain those goals.

While demography as a science strives for an objectivity and a realization of the truth that is not discolored by personal opinion or bias, population policy also involves moral choice (Wogaman 1973). One of the most persistent problems that one encounters in the population policy debate is whether policy measures should be voluntary or not. Perhaps the most controversial measure in this regard was the policy of the Gandhi government during the emergency of the mid-1970s in India, when sterilization was exacted by the law after a certain number of children had been born. It was advocated on the grounds of a lesser evil (the limitation of the freedom of persons to procreate) in face of the devastating poverty and hunger in the country. India's population has grown primarily as a response to better living conditions. The death rate has declined quite significantly in this century, but, as the birth rate was reduced very little, the population mushroomed. Secondly, voluntary programs to reduce the birth rate met with disappointing success. People who went ahead and had a large family were criticized for doing an injustice to their fellow citizens and putting pressure not only on the environment but on all social services. Thus, in a manner reminiscent of the "just war" theory, a coercive program of sterilization was decided upon.

Critics of the government policy countered, however, that while population control remains a serious issue, it was not at that time nor is it now so critical. There were, and are, more pressing factors such as land tenure, bonded labor, usurious interest rates, and food reserve distribution. And these are important not only in terms of justice but as a means of controlling population increases.

To have a plan that would be effective, it is necessary to review the motives by which people have children. Perhaps the most obvious motive concerns self-realization and personal satisfaction in conceiving and raising a child as both a sign and a creation of mutual love. At the same time, people in their mutual love and sharing of life together might wish to separate out sexual expression of personal intimacy with "unwanted pregnancy"—either for reasons of spacing births or for reasons of not having any (more) children.

Research has uncovered many other types of motivation, however, that enter into people's decisions to have children (Farughee 1979). These other motivations do not discount interpersonal and individual values, but they emphasize the often neglected radically social character of human sexuality. There are a number of social motivational factors in human sexual behavior. The first of these has to do with social and family welfare. In many peasant economies the welfare of the aged and the very young who are helpless, or of the sick and disabled, depends on the family structure. Traditionally, very little can be expected from the government or from nonfamily people. Thus, there is an incentive to have more children and, in a traditional agricultural society, more male children.

There are two other social motivations immediately tied to the welfare motivations, and they deal with infant mortality rates and the social position of women. When, as in many poor countries, public health is in a very poor state and infant mortality may reach 30 percent, parents know that of three children only two will survive to adulthood. And the remaining two would not be sufficient either to work for the family's food or to provide in old age. Also, in such societies male children are prized more than female. This bias towards the male partly derives from work ability and welfare significance. Furthermore, a daughter often ends up in the family circle of her husband, taking care of his parents. In addition, as women generally suffer from inferior social status, the security and status of a woman would derive from her children, rather than from his extended family should her husband die, take other wives, or leave her. In such a case, there may be an added incentive for the woman to become pregnant.

Many have remarked that a good deal of the population problem revolves around the social position of women. Priority must be given to changing it. This includes social legislation regarding discrimination, improved social services, and education to equip women with skills so that they not be so dependent on the male-dominated society for their welfare and security. More and more it is necessary to conceive of a population planning system in terms of the local society and culture and the concept of the family that is operative in that setting.

The social aspect of population growth has another dimension that was brought out very forcefully at the Bucharest Conference. This is the element of social values attached to ethnic and racial survival and well being. Minority groups, whether in the United States, the Soviet Union, China, or parts of Africa often possess a desire to flourish ethnically. A precondition of such flourishing, rather than being wiped out or absorbed by more dominant groups, is to maintain if not actually increase population. Thus, in a social sense, people are encouraged to have children and these births are seen as a social good accruing to the whole group.

Closely tied to the ethnic cultural survival is the desire of the group in question to attain a certain amount of political power. It has been argued in the United States, for example, that it is not in the political interests of blacks and other minority groups (who have already been despoiled of a good deal of their ethnic heritage) to limit their population. As the white population moves to zero population growth, the black population could move from 10 to 15 percent or more in terms of the spectrum of political power. The Soviet Union faces a similar problem. as the Russian population is just barely 50 percent of the total and the fastest growing segments are the Moslem peoples along the immense southern border. Thus, at Bucharest the Caucasian peoples were accused of racial and political motivations in their offer to sponsor birth-control programs in many parts of the third world.

With the benefit of hindsight, it is clear that population programs that neglect the social nature of human sexuality and underlying socio-economic conditions have little chance of succeeding. One reason that programs such as Planned Parenthood have been successful in first-world countries is that they in many ways correctly understood the quality of socio-cultural dynamics and matched the values of the people in those countries. In some areas, such as Germany, success has been unsettling; governments find the actual negative rate of population growth undesirable, and the idea has been put forth that it will be necessary to provide payments as incentives to have children in order to reverse the trend.

Whether to limit or to encourage births, some sort of incentives system seems to be generally necessary. Incentives, inasmuch as they constitute a use of pressure (if not force) to bring about a certain type of social behavior, raise many moral issues in terms of human liberty, the relation of individual choice to common welfare, and the rights of the family vis-à-vis the state. Indeed, there is no blueprint of a population program that is adequate for all cultures or universally accepted on an ethical basis. Planning is further hampered because many theories remain insufficiently tested, and data are such that a planner cannot be sure of the relative priorities that ought to be assigned to the various variables.

In summary, population is not a global problem regarding present-day food resources. But in a number of countries it poses a regional problem vis-à-vis local political economic systems. Many observers argue that the basic issue is to improve agricultural policy, both regarding the means to produce food and market mechanisms by which food is distributed. Without basic reforms in these areas, there is little likelihood the poor would become better off even if population decreased. More importantly, population poses a challenge regarding future quality of life, both globally and regionally. There is considerable discussion regarding what are, after all, truly effective birth control variables. A rather broad, all-encompassing strategy is called for. Clearly not all countries view the matter with equal alarm. In a World Bank survey (1984: 160–161) of 112 developing countries twenty-seven provided no support for family planning while forty-three supported it for health and human rights reasons only. There were only forty-two nations that supported family planning for demographic and other related reasons.

In his study on the matter, Arthur Dyck has evolved six basic areas of concern that any population program should address. His argument is based both on a notion of justice as well as what appear to be population-related variables (Dyck 1976). The first point he calls for is a good system of public health where adequate services are available to all. Within the ambit of a public health program, birth-control information as well as the necessary means to limit births would be provided on a noncompulsory basis.

Secondly, he emphasizes literacy and nutritional education programs that would especially emphasize women in the sense they are primary agents for the nutrition of children. Also, they are often more likely to be illiterate. In Dyck's opinion, these two policies taken together would have the effect of reducing infant and maternal mortality.

Thirdly, united to these first two points, is a program to bring about equality for women in general across all phases of the social order.

A fourth point emphasizes a program of political economic development especially in the area of agriculture. The agricultural sector in less-developed countries tends to be both the poorest sector in terms of individual income and also the sector in which more than half of the population makes its living now and will have to make its living in the future.

Fifthly, Dyck calls for social security systems that would provide for the welfare of the aged in ways that would not make them dependent upon the survival and prosperity of their children. Lastly, there is a call for the improvement of income levels in all sectors of the economy as well as more equitable income distribution. Income distribution itself is a population control variable.

After the Bucharest Conference, there seems to have been more widespread acceptance of the fact that policy measures such as these are all necessary if population is to be controlled. Single variable programs of whatever sort appear to have very little chance of success.

There are many variables involved in a demographic transition, where population growth rates begin to decrease. A number of these relate to the status of women. The quality of life is also important. Of all the social indicators that may be relevant, special prominence is due to income distribution. Growth must keep pace with population. But in market and semi-market economies, the basic components of human welfare are purchased and so income is a key variable. In an interesting study, Pan Yotopoulos brought out the insufficiency of per capita income as an indicator in discussing a demographic transition. When he combined the aggregate growth variable with an income distribution variable, analytical results greatly improved, reinforcing the position of the developmental distributivists (Farughee 1977; Yotopoulos 1977).

My position is that poverty, hunger, and population cannot be adequately analyzed in isolation but must be considered as part of both a socio-cultural and political economic system. Population growth and distribution is a necessary element in the explanation of poverty, but it is not sufficient. Population programs are clearly necessary to overcome poverty, yet at the same time much more is needed. What emerges by way of conclusion from the above discussion is that population poses a decidedly *relative* problem of scarcity for development. To what is the population/scarcity problem relative? It is relative

- to the characteristics of the structure of demand as related to aspirations regarding affluence and the material quality of life
- to projected future patterns of demographic growth, distribution, and migration
- to the socio-cultural milieu that constitutes the social nature of human sexuality and reproduction
- to natural resource endowment, conservation and reclamation
- to patterns of resource utilization and control

Scarcity can result from the above variables singularly or from an almost infinite number of combinations among them. What I want to insist on is that scarcity is in the last analysis a *social* fact. Both its strictly demographic as well as natural resource components are profoundly social. In the rest of this chapter I examine the natural resource base of scarcity in terms of a somewhat narrow focus on the population and environment equations (the so-called carrying capacity notion). In subsequent chapters I expand this analysis in terms of specifically social considerations of technology, power, and culture.

THE ENVIRONMENT AND POPULATION

For many years the environment has been viewed almost fatalistically, and it still is so viewed in many parts of the world today. Droughts and floods appear periodically, the soil may or may not give a good harvest. The attitudes of people in western culture toward nature have always been somewhat ambivalent. On the one hand, the power and beauty of nature fills one with awe and inspiration; on the other, nature is hostile and menacing—only the fittest can seemingly master nature and exploit it for their own purposes. And if nature has sometimes been unkind and cruel to the human species, people in their turn have not always refrained from ravishing nature. The central problem of ecology is to achieve a balance and harmony between people and the environment. Is this possible? Are population pressures too great? Are patterns of use distorted?

At this point I review the elements of environmental management that would complement the type of demographic policy outlined above. I begin this section with the basic environment: climate, water, and land. Then I round out the discussion with considerations on energy. As George Tuve has pointed out, energy, environment, population, and food are four very important issues that are inseparable in the sense that a treatment of one involves all the others (Tuve 1976). In dealing with ecological problems of the rural economy, I will attempt to touch upon these issues in their interrelatedness.

Climate

Everyone complains about the weather but seemingly no one can do anything about it. In some ways modern meteorology has not progressed much from the days of a ritual rain dance. Yet there is an exciting amount of new research going on. In its publication, *Climate and Food*, the National Academy of Sciences (1975) in the United States reviewed some of the main issues involved in climatology (see also Biswas and Biswas 1979; Bryson and Murray 1977).

One of the main problems at present is ignorance of the side effects on climate of many scientific innovations that are adopted for industrial use. For example, recently there has been considerable concern over the earth's atmosphere and the effects upon it of aerosol sprays, industrial wastes, and atomic tests. Much more research is needed to assess the impact of certain technologies upon weather patterns. Insofar as photosynthesis would be affected, the matter is of paramount importance to the rural economy. Fear of potential damage has prompted considerable legislation requiring environmental impact strategies. Such legislation adds an element of caution to public policy and has the advantage of steering people to first undertake pilot experiments. These are followed by a period of assessment, and then a decision for full-scale commitment to a certain technology or project, abandonment of it, or revisions.

Considerable advances have been made in climatology since the advent of satellite information systems that have greatly improved the art of weather prediction, facilitating in some cases crop protection and prevention of environmental destruction. For example, when water management can be improved through such advance information, then flood control is enhanced and losses reduced.

So far there has been little success in modifying and managing the climate by causing or preventing rain and raising temperatures. Behavior has mainly been reactive and adaptive, but there have been some very interesting developments. For example, the hothouse is an old idea, yet a group of agricultural engineers discussing the prospects of agriculture in the year 2001 (Food and Agriculture Organization 1977) speak of vegetable crops being grown in huge greenhouses located near markets. The greenhouse environment plus energy for other needs would be maintained by solar energy.

Another area of considerable research and development centers on plant photosynthesis. In the Soviet Union, for example, where most of the agricultural land lies north of the 49 degree latitude, and where there is a short growing period, attempts have been made to breed new varieties that are more efficient in photosynthesis.

Furthermore, considerable effort is being made to farm more intensively in areas where the climate is generally stable and more favorable. This involves making other agricultural inputs available to complement the good climate that is already given as a factor of production. Such needed complementary factors of production are items like irrigation facilities, fertilizers, and machinery. To cite but one example, in California nearly 75 percent of the rainfall falls in the north (Bain 1966). Southern California, especially the area stretching from Los Angeles to San Diego has an extremely mild and favorable climate and also good soil. In mass engineering projects, water has been brought from the north to the south through miles of aquaducts, canals, and tunnels; in addition, water has been brought from the Colorado River. All of these projects considerably upgraded the environment and converted rather marginal land to prime farmland. Yet at the same time, it is important to note that they were (1) very costly and (2) beset by problems of organizational politics, which at times distorted economic choices (Bain 1966).

In conclusion, there is little if any harmful effect on the climate that stems from rural economy, although there are potential bad effects from some types of industry, which seem to affect photosynthesis and plant and animal health, because they pollute the air. With regard to the climate, the rural economy has been characterized by adaptive behavior. Attempts have been made to alter the climate through greenhouses, and to improve reactions to the environment by new uses of satellite systems and by breeding new varieties of plants that are more adapted to environment and efficient in photosynthesis. Up to this point, attempts to transform the climate through measures such as cloud seeding have only been marginally successful (in terms of effects and cost efficiency). Efforts have accordingly concentrated upon adaptive management.

Water

While climate management has been adaptive, water management, which is one of the major problems of the rural economy, is increasingly proactive. It is a major ecological problem in general and also a formidable political problem. The problem in agriculture is to have good quality water available in the desired quantity at the right time. This is both a political, economic, and technical problem; it is also socially very volatile.

Most traditional agricultural societies have been plagued by either recurrent floods or drought or both. Floods and drought not only plague the rural economy by destroying crops and livestock but they make a wasteland of the environment itself. Agriculture that depends only on the hope of rainfall tends to have capricious history, marked by periodic famine and suffering (Chambers, Longhurst, and Pacey 1981). I have already mentioned the case of the California water management system that moves more than 13 trillion gallons of water a year. Despite costs and organizational problems, it has been highly successful in terms of flood control. Furthermore, in the late 1970s it protected the state's agriculture in some two years of quasi-drought and made it possible to increase production even though rainfall was but one-third normal levels. Such water management is both good ecological practice and good farming practice. But a project such as that undertaken in California is highly capital-intensive and, therefore, would be clearly beyond the reach of many developing countries.

There are numerous other means that can be adopted, however, even with labor-intensive methods. Traditional agriculture, such as has existed in China, has long been familiar with the techniques of terracing land and constructing reservoirs, ditches, and wells to control the availability of water. New methods of irrigation that employ sprinklers or the "drip method" have been effective in conserving water as well as in reducing salinity, which is higher with flooding irrigation. Flooding irrigation also tends to wash pesticides and other chemical residues into rivers and streams, causing ecological havoc by either polluting them and killing off fish and other life or, in the case of fertilizers, encouraging too much aquatic plant growth.

Flood and drainage control are two of the most difficult problems to solve. It would be worthwhile to examine the case of floods in India. *The Economist* magazine has noted that the floods in the late 1970s were the worst in living memory. In India, it reported at that time

> thousands of villages have been inundated, crops have been damaged in millions of acres of farmland, and millions of people have had to flee to high ground. The damage to property and livestock already runs into billions of dollars. Hundreds of people are known to have died but an accurate casualty count will not be possible for weeks, until stranded villagers can return to their homes. The present danger is that disease and starvation will strike the thousands marooned on islands in the middle of seas of pollution ["Savage Waters That Will Not Be Tamed," 1978: 59].

The Ganges Plain is potentially one of the richest agricultural areas in the world. Yet almost annually it is struck by flood disaster and a large percentage of crops perish. The warning system, however, has improved and, in the case above, thousands of lives were thought to have been saved because people had the time to evacuate.

In India, some 60 million acres, mostly in the north, are prone to flooding; so far only 23 million have been protected by dams and embankments. But the monsoon torrents of the 1978 floods also devastated many of these (it was caused by only a day and a half of heavy monsoon rain). Over the next five years, India was to spend $900 million on flood control measures. According to some experts, this fell short of the estimated $1,400 million needed for the Ganges Basin alone. In fact, over the past thirty years flood damage seems to keep increasing despite all past expenditures. Embankments are only part of the problem. Soil erosion in the catchment areas leads to the silting of river beds, which soon offsets the protective value of the embankments. The problem of silting up is especially severe in the

Himalayan foothills, where poor soil conservation management has seriously aggravated the problem. The area has been marked by rapid deforestation (to gather fuel as well as to expand cultivated acreage) and overgrazing by livestock. The floods owe as much to the hand of people as to the hand of nature.

It is clear from this example that even an historically well-known problem is not easy to control. In India significant expenditures have been made, but they have not produced significant results. Lack of coordination between erosion control and embankment construction have combined to undo the program. Plans have been proposed to put a halt to erosion, for instance, by planting fruit trees in the Himalayan foothill area. This project could have potentially helped cure the erosion problem and also provided much needed income to local peasants, enabling them to solve their fuel problems. But the plan broke down when put into practice due to persistent fuel shortages and to lack of infrastructure in transport and cold storage to market the fruit. (Already a vast percentage of Indian agricultural produce is wasted before it reaches the market.) An otherwise logical proposal made less than good sense in the actual given situation. In the meantime, one can expect more floods in succeeding years. In his study of India, John Mellor (1976) was extremely positive regarding the agricultural potential of this area. It could conceivably become a major food supplier for all of India as well as provide some items for export. Yet the transition is fraught with difficulties.

Water management is a very complex social problem, involving technical difficulties, multiple social objectives, property rights, and diverse roles for private and public sectors. Yet it is clearly possible to develop water systems that would use water resources more efficiently. The technical problems can be formidable, but so also are the social ones. In planning irrigation schemes, engineers and planners must necessarily consider the social structure as well as the natural environment (Howe 1982). They must build off local traditions of water management.

Finally, there are some international problems in water management deriving from rivers that cross borders. India's problems are also those of Bangladesh. In flood years, Bangladesh is liable to get more water than it wants; in lean years it competes with the port of Calcutta, which becomes silted up and needs a flow of water to wash it out. A similar problem exists between Lebanon and Syria (where Lebanon could control the flow of water) or between Syria and Iraq. According to some experts, international considerations also make Saudi Arabia reluctant to tap water from Iraq at a point just before fresh water runs into the Persian Gulf and mixes with the sea. Instead, in the Middle East there has been more experimentation with desalination, which is more costly but which affords more political independence. In general, however, the costs associated with desalinization tend to put it beyond the ordinary means for reclaiming a wasteland environment for use in a rural economic setting.

Land

The total area of the world is some 510,100,000 square kilometers; water covers the majority of the area and there are but 131,000,000 square kilometers of dry land surface. Of this area only about 15,000,000 square kilometers (12%) is cultivated and regularly under crops, 30,500,000 square kilometers (23%) is permanent meadow or pasture, and 41,500,000 (32%) is forest. The remaining 43,664,000 square kilometers of dry land (33%) is either built upon or is wasteland. Agricultural uses of land for cultivation, pasture, and forests covers about 57 percent of the dry land or 10,000,000 square kilometers. There are two primary land questions that are raised in the context of agricultural economics: increasing the quantity of land and improving the quality.

As can be seen from Table 3-4, there is considerable scope for expanding the amount of land under cultivation in both Latin America and Africa, both of which together barely use 25 percent of capacity. Part of the problem is the lack of knowledge of tropical soils and conditions. Also the quality of land is uneven. Europe and Asia have significantly less scope for expanding the arable acreage. The Soviet Union and North America, however, farm fairly intensively while retaining considerable room for expansion.

The intensity of farm activities is somewhat a function of population pressures on the land. There are varying notions of optimal farm size. In the United States, the farm population has shrunk to less than 4 percent of the population and farm size tends to be quite large. North America has generally followed the path of extensive farm technology: expanding production by bringing new land under cultivation with new mechanical inputs. In the Far East and Europe, more of an intensive technology has been used: expanding production through use of biochemical inputs (Japan, for example, on an average uses more than 400 kilograms of fertilizer per hectare) and multiple cropping. Optimal farm size in an economic sense is partially a function of the type of technology adopted and resources available. Overall, there seems to be a shift toward intensive farming, which promises higher returns on capital investment than does invest-

Table 3-4. Growth and Potential of Land Use for Agricultural Purposes (by Major Region, in 1000 Hectares).

	Land in Permanent Crops		Total Increase (%)		Estimated Ultimate Potential	Total Increase Potential	Percentage of World Total Potential Increase
	1966	1976					
World total	1,418,10	1,491,800	73,590	(5.19)	2,496,000	2,004,200	100.00
Developed countries	659,461	672,857	13,396	(2.03)	854,000	181,143	18.04
North America	220,954	232,097	11,143	(5.04)	—	—	—
West Europe	102,122	96,184	-5,684	(-5.57)	—	—	—
East Europe and USSR	276,559	278,574	1,975	(0.71)	—	—	—
Oceania	40,616	46,019	5,403	(13.30)	—	—	—
Other developed	19,170	19,983	813	(4.24)	—	—	—
Developing countries	758,743	818,943	60,200	(7.93)	1,642,000	823,057	81.96
Africa	173,375	185,610	12,235	(7.06)	466,000	280,390	27.92
Latin America	123,558	143,568	20,010	(16.19)	586,000	442,432	44.06
Near East	76,827	80,162	4,235	(5.510)	112,000	30,938	3.08
Asian centrally planned economy	132,432	141,266	8,834	(6.67)	204,000	62,734	6.25
Far East	251,538	266,329	14,791	(5.88)	272,000	5,671	0.56
Other developing	1,019	1,108	89	(8.73)	2,000	892	0.09

Source: Food and Agriculture Organization (1978).

ment in new lands where productivity may be poor. At the same time, some urbanization and industrialization patterns are taking over prime land.

With the emphasis on intensive farming technology, there is even more difficulty than usual in maintaining the quality of the land. In the past few years, one of the most alarming problems in the breakdown of a productive system has been advancing desertification. Some observers estimate this advance of some thirty miles (46 kilometers) a year; others are more skeptical (Eckholm and Brown 1976; Lappe and Collins 1978: 44 ff and Part II). But deterioration does take place, and specific conservation and reclamation policies are necessary to arrest it.

There are a number of causes of the land deterioration process: prolonged lack of rain, overgrazing, working the land too intensively, deforestation (e.g., clearing shrubs for firewood), and mismanaged irrigation, where the salt content builds up to the extent of ruining the soils. This process raises a number of important issues.

About 50 million people live in critical desert regions. In comparing the per capita cereal production in 1973-75 with 1950-52, most desert countries showed an alarming decline. Yet the desert can be managed in a productive way, as the case of the Negev shows. In the fall of 1977, a UN Conference was held in Nairobi on desertification. It called for an annual expenditure of nearly $500 million a year to end desertification (United Nations 1977). Such expenditures are rationalized in the economic sense in terms of otherwise lost productivity. According to UN estimates, cumulative degradation of rangeland and nonirrigated farmlands had reduced their combined annual productivity by more than $12 billion below potential. If damages due to waterlogging and salinity are added, the yearly losses total nearly $16 billion. It is argued that antidesertification investments would yield a handsome financial return. Such benefit/cost analyses are often spurious paper exercises. But they do serve to make a general point that is valid. In the late 1970s, major projects were begun in the Sudan, Somalia, and some areas of the Sahel that gave hope of turning the situation around. Yet the combination of lack of capital, management, and technical resources and adverse political conditions remained major obstacles, as events in the mid-1980s attest. The traditional methods of maintaining the quality of the land have been leaving the land fallow and crop rotation. These methods are still followed in many areas. But with proper soil analysis and the supplementation of soil deficiencies with biochemical inputs, much more can be achieved and even multiple cropping can be introduced. Problems of capital, management, and technology remain formidable. Yet it is precisely scarcity in these areas rather than a population/material resources scarcity that is the main problem.

A somewhat low-cost and readily available means of maintaining the quality of soils is through the recycling of organic wastes (Hobson and Robertson 1978; Rochlich 1981). As will be discussed below, recycling poses particular problems for modern commercial agriculture due to concentration of production units in stockyards and the consequent additional costs of waste transport and processing. Yet in developing countries, the organic waste is generally produced where it could be applied, with the exception of urban compost and sewage. In traditional Asian agriculture there has long been a system of local collection and application. While such organic wastes may not be of sufficient quality or quantity to replace chemical fertilizers, they could profitably be used in conjunction with them. Soil quality itself would seem to call for their use. Nonetheless, many problems remain: the logistics of collection, processing, and distribution of such wastes, knowledge of just how much and in what way organic wastes enrich the soil, and knowledge of what chemical nutrients should be used as complements in the production process.

The technology of soil fertility is still deficient in the area of tropical and subtropical soils about which so little is known (Hass, Carswell, and Cowler 1979; Hodder 1976; A. Kamarck 1976). One of the most publicized examples in recent years has been the opening up of the Amazon frontier in northern Brazil (Johnson 1979). This area has great potential in both farming and forestry. Yet practices of shifting agriculture (slash and burn) practiced with increasingly short intervals and poor logging practices have combined to degrade the ecology, both depleting the soil and destroying the forests. Up to this point, considerable research and experimentation has been carried out, but much remains to be done before efficient management systems of tropical agriculture emerge.

Land policies are a very complicated issue in almost every country. I leave ownership, control, and land reform to later chapters. One of the main problems I want to discuss here is the rural-urban relation. There are often complaints that urban and industrial uses are infringing upon prime agricultural land. This is true in many cases. But it is also critical that the rural economy be located near its markets. Proper economic analysis will always count the costs of waste, storage, and transport. Development planning must strive to harmonize urban and rural agricultural settlement patterns. To achieve such balance is a very complex economic and ecological question.

Other issues of land politics vary considerably from country to country. For example, in the United States some farmers are guaranteed a certain price for their product if they agree not to plant a certain percentage of their land. In Africa the land tenure system is linked to cultural factors of traditional tribal lands. And in India, there are many social problems connected with sharecropping or tenant farming. Political decisions and cultural values, therefore, are inextricably bound up with economic considerations and both affect the ecological quality of the environment. But surely water and land management policies are the most fundamental issues in improving rural ecology and in trying to harmonize environmental management with demographic policy.

PATTERNS OF ENERGY USE

Finally a word on energy. The most basic input in making the modern agricultural and food system "modern" is energy input. There is a tremendous dualism in energy use in world agricultural systems.

The U.S. food system is the most energy intensive of all. To grasp it in fact as a system, we need to take a look not only at the processes of food production but also processing, storage, and distribution. The U.S. food production system takes up about 16.5 percent of the nation's total energy use. The farm production level uses 2.9 percent; processing 4.8 percent; distribution 1.0 percent. Consumption and preparation both at home and in restaurants together make up another 4.3 percent and other uses are 3.5 percent. The increase of energy use in every agribusiness stage has more than doubled from 1940 to 1970. The U.S. system is often taken by some as a model of efficiency, yet basic calculations are sufficient to show that it is not necessarily so very energy or capital efficient. It should not become the model for the rest of the world. If the U.S. system were to become standard worldwide, food production would use up 80 percent of the world's present energy consumption and, according to some estimates, exhaust petroleum reserves in as little as thirty years. (Brown 1976: 112; Abelson 1975: 38).

There is an anomaly in the U.S. food system: Energy costs in a relative sense are somewhat low (only six cents out of one dollar of farm expenditures in the late 1970s), yet in total quantity (with reference to world consumption patterns) energy use is very high. The principal on-farm direct uses of energy are for crops rather than livestock and for items such as irrigation, crop drying, and machinery. The farm also consumes considerable energy indirectly in producing farm inputs such as fertilizer and pesticides.

The most serious challenge is to make the food system more efficient in its use of energy and also to find alternative, preferably renewable, sources of energy. For many U.S. products, energy input exceeds calorie yield. In more labor-intensive technology, on the other hand, the energy output exceeds the energy input. It is clear that many energy resources are both limited and nonrenewable and, therefore, that the agricultural systems that are energy intensive are not sustainable indefinitely nor can they become widespread in poor developing countries.

A number of solutions have been suggested. In a perceptive article, Moran Munasinghe has called for comprehensive energy policy that coordinates policy tools of pricing, physical controls, education and dissemination, and technical methods (including research and development) (Munasinghe 1983). In his view, pricing policy is first to be determined according to criteria of strict economic efficiency and then readjusted to better meet other (simultaneous) objectives of energy policy such as social priorities and basic needs, financial viability, conservation, and other specific issues such as regional or sectoral development and bureaucratic efficiency.

Physical controls are necessary to handle unforeseen energy shortages as well as to channel energy into socially desirable patterns of use. Education and public dissemination campaigns are necessary to shape public opinion and to elicit voluntary compliance.

New technical methods offer many exciting possibilities, particularly in the areas of renewable energy (Lindblad 1981) and the recycling of organic wastes (Rohlich 1981). There is also a whole phalanx of suggestions regarding substitute energy sources to be derived from the sun (United Nations 1979), sea, wind, and waste materials. There is no agreement that a totally renewable energy system is feasible and, if so, how much it would cost. There has been considerable ferment over alternatives (Leach 1976; Lockerate 1977; Makhijani 1975; Wortman and Cummings 1978, chs. 4, 5; Zeimetz 1975) but no completely adequate theoretical or economic solution has emerged. There is a consensus, however, that European and North American technology and energy use patterns would not be appropriate for developing countries, primarily because they are too capital intensive and labor displacing and would introduce both economic and social imbalances. Energy is a very scarce resource in most poor countries. Needs are often only met by imports (using scarce foreign exchange) and energy conservation is an issue of fundamental importance.

The shortages of energy in poor countries for household activities of cooking and heating have created grave problems for agriculture.

Table 3–5. Percentage Share of Energy Imports to Total Imports, by Value, and of Fuelwood Consumption to Total Energy Consumption, Together with an Index of Energy Consumption in Developing Countries, 1970, 1975, and 1982.

	1970			1975			1982		
	Energy Consumption Index	Energy/ Total Imports	Fuelwood/ Total Energy	Energy Consumption Index	Energy/ Total Imports	Fuelwood/ Total Energy	Energy Consumption Index	Energy/ Total Imports	Fuelwood/ Total Energy
Africa	100	3.0%	67.0%	126	6.5%	61.5%	177	9.3%	53.0%
Asia and Far East	100	5.3	24.0	141	11.7	19.0	191	19.6	16.0
Latin America	100	9.7	21.0	133	24.4	18.0	180	53.3	16.0
Total developing countries	100	6.3	28.0	135	14.3	24.0	185	21.4	20.0

Source: Food and Agriculture Organization (1985: 71).

As may be seen from the data presented in Table 3-5, from the period 1970-1982, the ratio of energy imports to total imports rose from 6.3 percent to 21.4 percent. The rise was sharpest in Latin America, where in 1982 energy accounted for 53.3 percent of all imports. At the same time, in 1982 fuelwood supplied 20 percent of developing country energy needs. The contribution of fuelwood decreased in all regions from 1970 to 1982. In Africa, however, it is still over 50 percent. This has important ecological consequences. In every developing region, deforestation has led to severe land management problems. For example, in China, household needs have led to the destruction of forests and protective brush covering in many places; the result has been serious erosion problems (Glaeser and Steidlmeier 1983). Further, the use of animal manures and other farm waste products for immediate household fuel has meant the ruination of biomass energy projects as well as a lower level of application of organic nutrients for soil. Developing country solutions to the energy problem still emphasize the role of animals in production as well as medium levels of technology to harness wind, water, solar, and biomass sources of energy in production, processing, and household consumption.

ECOLOGY, RURAL TECHNOLOGY, AND MANAGEMENT

As seen in the cases of India and China, the local energy problem is intimately connected with agricultural development and ecology. The issues cannot be separated. The preceding brief survey of natural resource endowment leads to a number of conclusions:

1. There are two types of population pressures on natural resources: (1) absolute, where population needs exceed potential natural resource carrying capacity and (2) relative, where population needs exceed the carrying capacity of a particular social management/technology set.

2. The population/environment question is not static. There are clear geographic environmental limits, but "carrying capacity" is necessarily a dynamic and variable notion.

3. Good ecology is also good agricultural management; it is a necessary complement to a population policy.

4. Natural resource management is the pivotal variable; in every part of the world, the potential exists to greatly enhance ecological quality and agricultural efficiency.

5. The four issues of climate, water, land, and energy are inseparable, and efficient management must attempt to set in place both comprehensive and integrated ecological and agricultural policies, which would not only harmonize the above four inputs but also harmonize the management of forests, grasslands, crops, and animals in production.

6. Environmental management poses many technical and economic problems. But it is rooted in sociohistorical patterns and organizational politics. These sociopolitical aspects of the issue are frequently the most formidable.

Agricultural economies that employ traditional technology relate to the ecological environment in a fundamentally different way than those specialized agricultural systems that are highly mechanized and employ high amounts of biochemical inputs (Hicks 1978). The main problem that the first technology set poses for the ecology is that of exhaustion and breakdown, stemming from overuse and lack of integrated management. Modern agriculture, however, also threatens the environment with breakdown by different types of overuse and pollution. There are two main ecological problems that are associated with the technology set of modern agriculture; agricultural wastes and the effects of agricultural chemicals.

The way in which poultry and animal meat is produced has changed considerably over the past decades. Whether for beef or for chickens, the production line has come more and more to resemble a factory. Chickens are raised in sheds containing thousands of cages, fattened on a programmed mix, and slaughtered when they have reached a certain optimal economic potential. With cattle and pork the process is similar. Cattle are brought from a range, and before being slaughtered, they are fattened in feedlots a few thousand at a time. The resulting problem is how to dispose of the waste manures (of which the normal steer produces several tons a year). Dumping the waste into lakes and streams only leads to pollution of those water outlets. Much more is being done to recycle manures into the soil as traditional agriculture has always done. In addition, progress is being made in converting wastes into energy (Jones and Ogden, 1984). Here the problem primarily involves the economic costs of transport and handling.

The problem of agricultural chemicals has probably received far more attention from consumer groups and nutritionists than from ecologists. But there is a problem in agriculture of chemical sprays killing off more in the environment than the pest that was the intended victim and thereby creating other ecological imbalances. In addition, when irrigation runoff sweeps with it chemical residues from the soil to nearby streams and lakes, it often happens that the local fish succumb to the poisons or that the new toxic influx contributes to the eutrophication of the lake or stream.

There is, of course, a positive side to technology. A tremendous amount of research is presently being done on how to control animal diseases and pests (Pimentol 1978). The estimated losses due to pests and diseases is very high. Cereal losses range from 24–46 percent, vegetables from 25–44 percent, and fruit from 29–36 percent. Losses due to animal diseases are extremely high, especially for beef and milk. Estimates of the potential nutritional benefits to be derived from pest control programs for rice and maize that succeed in correcting but 20 percent of current losses is well over a 100 million people fed per year (Harris and Lindstad 1976; National Academy of Sciences 1977: 77, 104–05). There are many problems however, (both technical and social), in achieving an intelligent and socially beneficial policy in this area of chemical inputs to agriculture.

Many of the past results and future projections are tenuous. One of the most alarming discoveries is that after certain pesticides are used against certain types of pests for a number of years, the pests begin genetically to develop resistance to the poison. In addition to chemical techniques, a number of biological techniques are being introduced. For example, one effort is to introduce methods that would sterilize the male of the species; another is to develop and introduce into the area a natural enemy of the pest that would then prey upon it. The troubling factor in much of this research is that so little is known of the secondary effects of such strategies. That is, in solving one problem is there a risk of creating a bigger one? It is not unusual that in trying to eliminate a pest more damage will actually be done to the pest's predators with the net result that the pest actually increases. Events such as the terrible plague of locusts in much of Africa in the late 1970s should make it clear that something must be done to control pests. Just how to do it is not clear.

Perhaps the most attention has been focused on the problem of the tsetse fly. It has been pointed out that nearly 75 percent of potential arable land in Africa is underdeveloped. In fact 4.5 million square miles in Africa (an area larger than the continental United States) is of limited use for human settlement and agriculture. It is infested by some twenty-two species of the tsetse fly, which plagues most of sub-Saharan Africa. It carries parasites and infects cattle and causes fatal sleeping sickness in humans who consume diseased meat. Projects have been underway to implement the sterile male technique (D. Smith 1977); this technique has been used successfully in parts of the United States and Mexico to eradicate screw-worms. Pesticides have been partially effective against some types of tsetse fly, but never fully so. The problem recently has been compounded by the development of resistant strains.

In addition to technology, there is a political context to pest and predator control policies. In parts of the world where naturalist movements are strong, notably in the United States, local agriculture has come into conflict with groups who object to the negative consequences of biochemical inputs or want to preserve certain species. In the western United States, for example, there is a considerable sheep industry. There is also a formidable coyote population (the coyote is a natural predator that feeds on rodents, rabbits, and in this case sheep) that causes thousands of dollars worth of damage each year. Until recently it had been the common practice of the sheep owners to control the coyote population by either shooting them or feeding them poisoned meat. Environmental naturalists protested and the coyote is now protected by law (Gee 1977). Ecology is in no sense merely a technical issue, it is sociopolitical as well.

The interface between rural development and technology is a complex management issue (Sims and Wright 1978). The first effect of technological innovation in the rural economic sector is the introduction of certain imbalances into the ecosystem, whether of pollution or of endangerment of certain species. The second effect, however, is in trying to correct imbalances that are present in nature by taking positive countermeasures. The above examples show that the forces of nature, whether pests, predators, or diseases, are extremely dynamic and resiliant. Secondly, compartmentalized problemsolving approaches do not work well due to unforeseen secondary effects. Thirdly, there are political problems deriving from various interest groups.

CONCLUSION

Four principal variables have been discussed in assessing the interrelation between population and resources and the reality of poverty and hunger. If food is scarce, these variables will have to be appraised and often redressed. Climate, water, land, and energy serve as the basis for management decisions and choices of technology.

Numerous authors cite the race between population growth and food supply, which in the most seriously affected countries is getting alarmingly worse. How are such observations to be interpreted? One might simply conclude that demand is greater than the supply of food. Such analysis would argue that the problem was primarily one of population pressures. In that case proper policy would primarily focus upon limiting births. The solution is enticingly simple. One would suspect that there was no international food surplus or further production potential to be derived from new technology and improved natural resource management. Numerous articles have gone through the arithmetic calculations demonstrating that there is more than enough (globally) for all people in the world today to eat well.

Taking hunger *locally*, however, the more important issue is how to increase local food supply. There are a number of countries where food is scarce. The main production problem lies in economically efficient and ecologically sound resource management. That is, the problem is more one of supply than excess demand. But there is more. If one takes the case of "poor" India, one observes that (in 1985) rice and wheat stocks totaled nearly 29 million tons. India itself has sold nearly 2,300,000 tons of rice and wheat from 1981 to 1985. In the coming year it is expected to sell 2 million more tons (U.S. Department of Agriculture 1985: 16). Such observations stimulate further questions regarding the structure of local agricultural production and the structure of markets and trade. If food is scarce, perhaps it is not *caused* by excess demand but rather by insufficient supply, inefficient management, poor distribution, and underdeveloped markets.

The difference in analysis is clear; the first position views hunger as a result of population pressures on the status quo of agricultural production, marketing and social organization, and the projected growth rates of this status quo. The second view states that the status quo systematically produces food scarcity and, further, that its projected growth will not trickle food benefits down to the poor even should a consistent surplus be produced.

In the second part of this chapter, I have surveyed possibilities of human living in the rural economic environment. The question of living in balance and harmony with nature is framed by three types of considerations: the characteristics of the actual physical environment, energy use patterns, and the level of technology, ecology, and management as manifested in various types of social organization. In these variables, one captures the principal types of relations that characterize human existence in nature. In environmental management there are, first of all, many possible opportunity sets. Good policy lies in making the most out of demographic, technical, economic, historical, and political constraints. To my mind the latter are more formidable.

Many observers have come to the conclusion that it is primarily the socioeconomic patterns that cause poverty and scarcity. Such social causes of poverty have been recognized as independent variables that themselves induce an expanding birth rate. Furthermore, in the view of Mark Cohen (Cohen 1977), population is not simply a dependent variable with respect to the carrying capacity of the earth but itself stimulates technological change and thus contributes to the dynamic nature of technology. Most observers seem to conclude, therefore, that the interrelationship between population, energy, environment and food is exceptionally complex. With this in mind, in the following chapter I discuss the technical transformation of the food system and the prospects for the development of scientifically based agriculture.

REFERENCES

Abelson, Philip, ed. 1975. *Food: Politics, Economics, Nutrition*. Washington, D.C.: American Association for the Advancement of Science.

Aiken, William, and Hugh LaFollette. 1977. *World Hunger and Moral Obligation*. New York: Prentice Hall.

Bain, Joseph Staten. 1966. *Northern California's Water Industry*. Baltimore: The Johns Hopkins University Press.

Biswas, Margaret K., and Asit K. Biswas. 1979. *Food, Climate and Man*. New York: John Wiley and Sons.

Brown, Lester. 1976. *By Bread Alone*. New York: Praeger.

Bryson, Reid A., and Thomas J. Murray. 1977. *Climates of Hunger*. Madison: University of Wisconsin.

Chambers, Robert, R. Longhurst, and A. Pacey, eds. 1981. *Seasonal Dimensions to Rural Poverty*. Totowa, N.J.: Allenheld, Osmun Publishers.

Cohen, Mark N. 1977. *The Food Crisis in Prehistory: Overpopulation and Origins of Agriculture*. New Haven, Conn.: Yale University Press.

Dyck, Arthur. 1976. "Population Policy." Harvard Divinity School. Mimeo.

Eckholm, Eric, and Lester Brown. 1977. "Spreading Deserts—The Hand of Man." *War on Hunger*, August, 1–11 and September, 1–8.

Ehrlich, Paul R. 1976. *The Population Bomb*. rev. ed. New York: Ballantine.

Farughee, Rashid. 1979. *Sources of Fertility Deadline: Factor Analysis of Inter-Country Data*. Washington, D.C.: World Bank.

Food and Agriculture Organization (FAO). 1977. "Agriculture in the Year 2001." *Food Engineering*, September, 121–24.

_____. 1978, "How Much Good Land Is Left?" *Ceres*, July–August, 14–15.

_____. 1985. *The State of Food and Agriculture, 1985*. Rome, Italy: Food and Agriculture Organization.

_____. 1985. *Fifth World Food Survey*. Rome, Italy: Food and Agriculture Organization.

Gee, C. Kerry. 1977. *Sheep and Lamb Losses to Predators and Other Causes in the Western United States*. Washington, D.C.: U.S. Department of Agriculture Economic Research Service.

Glaeser, Bernhard, and Paul Steidlmeier. 1983. "Implementation Problems of Rural Eco-development Policy in China." *Internationales Aisenforum* 14, no. 1: 55–79.

Hardin, Garrett. 1973. *Exploring New Ethics for Survival: The Voyage of the Spaceship Beagle*. New York: Penguin.

Harris, Kenton L., and Carl J. Lindstad. 1976. *Postharvest Grain Losses: Assessment Methods*. London: London Association of Cereal Chemists.

Hass, E., G. H. Carswell, and H.W. Cowler. 1979. *Agriculture in Semi-arid Environments*. Berlin: Springer Verlag.

Hicks, C. S. 1978. *Man and Natural Resources: An Agricultural Approach*. London: Croom, Helm.

Hobson, P. N., and A. M. Robertson. 1978. *Waste Treatment in Agriculture*. Essex, United Kingdom: Applied Science Publishers.

Hodder, B. 1976. *Economic Development in the Tropics*. London: Methuen.

Howe, C. W. 1982. "Socially Efficient Development and Allocation of Water in Developing Countries: Roles for Public and Private Sevtors." In *Managing Renewable Resources in Developing Countries*, ed. C.W. Howe, 95–127. Boulder, Col.: Westfiew Press.

Johnson, Peyton. 1979. "Fighting the River Frontier." *Ceres*, July–August, 23–30.

Jones, Harold B., and E.A. Ogden. 1984. *Energy Potential from Livestock and Poultry Wastes in the South*. U.S. Department of Agriculture, Economic Report No. 522. Washington, D.C.: U.S. Government Printing Office.

Kamarck, Andrew. 1976. *The Tropics and Economic Development*. Baltimore: The Johns Hopkins University Press.

Lappe, Frances Moore, and Joseph Collins. 1978. *Food First*. 2d ed. New York: Ballantine.

Leach, Gerald. 1976. *Energy and Food Production*. London: PIC Science and Technology Press, Ltd.

Lindblad, C. J. 1981. "The Potential for Renewable Energy Technologies in the Rural Postharvest Food System in Developing Countries." *Research and Development Abstracts* 9, no. 4: 63.

Lockerate, William, ed. 1977. *Agriculture and Energy*. New York: Academic Press.

Makhijani, Arjun. 1975. *Energy and Agriculture in the Third World*. New York: Bollinger.

Mellor, John W. 1976. *India and the New Economics of Growth*. New York: Twentieth Century Fund.

Munasinghe, Moran. 1983. "Third World Energy Policies, Demand Management and Conservation." *Energy Policy* 11, no. 1: 4–18. World Bank Reprint Series No. 255.

National Academy of Sciences. 1975. *Climate and Food*. Washington, D.C.: National Academy of Sciences.

_____. 1977. *Supporting Papers: World Food Survey.* Vol. 1. Washington, D.C.: National Academy of Sciences.

Paddock, William, and Paul Paddock. 1978. *Times of Famine.* Boston: Little, Brown and Co.

Pimentol, David, ed. 1978. *World Food, Pest Losses and the Environment.* Boulder, Col.: Westview Press.

Rohlich, G.A. 1981. *Food, Fuel, and Fertilizer from Organic Wastes.* Washington, D.C.: National Academy Press.

"Savage Waters That Will Not Be Tamed." *The Economist*, September 9, 1978, 57.

Simmons, George B. 1979. "Family Planning Programs or Development: How Persuasive Is the New Wisdom?" *People*, September, 101-10.

Simon, Julian. 1981. *Population: The Ultimate Resource.* Princeton, N.J.: Princeton University Press.

Sims, Laura S., and Helen Sinciklas Wright. 1978. "An Ecological Systems Perspective: Its Application to Nutrition Policy, Program Design, and Evaluation." *Ecology of Food and Nutrition* 7, no. 3: 173-9.

Smith, Deborah. 1977. "Challenging the Tse-Tse Fly." *War on Hunger*, August 8-14.

Teitelbaum, Michael S. 1974. "Population and Development: Is a Consensus Possible?" *Foreign Affairs* (July): 742-60.

Tuve, George. 1976. *Energy, Environment, Population and Food.* New York: John Wiley and Sons.

United Nations. 1977. *Report on the Conference on Desertification.* New York: United Nations.

_____. 1979. "The Solar Game Stakes." *Development Forum* 7, no. 6: 8-9.

_____. 1981. *World Population Prospects as Assessed in 1980.* New York: United Nations.

U.S. Department of Agriculture. 1985. *South Asia: Outlook and Situation Report.* Washington, D.C.: Government Printing Office.

Winrock International. 1981. *The World Livestock Product, Feedstuff and Food Grain System.* Morrilton, Arkansas: Winrock International.

Wogaman, Philip J. 1973. *Population Crisis and Moral Responsibility.* Washington, D.C.: Public Affairs Press.

World Bank. 1984. *Population Change and Economic Development.* New York: Oxford University Press.

Wortman, Sterling, and R. Cummings, Jr. 1978. *To Feed This World.* Baltimore: The Johns Hopkins University Press.

Yotopoulos, Pan A. 1977. "Demographic Transition." *Food Research Institute Studies* 26, no. 2: 1-15.

Zeimetz, Kathryn A. 1975. "Growing Energy, Land for Biomass Farms." U.S. Department of Agriculture, Economics, Statistics, and Cooperative Service, Agricultural Economic Report No. 425.

4 THE PROMISE OF TECHNOLOGY

The population/natural resources equation cannot be adequately evaluated apart from the technological transformation of the economy. The economy has a double task: to maintain a rate of growth that matches the basic survival needs of a growing population and to fulfill the population's expectations regarding a certain quality of life. This chapter discusses the potential technological transformation of production, marketing, and consumption patterns within the context of farming systems.

The world agricultural and food complex is not one neat system. It is, in fact, composed of many systems. At first glance there seems to be a large potential for expanding food production in the developing countries. But there is tremendous regional diversity. Studies conducted by the National Academy of Sciences (1977a; 1977b) and the Food and Agriculture Organization (1985), and the USDA's monitoring of agricultural and food production (U.S. Department of Agriculture 1983) have confirmed the alarming data already noted in Chapter 3. In many areas (primarily in Africa), notwithstanding technological progress, population growth is in fact outpacing food production and supply. Although in a global sense and in the long run one may speak of the technical potential to solve the food problem, in the short run and in the local or regional sense the hunger problem is not uniform and a general technical solution has proven rather elusive. Specific attention must be given to the many diverse local farming systems. Also, while food reserves and aid may be used in the short run to solve the more pressing problems of supplies here and now, in the long run agricultural development and changes in rural structures and patterns of resource use are needed in the poor countries themselves to raise them to a level of food security. Is such development and change possible?

For some time the agricultural economics and development literature has been skewed. It has tended to favor narrowly conceived economic strategies focusing primarily on increasing production and macro policy instruments. Macro production policies are, of course, of fundamental importance, but, in and of themselves, they are not adequate. Accordingly, increasing attention is now being given to designing comprehensive and integrated approaches to development that would explicitly correlate micro and macro policies and link production strategies with marketing and consumption policies as well as with the building of appropriate infrastructure.

Two shifts characterize recent empirical research. These emphasize the household as the basic unit of analysis, on the one hand, and adopt a farming systems approach, on the other. Inderit Singh, Lyn Squire and John Strauss have provided a concise survey of agricultural household models. These models combine analysis of producer and consumer behavior rather than treating them separately and, in so doing, assess their implications for policy (Singh, Squire, and Strauss 1985). I return to this point in Chapter 8.

The farming systems approach is more relevant to the immediate goal of this chapter to assess the promise of technology (Norman 1982; Toulmin 1983). The classification of farming systems is not an easy matter, whether in terms of ecological characteristics or agricultural uses (Grigg 1974). In developing countries the key differences are between temperate zone and tropical agriculture. In temperate zones, both cultivated areas and yields per unit of land could be significantly increased by employing present levels of technology. The procedure in tropical areas is less clear, yet present investment in research promises to develop newer technologies that would be significantly more productive.

Modern technology embodies tremendous promise in the battle against poverty and hunger. But technology itself only exists as part of a social system. In addition to ecological and biological constraints, modern agricultural technology faces economic, political, and social constraints. It is absolutely vital to develop the technology to increase production in tropical agriculture, for example. But that is not all. Recalling that the poor and hungry in today's world are principally those who do not command the necessary resources to either *produce* what they need or *purchase* it, it becomes clear that technology choice must explicitly link production strategies with resource transfers and income-generating public policy choices. Given the population base of most developing countries, that task is formidable indeed (Johnston and Clark 1982: ch. two). Policies to control population growth remain very important. But more than mere population policy is involved. In fact, it must be integrated with intersectoral planning, fiscal policies, and human resource development. As technology travels from laboratories and experiment stations to the lifeline of the social system it poses both normative questions (regarding human development and the quality of life) and institutional questions (which touch processes of absorbing, adapting and disseminating technical progress). The principal production system in developing countries is the small household-based farmer who typically operates a mixed farming system combining crops and animals. Can such a system be technologically transformed? The main questions upon which economic development analyses have focused are the absorption, adaptation, and dissemination of technology at the local level. In what follows I discuss these points as they affect production (factor accumulation and allocation), marketing, and consumption systems.

TECHNOLOGY AND FACTOR ACCUMULATION

This section presupposes the discussion of the potential of technology for natural resource management presented in Chapter 3. I concentrate on technology as related to other important production factors: labor, management, and capital. What is the role of technology in accumulating these other factors? I organize my remarks around the two main participants in the local farming system: the rural laborer and the farmer manager.

Most developing countries are characterized by a large rural population and work force. Typically, productivity is very low and the standard of living hovers around subsistence. At the same time, capital for investment is in scarce supply. In the more developed nations the agricultural labor force is expected to decline sharply (by 88 percent) over the 1970–2000 period. In developing countries it is expected to increase by 26 percent. The nonagricultural labor force, by contrast, will increase in both by 67 percent and 219 percent respectively (Food and Agriculture Organization 1977).

Such statistics can be somewhat misleading if population distribution between urban and rural sectors is not explicitly taken into account. The vast majority (60–70 percent) of the population in developing countries is rural. Furthermore, it will most likely have to find employment in that sector in the coming years even though urban and nonagricultural employment may be expected to grow significantly. The conclusion is inescapable that even under the optimistic assumptions, the developing countries (excepting Latin America) will for the most part remain predominantly rural societies into the 21st century. The Food and Agriculture Organization (1985: 81) estimates that by the year 2000, Asia and Africa will be 60 percent rural, while Latin America will only be 25 percent rural.

In rural agricultural development, there is some potential in substituting labor for capital in poor countries. Indeed, such a procedure has been followed in using surplus and slack labor in labor-intensive capital construction projects (mainly conservation, irrigation, and infrastructure) as well as in other public works. Many countries have a comparative advantage in labor, and the appropriate strategy would be to select a technology set that complements and utilizes this abundant resource and conserves scarce resources. There is no global estimate on how much these strategies would increase production, yet one may suppose that the results would not be negligible. And the income situation of workers and families would be improved, which suggests that as production increases market potential would be enhanced.

The growth of the agricultural population and of the rural labor force in developing countries obviously brings with it a number of problems. These include providing for the employment and welfare of those in the rural sector and improving the productivity of rural labor in order to meet the needs of the urban population as well as those of other sectors of the economy. The actual statistical picture is not very bright. In the 1980s as compared with the base 1967-71, the average production of agricultural workers has declined in much of Africa, while it has slowed in Latin America and the Far East (U.S. Department of Agriculture 1983: 12, 84, 122). If this trend were to continue it could indicate a decreasing flow of a factor and product surplus from the rural agricultural sector to other sectors of the economy. While a country might adopt a labor-intensive technology so as to both guarantee employment to the rural masses and to conserve capital, it must at the same time take measures to increase productivity. Deciding on policy to economically rationalize the labor/output ratio is the key element to such planning.

Regarding worker productivity in various agricultural systems, it can generally be said that productivity increases together with increased applications of science and technology to the system (granted diminishing returns). But laborers must know how to use new inputs (e.g., machinery and agricultural chemicals) and farm efficiently with them. This may be clear enough in itself, but there are many formidable obstacles to such human resource development.

The mam point is the quality of labor inputs. Poor health and nutrition impede the training as well as any top-level performance of the labor force and thus represent an opportunity cost to many developing countries. Also, new techniques, such as those embodied in the Green Revolution, biotechnology, and information technology, call for increased literacy and training if they are to be successful.

The path to improving the quality of the rural labor force calls for simultaneous efforts in the areas of nutrition, public health, education, and extension. Such efforts will pay off in increased productivity and should eventually provide a path to capital accumulation. To conclude, the prospects for the rural laborer are beset with problems. This is especially true of the landless. Their chances of finding employment with landed farmers are seasonal at best. Further, it seems unlikely that either public works or rural industries will be able to take up the slack. I return to the question of the poor who have no resources later when I discuss power. For now I wish to underline the fact that the choice of technology is crucial for the welfare of this group.

Most discussions of the technological transformation of traditional agriculture center upon farmers who have some resources. The question is how to make those farmers more efficient managers. In its most general sense management involves two principal functions: administration and entrepreneurship. While these functions may be combined in the case of a small farm, they are in fact often separated. Management is a factor that runs throughout the entire production process and represents a set of decisions about the way other inputs are handled. How is "management" accumulated as a production factor and how does technology affect it? The first point to consider is economic efficiency.

There are three main components to the notion of economic efficiency: technical efficiency, price or allocative efficiency, and social efficiency. While the first two are more purely economic in character (at least in the academic sense) the latter involves the social goals of the economy, and I leave it for later chapters.

Technical efficiency refers to maximizing outputs from a given set of inputs. The point is to improve factor productivity. Take the example of comparing two farmers who possess two farms identical in every respect and who use exactly the same set of inputs under the same conditions. If one farmer produces 3.0 tons per hectare and the other produced 2.0 tons per hectare, one would say the first is more technically efficient. Perhaps the difference between the two farmers is to be found in timing, education, or whatever, but the one who achieves higher output for an equivalent set of inputs is more technically efficient.

Price (or allocative) efficiency refers to the situation where, for a given output that is the same in all respects for each of the two farmers, one is more successful than the other in maximizing profits or in minimizing costs. It is clear that two farmers may produce the same thing, but one saves on costs by substituting labor for machines, or gains in profit by selling his produce when the market is at a more favorable position.

The farm manager faces three general types of questions: (1) What to produce? (choices between the combinations of different possible products); (2) How to do it? (choices between various possible combinations of inputs); and (3) For whom? (the assessment of various market outlets and their prices). The economic logic of how a farmer approaches output/output and input/input questions and combines them in a dynamic set of input/output decisions in the light of competitive and/or supported markets has been set forth with clarity by Peter Timmer, Walter Falcon, and Scott Pearson and need not be repeated here (1983). The point I stress is that what must finally be assessed is the *social* logic of management. This definitely includes economic (market) logic but also incorporates political and cultural factors.

What sort of technologies are appropriate for the developing world? Will farmers adopt them? The word appropriate is not easy to define in this case. It is necessarily a dynamic concept that changes along with human, ecological, political, and other conditions in a country as well as across the range of production and marketing systems considered. The literature on appropriate technology is vast and growing rapidly. Here I can do no more than refer to it in a cursory way. Yet this suffices to make the point that it is very difficult to acquire the technology needed for development (Riedjik 1982; United Nations Conference on Trade and Development 1982). The ability to *acquire* technology, either by purchasing it or generating it, is severely constrained by capital and human resources. The ability to *absorb* it (with or without further modifications) is likewise constrained by human resources and development infrastructure as well as by the perception of risk and other economic and social factors.

Only by being efficient in an economic sense will a farmer be able to accumulate capital and open the door to improving his or her technology set. How does a farmer improve efficiency as a manager? Clearly the most general answer is that of experience: One learns by

Figure 4-1. Constraints to Small Farm Household Agricultural Management.

Economic	Cultural
• risks	• traditions
• fixed costs	• values/social paradigms
• supply of inputs	• agronomic practices
• tenancy status	• social institutions
• information	• knowledge
• labor supply	
• agribusiness	
Political	**Technical**
• public economic and rural policies	• pests, weeds, etc.
	• soil quality
• infrastructure	• water
• legal process	• variety
• public order	• new research
• political institutions	• extension

doing. But in a more scientific way, some of the elements of managerial ability can be taught.

Figure 4-1 outlines the four sets of constraints to agricultural management: (1) economic, (2) cultural, (3) political, and (4) technical and biological. It is clear that while education cannot simply remove such constraints it can make inroads in teaching people how to anticipate and handle them.

The issue of the adoption of agricultural innovations in developing countries is indeed complex. Gershon Feder, Richard Just, and David Zilberman have provided a good survey of economic factors (1982). At the individual farm level, adoption is a dynamic process influenced by a number of economic factors: (1) assessment of risks, (2) fixed costs, (3) supply constraints of labor, credit, land, and other variable inputs, (4) tenancy status, and (5) information (extension). They analyzed these factors in light of the management objectives and judgments of the farmer. The evidence supports the conclusion that small farmers *can* be economically efficient and "rational" (in the neoclassical sense) in adapting new technology. But not automatically so.

Political and cultural factors also enter management decision-making in a dynamic way. Cultural values and traditions set the context for economic logic as they define the ultimate purposes of economic activities. Also the political milieu of consultants, bureaucratic planners, extension agents, logistics, social infrastructure, and the overall quality of local and national governments have a definite impact upon assessing whether it is *socially reasonable* to adopt certain sets of innovations. For innovations to be adopted, the *total social calculation* of economic, political, and cultural benefits and costs must be positive. The above study provides many valuable insights, but it does not succeed in clarifying the total social calculation in adopting technical innovations.

In developing countries increasing attention is being paid to nonformal education and extension services as vehicles for transmitting to the local populace some basic management skills. Both the Food and Agriculture Organization (1979b) and the World Bank (Coombs 1974) have given increasing attention to this process. One of the most effective methods employed has been the demonstration effect. This method combines instruction in farm management with actual implementation on the local scene. One advantage of this method is that people may concretely see the good points of changing. But also the new management techniques themselves can be changed and adapted to local conditions of culture, traditional agriculture, and physical characteristics.

In studies of technical innovation among small farmers in Nigeria, a number of institutional factors emerged as important, namely the suitability of the proposed technology with reference to the existing values of farmers and the method of organizing and disseminating information. Innovations, it was found, must correspond to the type of farming system as well as to the resource endowment. The possibility of partial adoption has proven to be important, as farmers gradually become convinced of the advantages of the new technology over the old. At the same time, enabling mechanisms such as the provision of credit and an adequate distribution and extension system are essential.

Successful technical innovations seems to hinge on several key variables: the farm household's aspirations in terms of security and economic well-being, understanding of the principles of farming and a local farming system, and awareness of the different packages of innovations available together with their organizational and institutional frameworks.

Table 4-1 presents an overview of resource use in agriculture for selected countries. The amount of good arable land is limited. As noted in Chapter 3 (Table 3-4) Africa and Latin America would seem to have the most room for expansion by converting forest lands to agriculture. Irrigation, fertilizer application, and the use of machinery are very low in Africa and in most of Latin America. Because of a large rural population, mechanization may be less important. Asia has made the most commitment to fertilizer and irrigation. Also its official commitment to agriculture, while smaller in per capita terms, is larger in aggregate terms.

The pivotal variables seem to be research into tropical agriculture, irrigation, and chemical inputs. I discussed irrigation in the preceding chapter. Here I confine myself to fertilizer, leaving research into new technologies for the next section.

World fertilizer supplies in 1984 stood at approximately 126 million metric tons. Nitrogen fertilizer accounted for 67 million tons of this volume, phosphate 33 and potash 26. The USDA (1986: 11–15) forecasts that production of the three plant nutrients will increase 40 percent by 1990 and consumption will increase by 33 percent. Potash supply is expected to exceed demand. About 80 percent of increased production will come from Canada and the Soviet Union, while production will also rise in Latin America and the Near East. Thirty percent of increased phosphate production will come from Morocco and Tunisia, while the Soviet Union will account for 20 percent. It is expected that India, China, and Mexico will also significantly increase output. Asia is expected to be the largest deficit area for phosphates.

Nitrogen fertilizer production will grow in developing countries with plentiful natural gas resources: Indonesia, Saudi Arabia, Mexico. China, India, and Argentina are also significant producers.

The one area of the world with undeniably bleak prospects is Africa. It accounts for less than one-half of one percent of global nitrogen and potash production and only slightly over one percent of consumption. African phosphates (primarily from Morocco and Tunisia) account for 6.5 percent of production and 1.7 percent of consumption. These trends are expected to continue. Latin America accounts for 5–6 percent of the consumption of the above nutrients, while Asia accounts for 17 percent of nitrogen consumption, 13 percent of phosphate and 6 percent of potash. Asia is expanding both production and consumption most rapidly.

Aside from the managerial capacity to use fertilizer and the capital problems associated with the procurement of adequate supplies of fertilizer, other complementary inputs (such as irrigation) are often lacking. Furthermore, the logistical infrastructure needed to distribute them properly is generally weak. When supplies arrive late, when

Table 4-1. Resource Use in Agriculture, Selected Countries by Region, 1982.

Country	Arable Land (Forest) as Percentage of Total	Percentage of Arable Land Irrigated	Fertilizer Use (kg per Ha) of Arable Land	Tractors per 1000 ha of Arable Land	Official Commitment to Agriculture $ per Caput	Agricultural Population per Ha of Arable Land (and ag. labor force as % of that population)
Bangladesh	68 (16)	20	51	1	7.6	8.5 (34)
China	11 (14)	44	155	8	0.2	5.5 (46)
India	57 (23)	24	35	3	2.0	3.6 (38)
Malaysia	13 (67)	9	102	2	28.5	1.5 (35)
Pakistan	26 (4)	72	62	5	3.2	2.4 (27)
Philippines	38 (41)	12	30	2	8.5	2.0 (35)
South Korea	22 (66)	54	282	3	4.5	6.5 (39)
Thailand	37 (31)	18	18	6	7.1	1.9 (44)
Bolivia	3 (52)	4	1	—	3.4	0.5 (33)
Brazil	9 (67)	3	37	5	2.8	0.6 (32)
Colombia	5 (57)	6	55	5	8.4	1.2 (30)
Ecuador	9 (52)	21	29	3	6.6	1.5 (32)
Mexico	12 (25)	22	78	7	6.3	1.1 (29)
Paraguay	5 (52)	3	4	2	18.0	0.8 (32)
Peru	2 (55)	34	27	4	10.2	2.0 (26)
Venezuela	4 (39)	8	41	11	—	0.7 (31)
Botswana	2 (2)	—	1	2	45.1	0.6 (46)
Cameroun	15 (54)	—	6	—	17.2	1.0 (45)
Ghana	12 (38)	1	10	1	2.5	2.2 (36)
Ivory Coast	12 (26)	1	9	1	16.6	1.7 (49)
Kenya	4 (4)	2	29	3	10.4	5.8 (37)

Nigeria	33 (16)	—	7	—	1.5 (37)
Senegal	27 (28)	3	4	36.9	0.8 (41)
Tanzania	6 (47)	1	4	10.1	3.1 (40)
Zaire	3 (78)	—	1	1.7	3.5 (41)
Zambia	7 (27)	—	15	15.3	0.8 (36)
Zimbabwe	7 (62)	4	53	17.5	1.6 (32)
Algeria	2 (2)	5	21	0.1	1.2 (22)
Egypt	2 (—)	100	335	3.4	8.7 (28)
Iran	8 (11)	25	65	—	1.1 (28)
Iraq	13 (3)	32	15	—	1.0 (24)
Jordan	4 (—)	9	35	4.2	1.1 (24)
Morocco	19 (12)	6	25	12.1	1.3 (27)
Syria	32 (3)	10	27	5.6	0.8 (25)

Source: Compiled from Food and Agriculture Organization (1985: Annex, Table 12, pp. 166–171).

a farmer lacks proper instruction and cannot read or understand directions, and when irrigation facilities are lacking, a fertilizer program may easily end in ruins (Waterston 1979).

I leave most macro policy issues to the final chapters, but one point deserves to be emphasized here. If traditional farmers are to accumulate an investible surplus, what is needed in developing countries is a domestic policy set that allows farmers to make a profit. In that way they would be stimulated by incentives and could also purchase needed inputs. The typical micro-level farm system is based upon the household. There are very powerful social, political, and economic reasons for an agricultural policy to respect this decision-making unit. The overwhelming evidence from rural research is that small farmers *can* be economically rational and that they do respond to the promise of improved technology. The most important thing for policy is to address their motivation and incentives and to facilitate their intelligent functioning. The small farmer can become a more efficient manager if institutional obstacles to managerial knowledge, technology, and capital accumulation are overcome. This issue is socially complex, but it definitely includes getting prices right. In addition, there is a need for extension programs and more efficient rural credit channels from local financial institutions. There are obvious problems of resource accumulation in international rural development today. The main obstacles are institutional rather than technical.

TECHNOLOGY AND RESOURCE ALLOCATION

The economics of poverty comes more sharply into focus when one considers the problem of allocation of resources: what to produce, how, and for whom? The farm-level managerial aspects of these questions have been presented above. My focus in this section is to survey the contemporary prospects of a farming systems' production possibility set.

In this section I concentrate on food production, although many of the points are valid for agriculture in general. A long-run solution to the problem calls for local and regional staple-food security (combining local supply with imports) if not self-sufficiency. Food aid and commercial trade in food products will continue to be important, but attention must be given to basic security in staple food-stuffs in poor countries for a number of reasons.

The first reason is that in an aggregate technical sense the underdeveloped areas promise a greater return for new investments and inputs such as fertilizers than the developed areas, which already face significant diminishing returns to scale and higher costs for further increased productivity.

Secondly, the continued high-level dependence on imports for food drains off scarce foreign exchange from other vitally needed development investments and thus the opportunity costs of imported foods remains comparatively high.

Thirdly, continued reliance on food aid (although its actual costs in a particular case may not be at issue) can function as a disincentive to local agriculture. It does not encourage local farmers to develop agriculture to its full potential. Aside from harming agricultural production, this policy will not expand jobs and, as a result, will keep the rural population poor. In so doing, it will hinder the development of internal markets.

Finally, such a policy of reliance on food aid and imports to meet the basic demands of subsistence tends to lock a developing country into patterns of dependence, where food could be used as a political weapon.

To grasp the actual potential for staple-food self-sufficiency, it is instructive to review the past record and the future potential for food production. Not all products are equally important for the human diet. In developing countries, nonmeat products account for nearly 90 percent of calorie intake; cereals account for about 55 percent. In developed countries, animal products assume more importance as the level of affluence rises, yet even there, nonmeat products account for roughly 75 percent of calorie intake (cf. Fig. 4-3). There are roughly 80,000 species of edible plants on the earth. At one time or another some 3,000 have been used for food. While some 150 have been cultivated on a large scale, less than twenty crops currently provide almost 90 percent of the world's food (U.S. Congress, Office of Technology 1983: 6).

The first question to face regarding factor allocation and food supply is what do people actually eat and—equally important—what are they *willing* to eat. Many studies on hunger focus upon grain, for it is the main component of poor diets. Yet this leaves 40-45 percent of food intake unaccounted for. Policy based on such reductive analysis has many shortcomings (Mayer and Dwyer 1979). Each of the major components of the human diet must be examined in terms of potential future demand and supply. Furthermore, in food planning one should keep in mind other alternatives than the first-world diet. There are five principal food groups: (1) cereals, (2) meats, eggs, and milk, (3) vegetable, fruits, root crops, and pulses, (4) fish, and (5) oil crops and nonconventional foods.

What is the production potential of these food groups? The starting point of analysis is traditional agriculture. During the past century very significant progress has been made in achieving higher yields through processes of selection and breeding. This process culminated in the breakthroughs summarized under the rubric of the Green Revolution. The success of new varieties of plants has been very much linked to complementary inputs such as irrigation, fertilizers, and pesticides. In a lesser way, breakthroughs have been achieved in animal husbandry, breeding, and selection of feeds. The Green Revolution is not without its problems. Most notable are its geographic limitations, the cost of necessary complementary inputs, equity considerations, and problems of funding. But it holds great potential.

At the same time, new developments have been taking place that are termed a "biorevolution." (Buttel, Kenney, and Kloppenburg 1985; Kenney and Buttel 1985.) According to proponents, the biorevolution represents another quantum leap in agricultural technology. Its points of contrast with the Green Revolution are summarized in Table 4-2. The biorevolution overcomes the geographical as well as commodity limitations of the Green Revolution. It also promises less input problems. Even though it is easily extended to the entire population, however, it will not provide an automatic solution to equity problems. One reason for this is that this new technology has been developed more through private enterprise than public funding. Its distribution will accordingly be on market terms. The rural "resource poor" will not necessarily constitute an attractive market. Nor will research be necessarily geared to the production needs and conditions of the poor.

In aggregate terms, the production potential of the biorevolution is very promising indeed. There are eight areas of application, (U.S. Congress, Office of Technology Assessment 1983: 4-5).

1. Promoting underexploited plant species, especially native species already adapted to local climates and conditions. This is highly important for tropical agriculture.
2. Developing multiple cropping and intercropping systems suitable for specific tropical environments as a way to maximize land productivity.
3. Designing integrated agricultural systems that take advantage of the special benefits provided by leguminous (nitrogen-fixing) trees.
4. Cultivating "green" fertilizer (e.g. the azolla plant) for rice production.
5. Using underexploited animal species to meet local needs for high protein food as well as to provide local populations with innovative cash crops.
6. Exploring the use of natural mineral soil amendments, e.g., zeolite minerals, that improve soil properties and extend fertilizer efficiency.

Table 4-2. Comparison between the Green Revolution and the
Biorevolution.

Green Revolution	Biorevolution
1. Selection; traditional plant breeding	1. Genetic alternation at cellular and molecular levels
2. Limited geographic area	2. Large geographic sphere
3. Irrigation/petrochemical inputs	3. Varied (lower cost) inputs possible
4. Limited rural population	4. Entire rural population
5. Limited number of commodities; confined to plants	5. General application to any living organism; including animals, plant tissues, agricultural products
6. Rural resource-poor not an attractive market; high equity problems because of narrow distribution	6. Rural resource-poor not an attractive market; potentially less equity problems because of wider distribution
7. Predominantly public based research	7. Predominantly private based research
8. Medium R&D infrastructure costs; low return on investment	8. High R&D infrastructure costs; higher return on investment
9. Public funding problems	9. Corporate commitment to funding
10. Technology transfer via international public research institutes; public character of discoveries	10. Technology transfer via private capital and market consolidation; legal/market framework of patents and proprietary information
11. Welfare/equity pegged to public policy processes	11. Welfare/equity pegged to corporate interests

7. Reducing the need for commercial nitrogen fertilizer by innoculating suitable crops with beneficial soil bacteria—rhizobia—that biologically take nitrogen from the air and convert it to a usable form for the plant.

8. Increasing a plant's capacity to absorb nutrients by encouraging the growth of beneficial micro-organisms—mycorrhizal fungi—that live in association with some plants.

In a recent study, the U.S. Office of Technology Assessment (1984; 1986: 33-85) identified 28 emerging agricultural production technologies (12 animal-related and 16 focusing on plants, soil, and water.) The principal results are presented in Table 4-3. The methodology employed was based upon several probable scenarios of research, extension and adoption over the years 1982-2000. For the most likely environment, growth rates average a little over 1.1 percent per year, the exceptions being poultry meat production (2.3%) and milk production (5.6%). Scenarios may be quite diverse in devel-

Table 4–3. Estimates of the Effects of New Agricultural Technologies on Crop Yields and Animal Production Efficiency, 1982–2000.

	Actual 1982	No New Technology Environment 2000	% change	Most Likely Environment 2000	% change	More New Technology Environment 2000	% change
corn (lbs./acre) (mt/ha)	6,328 7.11	6,944 7.80	(9.73)	7,728 8.68	(22.12)	8,400 9.43	(32.74)
cotton (lbs./acre) (mt/ha)	481 (est.) 0.548	511 0.57	(6.24)	564 0.63	(17.26)	571 0.64	(18.71)
rice (lbs./acre)[a] (mt/ha)	6,300 7.07	6,540 7.35	(3.81)	7,440 8.36	(18.10)	8,040 9.03	(27.62)
soybeans (lbs./acre)[a] (mt/ha)	1,800 (est.) 2.02	2,100 2.36	(16.67)	2,220 2.49	(22.22)	2,220 2.49	(22.22)
wheat (lbs./acre)[a] (mt/ha)	2,160 2.43	2,460 2.76	(13.89)	2,700 3.03	(25.00)	2,760 3.10	(27.78)
Beef lbs. meat/lbs. feed[b] calves per cow	0.070 0.88	0.066 0.98	(–14.29) (11.36)	0.072 1.0	(29.00) (13.64)	0.073 1.04	(32.85) (18.18)
Dairy lbs. milk/lbs. feed[b] milk per cow per year (1000 lbs.)	0.99 12.3	0.95 15.7	(–4.04) (27.64)	1.03 24.7	(4.04) (100.01)	1.11 26.1	(12.12) (112.2)

Poultry							
lbs. meat/lbs. feed[b]	0.40	0.53	(32.50)	0.57	(42.50)	0.58	(45.0)
eggs per layer per year	243	260	(7.0)	275	(13.17)	281	(15.64)
Swine							
lbs. meat/lbs. feed[b]	0.157	0.17	(0.28)	0.176	(13.38)	0.18	(14.65)
pigs per sow per year	14.4	15.7	(9.03)	17.4	(20.83)	17.8	(23.61)

a. Corn was converted to pounds at 56 lbs. per bushel; rice, soybeans and wheat were converted at 60 lbs. per bushel (1 lb. = 2.2 kg; 1 ha = 2,471 acres).

b. Measures pounds of meat or milk produced per pound of feed consumed by the animal.

Source: Table based on U.S. Congress, Office of Technology Assessment (1986: 80).

oping countries as well as in tropical regions. Yet such estimates are useful in demonstrating that technology is by no means stagnant.

In fact, Table 4-4 summarizes growth in cereal output in developing countries using conventional and Green Revolution technologies. It can only be expected that biotechnology would enhance that performance. The highest growth in yields is found in East Asia and the lowest in Africa, which correlates with patterns of resource use in agriculture noted earlier.

The Office of Technology Assessment also points out that modern information technology is transforming agriculture. This includes telecommunications, which links farmers to weather and price information as well as to researchers, other farms, and related institutions. Secondly, communication and information management on the farm itself is involved, using a central computer system. Finally, this is linked to local area networks providing monitoring and control technologies, managing equipment, livestock identification and feeding, wastes, crops, storage, and so forth. While such a system may be a long way off for third-world farmers, it need not be for extension services in those areas. To return to the five food groups, the technological picture emerges as quite promising.

Cereals

One way of further increasing food grain production is to devote more production resources to it. As was shown, roughly 67 percent of the world's presently used acreage is devoted to food crops. The other 33 percent is taken up with nonfood crops such as tobacco, cotton, and so forth. There are serious tradeoffs between (1) immediate food needs and (2) wider development needs in terms of local industry (e.g., cotton and jute for textiles) and of trade in order to earn foreign exchange. For example, there are potential conflicts in the use of grain (Figure 3-1). Worldwide grain used for livestock feed roughly parallels human consumption. Regional disparities in this "competition" between humans and animals is enormous. It underlines a link between desired more affluent lifestyles and technology choice. There are two main avenues to expanded grain production: expanding the acreage and farming more intensively. For poorer countries, the most promising way out of the impasse is found in new, green, biorevolution, and information technologies. They hold the promise of more intensive farming. Growth in yields for the period 1960-84 are presented in Table 4-5. The highest overall yields are found in East Asia. This is not surprising, given their use of fertilizer and irrigation reported in Table 4-1. Africa is clearly the worst off of all developing regions. Nevertheless, Africa

TABLE 4-4. World Agricultural Production, by Commodity and Region, 1973–1983 (by million tons).

	World			Africa			Latin America			Far East Developing Market Economies			Asia Centrally Planned		
	1973	1983	Annual Rate of Change (%)	1973	1983	Annual Rate of Change (%)	1973	1983	Annual Rate of Change (%)	1973	1983	Annual Rate of Change (%)	1973	1983	Annual Rate of Change (%)
Total															
cereals	1375.3	1643.1	2.37	39.8	45.2	1.14	74.6	98.5	3.11	225.3	316.3	3.37	140.9	372.8	3.91
wheat	376.2	497.0	3.16	46.8	48.7	0.21	12.1	19.4	3.94	32.7	57.2	6.20	35.8	62.5	7.15
rice	335.9	450.1	2.86	49.7	59.6	1.75	11.8	14.8	2.72	150.7	208.5	3.22	139.9	193.6	3.09
root crops	590.9	555.4	-0.36	69.4	82.8	1.93	45.1	41.7	-0.36	410.4	580.8	3.85	168.2	159.4	-0.39
potatoes	312.4	287.7	-0.53	2.0	3.7	5.70	8.6	10.1	2.29	65.3	131.4	7.09	32.9	52.2	4.19
cassava	100.0	115.2	2.17	39.5	46.9	1.87	31.9	28.1	-0.89	247.7	371.5	4.65	3.5	6.7	8.33
vegetable															
oil crops	39.9	53.6	3.97	3.6	3.7	—	3.6	6.5	5.79	89.36	145.4	4.96	4.5	7.8	7.19
soybeans	59.2	79.3	3.97	0.9	2.0	8.9	6.1	20.2	11.03	9.07	15.9	5.47	8.7	10.3	2.50
pulses	42.3	44.7	0.41	42.9	53.9	1.67	4.5	4.8	1.05	127.3	147.8	0.83	6.7	6.5	-0.30
coffee	41.9	55.5	2.85	13.8	12.4	-0.82	2.4	3.7	3.72	0.3	0.5	7.68	0.01	0.02	6.11
cocoa beans	14.0	16.1	1.50	9.6	8.8	-0.54	0.4	0.6	3.97	0.02	0.09	19.72	—	—	—
tea	14.6	20.8	3.52	1.5	2.2	3.79	0.04	0.06	1.49	0.8	0.9	1.72	0.22	0.45	7.55
cotton lint	14.0	14.4	1.22	0.5	0.5	-0.01	1.8	1.3	-2.60	1.9	1.8	-0.57	2.6	4.6	5.38
tobacco	49.3	59.6	2.01	0.2	0.3	2.84	0.6	0.7	1.66	0.9	1.2	2.73	1.0	1.4	5.50
total meat	105.5	140.5	2.90	3.7	4.9	3.30	10.8	14.8	3.56	3.8	6.2	5.11	10.1	17.9	6.86
total milk	413.2	495.2	1.65	6.4	8.4	2.92	27.2	35.8	2.55	33.4	48.7	3.72	2.7	4.5	5.03
total eggs	21.6	29.3	3.22	0.4	0.8	6.05	1.6	2.7	6.19	1.1	2.2	7.53	2.4	3.9	5.24
fish															
freshwater	7.3	9.3	2.50	1.3	1.3	0.21	0.2	0.3	6.19	2.4	2.9	2.13	1.3	2.3	4.86
marine	48.4	57.8	1.57	1.9	2.1	0.14	4.5	8.1	6.43	6.2	8.7	3.22	3.8	4.8	1.56
sugar	76.4	97.7	2.65	2.9	3.9	3.51	23.2	28.6	1.91	8.6	17.1	5.72	2.8	5.3	7.0
bananas	32.6	40.2	2.59	3.5	4.3	1.98	17.3	18.2	0.84	8.7	13.8	5.55	1.2	1.6	4.32

Note: Production figures are rounded and may yield different calculated rates of change than the official rates presented here.
Source: Derived from the Food and Agriculture Organization (1985: Annex Table 1, pp. 126–133).

Table 4–5. Growth in Yields of Cereal, 1960–1984 (average annual percentage change).

Region	Years	Wheat	Maize	Rice [a]	Millet	Sorghum
Developing countries	1960–70	3.54	2.47	2.20	3.19	3.53
	1970–84 [b]	3.87	2.91	2.44	0.13	1.43
By region						
East Africa south of Sahara	1960–70	2.28	0.96	1.10	1.11	0.68
	1970–84	2.73	-0.58	-0.42	-1.00	-0.90
West Africa south of Sahara	1960–70	1.10	1.76	0.15	-0.41	-2.87
	1970–84	1.86	-0.26	1.55	0.03	2.31
East Asia and Pacific	1960–70	6.40	4.30	3.30	7.18	8.82
	1970–84	6.38	4.73	2.85	3.58	4.04
South Asia	1960–70	3.59	1.09	0.89	2.05	0.16
	1970–84	2.86	1.03	2.15	1.40	3.20
Middle East and North Africa	1960–70	1.91	5.00	3.29	1.24	-1.13
	1970–84	0.87	1.87	0.96	5.51	-0.48
Latin America and the Caribbean	1960–70	0.47	1.74	-1.33	-2.46	2.09
	1970–84	2.42	2.19	1.64	-0.12	2.58
Industrial market economies	1960–70	2.22	3.67	1.63	-3.77	2.71
	1970–84	1.56	1.88	0.42	0.16	0.29
East-European nonmarket economies [c]	1960–70	4.07	3.94	5.34	2.35	—
	1970–84	0.73	2.81	0.59	-2.37	-1.48

a. Including rice in terms of paddy.
b. Preliminary estimates for 1970–84.
c. USSR and Eastern Europe.
Source: World Bank (1986: Table B–3, p. 60).

might be expected to grow quickly once the required resources were marshalled. The case of China is illustrative.

China's rice yield increased from 4.13 mt/ha in 1980 to 5.51 mt/ha in 1984; this compares with 7.07 mt/ha in the United States in 1982 and a projected 8.3 mt/ha in the year 2000 (given the most likely environment). Similarly, China's wheat yield increased from 1.9 to 2.9 mt/ha; this compares with 2.4 mt/ha for the United States in 1982 and a projected 3.03 mt/ha in 2000. China's 1982 corn yield was 3.27 mt/ha compared with 7.12 for the United States and 8.68 projected for 2000. While the new technologies are promising, the dilemma of how to finance their adoption remains unsolved. The market is, after all, geared to *exchange*. The main obstacles to increasing cereal production are the acquisition of technology and the lack of capital and managerial expertise needed to apply the most efficient input package. Input supply problems are made even more complex in that they entail questions of affluent lifestyle.

Meats, Eggs, and Milk

One of the most contested questions in recent years has concerned the quality and composition of diet and, more specifically, the amount of meat necessary for good nutrition. The main categories of meat production are beef, sheep and goats, pork, and poultry. Beef and pork are clearly the leaders in consumption accounting for a little more than 33 percent each; poultry is third with about 20 percent of the total. The per capita production varies considerably over various regions of the world, reflecting both cultural restrictions and dietary preferences as well as levels of affluence.

The productivity of nearly all animals, but especially of cattle, pork, and poultry (the main food groups) has been projected to rise significantly during the period extending to 2000 (Table 4-3). Conceivably, this can mean increased competition for land resources between feed for meat production (and export) and food grains for local populations (feed/meat data are summarized in Table 4-3). Poultry are about six times as efficient as beef and three times as efficient as swine. However, other technology sets are available. Considerable evidence suggests that ruminant animals are the most efficient of all (DeBoer and Fitzhugh 1983; Fitzhugh et al. 1978).

A food vs. feed competition would have far-reaching consequences in the poor countries. But such a competition need not take place. From a technical point of view, animals, especially ruminant animals, and poultry can be harmonized with cereal and vegetable production for direct human consumption. People need not give up on meat production. Noncompetitive feed resources are available and can also be significantly increased to allow a high rate of animal and poultry productivity. Animals and poultry are an integral and critical part of the natural ecosystem that must be preserved. The technological know-how is not out of reach. Enough is already known to proceed advantageously if properly managed.

The contribution of eggs and dairy products to meeting nutritional needs varies considerably, depending on dietary preferences as well as storage and processing facilities. Yet there is important potential for increasing food production in these areas. New agricultural technology (Table 4-3) promises yields from present 243 to future 275 eggs per layer. Milk cows are expected to double production from 12,000 to 24,000 pounds of milk. Such gains will not be realized immediately in developing countries. In Africa milk production grew at an annual rate of 2.9 percent from 1973-83 but lagged behind population increases. Egg production grew at over 6 percent and meat at 3.3 percent. In tropical areas there are surely formidable technical problems for livestock and crops alike. But it would be incorrect to deny future potential.

In producing these items, there would seem to be considerable leeway for traditional small producers and household production in rural areas as well as for introducing new methods of processing so that what production there is would not be lost through spoilage. Small farm households in developing countries typically raise vegetables and fruit. In addition they keep two to three pigs, ten to twelve chickens and, if well off, a buffalo. In addition, one frequently finds, rabbits, goats, and even fish ponds. These household animals may be fed some grains, but they generally forage. It seems, therefore, that within the context of existing technology, resources, and patterns of distribution production of eggs and milk could dramatically increase.

Vegetables, Fruits, Root Crops, and Pulses

Vegetables, fruits, root crops, and pulses account for roughly 20-25 percent of the world intake of calories and protein. Thus, while cereals account for nearly half the world diet, the next 15-20 percent derives from these other fruit and vegetable products. Over the period 1973-1983, root crops decreased 0.36 percent, while pulses increased 0.41 percent on the world scale.

In Africa, however, where food production per capita has been declining, pulses grew at 1.67 percent and potatoes at 15.7 percent from 1973-83, but this was not enough to offset the low growth in the area of cereals (Evenson and De Boer 1978; Goering 1979). Citrus fruits declined and bananas grew at only 1.9 percent per year.

Many of these crops would seem to be grown for home consumption and may well escape the statistician.

It may be seen that production of these crops in developing countries does not manifest the same glaring disparities as for other products. The real difference between the two in this area emerges in the lack of development of processing potential in poor countries. Most of these items are highly seasonal and therefore are more susceptible than foodgrains to spoilage, due to lack of storage and processing facilities. Waste in these terms has been estimated to be as high as 30 to even 50 percent of what is produced (National Academy of Sciences 1977b: vol. I). These estimates are very broad; nonetheless, they highlight an important policy issue.

Fish: Mariculture and Aquaculture

In recent years there has been considerable discussion of fish farming, notwithstanding the fact that in the aggregate fish products form a smaller part of the human diet, with notable exceptions as in Japan. More than 95 percent of present food supplies are derived from the land. That the ocean holds fantastic potential is unquestionable (Simmons and Fryer 1978). From 1974–1983, the world fish catch increased at an average rate of 1.8 percent per year. Between 1950 and 1960, the world catch doubled; and it did so again from 1960–1970. From 1945–1970, growth in the world fish catch averaged about 7 percent a year. (Food and Agriculture Organization 1979a.) But since that time, the world catch has hovered around 70 million tons. From 1979–1983 growth picked up to 2.1 percent.

About one-fourth of the usable catch goes into feeds for animals and the rest is for human consumption. The spectre of over-exploitation of the sea hangs over the fishing industry as larger and larger vessels with sophisticated equipment roam the oceans. Ocean management looms as a major problem as most countries have extended their boundaries to the 200 mile limit. With respect to future world catches, there are limits to various types of technology. Conventional measures do not hold great promise. Mariculture (farming the oceans) remains in its infancy. Yet this potential must be added into the population/food equation.

There also has been renewed interest in the economics of aquaculture (raising fish in ponds and tanks), most notably with regard to carp, milkfish, and trout. It is clear that this potential is yet to be tapped (Bell 1978; Brown 1977). Biotechnology is also entering this area ("How Genetics May Multiply the Bounty of the Sea" 1985). Research is concentrating upon stimulating faster growth of fish, as well as on resisting diseases and managing polluted environments.

Oil Crops and Nonconventional Foods

A final area of discussion in the supply of foods deals with noncon-ventional foods, that is, foods that either are natural products but not normally consumed and new foods that are formulated from a combination of natural products. At present such foods do not form a large part of the world diet; many of the new foods are combina-tions of oilseeds and cereal grains (see Berg 1972, for a general non-technical description). The main oilseeds are soybeans, groundnuts, cottonseed, sesame, and sunflower seeds. Soybeans and groundnuts especially are very rich sources of calories and proteins.

The soybean, whose major producers are the United States, Brazil, and China, constitutes roughly 40 percent of the world oilseed pro-duction. China's yields have risen from 1.1 mt/ha in 1980 to 1.26 in 1984. In the United States the 1982 yield was 2.02 mt/ha with a projected yield of 2.49 mt/ha in the year 2000 (Table 4–3). In the West, the primary use of meal from soy and other oilseed products, has been as animal feed. In the East Asian diet, however, soy cakes form a significant part of the human diet. Soy is used in the United States in flours, milk substitutes, and in textured meat-like products. Yet it still forms a relatively small part of the diet even though it is highly nutritious. In developing countries, oil seeds are being dis-cussed as alternatives primarily because they represent relatively cheap sources of protein nutrition, as opposed to high meat diets.

What can one conclude about technology and resource allocation from this survey of the production situation of the principal food crops?

1. Both nations and individual farmers face an array of choices regarding what to produce and how to do it.

2. In none of the five food groups discussed is present technology at a loss to significantly increase supply (either with respect to pro-duction or post-harvest activities). Future technologies are even more promising.

3. The potential contribution of technology is frequently unrealized not because adequate technology itself is lacking but because other social factors impede its adaptation, absorption, and diffu-sion. The principal economic obstacles are lack of capital and managerial expertise.

Thus far I have discussed the promise of technology for resource accumulation and allocation. In both cases the promise is very great.

Why is it not realized? Technology does not exist in a vacuum nor does it "apply itself" automatically; to function appropriately it must be set within an efficacious social strategy. In my view the components of that strategy are as follows:

1. The small farmer (household) as the basic unit of production. This is necessary for a wide variety of reasons including social viability, political stability, income distribution and welfare objectives, and efficient economic production. It does not preclude forms of cooperation (such as cooperatives) so as to take advantage of economies of scale or social forms of management based upon extended family or tribe.

2. The small farmer household will typically engage in mixed crop and animal farming systems that promise technical efficiency, good economic return, family security, and other social and cultural values (De Boer and Fitzhugh 1983: 3, 75–81).

3. A basically decentralized market system that respects the economic logic of incentives regarding what to produce, how to do it (including adopting new technology), and for whom. Market prices serve to (1) pull together and communicate information on the various possibilities of exchange and (2) to indicate the opportunity cost of various strategies. This does not preclude a government role in macro policy and planning issues particularly in areas of market externalities. Rather, it seeks to forge a complementarity between the government's policies and the dynamics of markets.

Technology and Food Marketing

In assessing the promise of technology, it would be entirely too narrow to limit discussion to production. Modern technology is also transforming markets in astounding ways. There are many major market participants to consider; they span suppliers, farmers, processors, wholesalers, and retailers in both national and international areas. Market distribution mechanisms are to be understood here in terms of the dynamics of supply and demand, as is expressed in a general economic model. In what follows, I review the nature of markets and how technology can improve them.

What is a market? A market exists when buyers, who wish to exchange some resource, good, or service or its equivalent (in money) for another resource good or service, are in contact with sellers wishing to exchange similar items. A market is defined in terms of the fundamental dynamics of supply and demand and is not necessarily confined to any geographical location. The concept of a market includes functions of processing, storage, and transfer. In a free market economy, the price system inherent in the market is the mechanism by which resources are allocated. The term "free market economy" refers to an operating characteristic of the exchange system: that the allocative decisions of exchange are made by private entrepreneurs and participants, not a central authority or government. Thus, the majority of decisions are "free," decentralized, and private. Socialist systems develop controlled exchange systems through their planning mechanisms; the scope for private initiative is severely diminished.

Marketing as a specialized activity in agriculture primarily results from production specialization and new divisions of labor. In a system characterized by subsistence agriculture, the producer, "marketing," and consumer functions may all be combined in one person or family. As agriculture develops beyond subsistence a market orientation develops: a sense of producing a surplus and of trading one's surplus product with someone for something else. In traditional societies informal barter markets may dominate; cash markets are not uncommon. It often occurs that one day a week will be the day the farmers go to the village with their products to sell or trade. The Conference Board has estimated that farmers who have between one and ten hectares generally market around 50 percent of their product, and of this portion anywhere from 20-50 percent is generally wasted due to problems such as poor storage (Conference Board 1977).

Modern commercial agriculture differs markedly from traditional agriculture because it tends to be much more specialized in terms of product line and also (on the part of the producer) is less interested in producing for home consumption (being willing to procure what is needed in the market itself). Food marketing covers the many stages that food goes through from the time it leaves the farm gate to the moment it is picked up by the final consumer. The result is that there are many markets, prices, and exchanges involved.

The first stage for the farm commodity is transportation to the processor, who may combine the product with other ingredients to form new foods or simply process it into a more usable form such as frozen orange juice concentrate. From the processor the new product goes to the wholesaler, where the product is packaged in a form suitable for consumer needs (either institutional or family). Increasingly, in developed countries the processing and wholesale segments of the process are becoming integrated vertically. From the wholesaler the food product goes to the retailer; food stores and supermarkets are still the pipeline for about 80 percent of food sold according to the Conference Board study cited above. But institutions and prepared food outlets are gaining an increasing share of the market, especially in the developed world. The middlemen (those between the farmer and the final consumer) are increasingly important in modern agribusiness. Their new techniques of food engineering are instrumental in saving a considerable amount of food and agricultural products from being wasted. Furthermore, through modern transport and distribution, they have been successful in internationalizing many markets that before were only local in scope. This internationalization of markets has, of course, had impacts on the nature of the agricultural product itself as the product has to be able to sustain shipping and handling.

The farmer has to know what the marketing middlemen are looking for (whether a certain species of tomato or a type of orange suitable for orange juice concentrate). The middleman in turn has to be aware of the changing nature of consumer demand. In the United States, for instance, with the change in work patterns and the use of leisure time, an increased demand for formulated and prepared foods has evolved. Higher incomes have stimulated a demand for higher quality cuisine and specialty foods. There are risks and uncertainties in estimating consumer behavior in terms of prices, incomes, and substitution effects. A new product such as "beefaloe" may be a sound product nutritionally as are soy-beef burgers. But if marketing agents fail to meet consumer preferences, they must absorb the loss.

Each marketing stage involves many submarkets in terms of inputs: energy, transport, packaging materials, and advertising. For this reason the food and energy crises of the mid-1970s interacted to exert a double effect on the rise of food prices. Since then, even though food production in the farm sector has recovered in terms of quantity produced, prices have continued to rise somewhat due to energy, transport, and processing costs.

Marketing is dynamic and as consumer preferences change, there are always new opportunities for marketing entrepreneurs to carve out new markets such as natural foods. How can marketing be improved? The promise of technology here is as powerful as it is in production itself. Figure 4–2 indicates typical market problems of traditional, transitional, and market-oriented economies as they are affected by political/economic and socio/cultural forces. This figure also presents some modern market structure alternatives that may be used to confront various market problems. In what follows, I discuss some of the leading points that affect transitional agricultural economies.

Figure 4-2. Some Typical Marketing Problems and Potential Solutions.

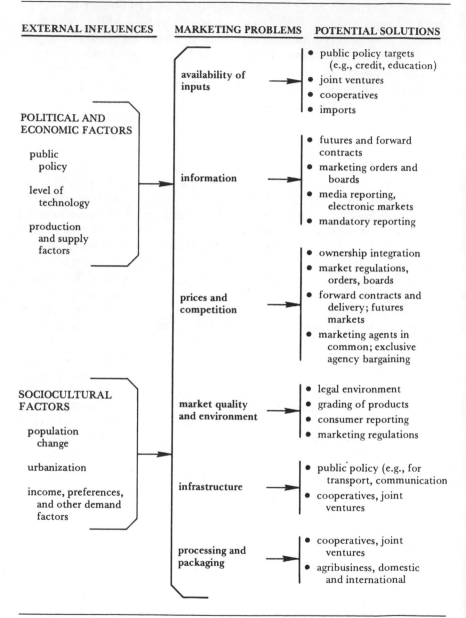

EXTERNAL INFLUENCES   MARKETING PROBLEMS   POTENTIAL SOLUTIONS

POLITICAL AND ECONOMIC FACTORS

public policy

level of technology

production and supply factors

SOCIOCULTURAL FACTORS

population change

urbanization

income, preferences, and other demand factors

availability of inputs

- public policy targets (e.g., credit, education)
- joint ventures
- cooperatives
- imports

information

- futures and forward contracts
- marketing orders and boards
- media reporting, electronic markets
- mandatory reporting

prices and competition

- ownership integration
- market regulations, orders, boards
- forward contracts and delivery; futures markets
- marketing agents in common; exclusive agency bargaining

market quality and environment

- legal environment
- grading of products
- consumer reporting
- marketing regulations

infrastructure

- public policy (e.g., for transport, communication
- cooperatives, joint ventures

processing and packaging

- cooperatives, joint ventures
- agribusiness, domestic and international

Note: Any item listed in the first column under "political and economic factors" and "sociocultural factors" could relate to any one of the six marketing problems listed in the second column.

Source: Derived from U.S. Department of Agriculture (1972).

The first way of improving marketing is transport. For many agricultural products, ease of transport is important in order to prevent waste and also to open up new markets. A good highway and rail infrastructure are absolutely basic to food marketing and to a robust agribusiness sector. Increasingly, too, as agricultural markets become internationalized, ocean shipping and air freight are becoming important to the expansion of agribusiness marketing. As market size is increased, agricultural producers and marketeers can increasingly profit from specialization. Areas that have a comparative advantage in vegetables and fruits, for example, generally produce more than local markets can absorb. Until new markets are opened up, the farm sector must be content with planting alternative crops that are less valuable.

Closely linked to the improvement in transport are innovations in the area of storage of agricultural products. Refrigeration and freezing have revolutionized both agritransport and agristorage and have been the basis of rapidly expanding markets. In many poor countries, where anywhere from 15–50 percent of a harvest may go to waste, food processing could actually turn the hunger picture around as well as provide a venue for earning foreign exchange in terms of exports. Less expensive means of preservation are also available in terms of traditional drying of products and canning. These procedures have been extremely important for both fruits, vegetables, and meats. Innovations in powdering products (milk and potatoes for instance) have also contributed considerably to the building of new markets. Tremendous advances have been and continue to be made in processes of preservation, methods of handling, and materials for packaging (plastic especially) to reduce spoilage and waste.

Thirdly, maintenance of quality is highly important to any functioning market, and thus marketing can be made significantly better by improving the quality of sorting and grading. This is especially true in the area of fruits, vegetables, and meats. In formulated foods, it is much easier to achieve quality control in the production process itself.

A number of other items are also quite important for improving the quality of the market. They include more efficient collection and dissemination of market information either on the part of the government or marketing institutions. Also streamlining procedures to enter into markets, especially between states or countries, is of considerable importance. These procedural matters particularly concern customs' inspection of products and impositions of any taxes or regulations such as labeling in terms of nutritional content. In developing countries, where marketing is not so far along, it is important to improve conditions of sale, access to credit, and the competitive conditions of the market by restricting monopolies.

Perhaps the central problem in agribusiness trade is the volatile nature of prices. Increased productivity and the continual production of surpluses, as in North Atlantic countries, tends to drive prices down. Yet the price of inputs into the first-world food system, which is highly energy-intensive, has tended to drive prices up. Government protection of farmers' income is another component to the price spiral. Thus, agricultural prices represent a conglomeration of economic and political influences, all of which complicate the entry of the poor into the international marketplace.

In analyzing a farmer's production decisions, one of the greatest difficulties is to anticipate future costs and prices with a minimum of error. As much as possible, farmers would like to know beforehand the nature of the future markets they will face for inputs such as seeds, fertilizers, and fuel, as well as the price their final products will fetch on the market when the production process is completed. With worldwide uncertainties such as weather, politics, and economic conditions, the inherent risks are enormous. It is not surprising, therefore, that market mechanisms have emerged to circumvent these risks as much as possible. These mechanisms are rooted in a modern technological infrastructure.

The first mechanism, which is widely used in the marketing of fruits and vegetables that are highly perishable, is that of a forward contract. Before the farming season the farmer will enter into contract with a processor such as a canner or a wholesaler of fresh fruit and vegetables to supply so many tons of the product in question or to plant so many acres with specific price conditions. Thus, the farmer can lock in a profit and the canner can lock in supply without worrying about the day-to-day fluctuations of the spot price or the abundance or scarcity of various products in the year. In eliminating some of the market risks, the farmer also may be foregoing the possibility of maximizing profits should the market price rise way above the contract conditions. This sort of forward contract is straightforward enough. In practice, however, it is clearly possible that the small farmer will be caught in a price squeeze between input suppliers on the one hand and low prices for their products offered by the oligopolistic processors (Lappe and Collins 1978: chs. 35–36).

The so-called futures market for specific commodities, notably grains, some livestock, and precious metals, is a more sophisticated market mechanism (Tewels, Harlow, and Stone 1974). There are two major activities in the futures market: the hedging of farmers and inventory holders and speculation. As has been noted, farmers as well as processors who need a specific inventory are continually wracked by the volatile fluctuations in price and supply that characterize the farming world. They both have an interest in either locking in a price or locking in a supply and so they enter the futures market to hedge their risks. The futures market is a major management tool at their disposal—it is a market where future market positions are bought and sold on the basis of expected or desired profitability. It is a primarily financial market rather than one for physical movement of products.

The necessary component of hedging is that someone be willing to absorb the risks associated with price and supply fluctuations. Speculators do just that. They may be gamblers, but more importantly speculators are providing a form of insurance to farmers and inventory holders based upon their own studies of market conditions and the anticipation of future supply and demand movements of the market in question. Speculators provide a service that producers and processors are glad to purchase.

The existence of the futures market provides three basic benefits for farmers and other hedgers. First and foremost, this market can protect them from adverse price fluctuations (while at the same time they forego the benefits of favorable price upturns unless they liquidate their position and establish another in the market).

The second major benefit to hedgers is the enhanced access to credit that comes with futures transaction. Most capital outlays for the farmer occur six to eight months before the harvest; there is often a problem with cash flow. But in using the futures market, the farmer can present his future sales as security to creditors, thus facilitating the process of obtaining a loan.

Finally, a farmer who hedges gains the advantage of increased marketing options: He or she no longer is constrained to sell at harvest, take it or leave it. But one can gauge sales according to what seem to be more favorable market conditions (in terms of comparative costs such as storage and insurance).

The problems with the poor of the world using the futures market are more practical in nature and focus upon knowledge of the sophisticated nature of the market, as well as the lack of financial reserves. In today's world the futures market is not a tool the poor can be realistically expected to use. In fact, at times it seems to be a structure that uses them. They cannot form it but can only react to it. There is a profound dualism in both the structures and welfare functions of present-day agricultural marketing.

Ideally, the speculator operates within the same supply and demand setting as the farmer. Yet as regards knowledge of the market, he or she would seem to be more of a specialist in its dynamics and orientations. It is put forth by critics of speculators that, by acting in concert, they manipulate price movements in their favor, causing unwarranted price fluctuations such as would not otherwise occur. These critics argue that the price movements create benefits for no one but the speculator. The suit brought by the Commodity Futures Trading Commission against the Hunt family over soybeans in the late 1970s, as well as its numerous other attempts at regulation, provide a case in point.

Some activities of speculators can be seen as stealing bread out of the mouth of the poor. Yet there is a potentially positive function to the market. Indeed, even though many poor farmers cannot use this market, the marketing agencies for poor countries could well use the futures market to ensure a proper inventory of food supplies and hedge themselves against the risks of price and supply fluctuations (Lebech 1979).

If the above discussion indicates general ways in which marketing might be improved by contemporary technology and management expertise, it is also important to ask whose responsibility market development is. First of all, it is the responsibility of marketing enterprises, such as agribusiness firms involved in food engineering, transport firms, warehouses and storage enterprises, and packagers. Indeed, the general underlying philosophy in OECD countries is that letting the market function will, as firms seek profitability, lead to better and more efficient market structures.

Farmers' cooperatives to sell products or to purchase inputs are also a potentially important component in the process. The market must guarantee farmers a sound rate of return if adequate supplies of a product are to be expected. Producer cooperatives can do much to stabilize the lines of supply in the farm movement.

Consumer cooperatives also are becoming increasingly important in the farm marketing process. The consumers are no longer content to take what they find in the market at the going price. Instead, they are asking for clearer information (labeling and unit pricing), higher quality of product and lower prices. As they make their consumer preferences known, this will in turn have its effect on suppliers of agricultural products.

Local and national governments also have a considerably important role to play in the marketing process whether by maintaining competitive conditions in the market, establishing marketing orders, marketing boards, or by setting up an infrastructure that enhances market functions. The government is often charged with procedures of inspection as well as with enforcing contracts between marketing agents. Furthermore, through tariffs, duties, and quotas, it can influence the size of the international market. Finally, one of the most important things a government can do to enhance the functioning of the market is to maintain the value of the currency, which is the medium of exchange upon which confidence in the market system rests.

TECHNOLOGY AND CONSUMPTION

As has been noted, food consumption demand derives from various needs, principally physiological, psychological, and sociocultural. There are two main sources of the increasing demand for agricultural products in today's world. One is increasing population and the problem of meeting subsistence needs. The other, and perhaps more important in the long run, is the demand that stems from affluence. It includes meats and feeds to produce meats, and fruits and vegetables being supplied internationally on a year-round rather than simply on a seasonal basis.

There are, of course, a number of potential food sources that technically can be combined in a vast variety of ways to yield the goal of adequate nutrition. Developing and developed country diets differ enormously in components and affluence. A wide array of diets is possible. The most appropriate approach would seem to be to supplement the deficiencies of traditional diets, providing the requirements of protein, calories, vitamins, and minerals. Traditional diets in East Asia, India, Mexico, and other regions can be improved relatively easily. There is no need to mimic the first world. An optimal diet in this regard would only suffer the constraint of availability; that is, whether the desired products may be produced locally or need to be imported and whether people have sufficient means to purchase them.

Secondly, one can see that each potential diet reflects a different price range and varying quantities of different commodities consumed. While nearly all diets contain similar items, it can be seen from Figure 4-3 that the proportionate share of the diet represented by each item can vary enormously.

Thirdly, if one looks at developing regions themselves, one may observe considerable differences in dietary patterns and the supplies of essential proteins and calories. Latin America reflects the most significant departure from other regions reflecting tastes biased towards a greater consumption of meat (see Fig. 3-1).

To conclude, there are a tremendous number of dietary patterns that are available. Any diet must meet physiological, psychological,

Figure 4-3. Dietary Patterns in the Developed and Developing Countries (Percentage Share of Food Groups in Per Caput Calorie Supply).

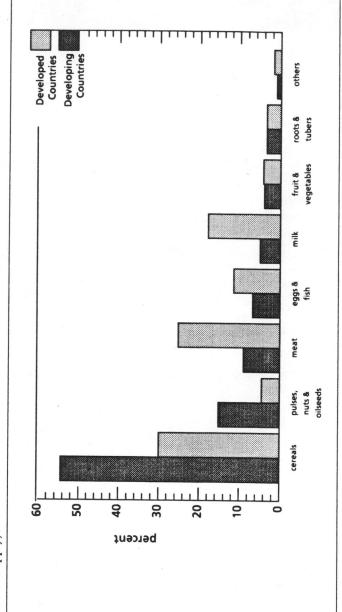

Source: Derived from Food and Agriculture Organization (1977: 24ff; 1986: 78–82).

and sociocultural constraints. In addition, any diet must meet the constraints of a budget. In talking of an adequate diet, therefore, one need not, and perhaps should not, think of imitating first-world dietary patterns.

Technological innovations should begin with existing diets. A wide variety of new foods and formulated foods are being experimented with as human food and also as animal feeds (Mayer and Dwyer 1979). They have considerable potential as dietary supplements. There are four main types of products that command attention: single cell proteins (algae, yeasts, and bacteria); fish protein concentrate (derived from grinding fish after the oil and water is removed and then using it in combination with, for example, white wheat flour); leaf protein concentrate (produced by mashing leaves and pressing out their cell sap); and synthetic amino acids (chemically synthesized and used in food fortification). All of these new foods present questions regarding nutrition, relative costs, and dietary appeal. Perhaps, at this time, the line of research is more important than these particular products are in themselves. For this line of research represents the possibility of transforming traditional diets into more nutritional eating patterns at relatively little cost (when compared with affluent diets) and, by so doing, making use of items that now are largely wasted.

CONCLUSION: PROMISE AND PRIORITIES

In today's world there are growing requirements for food supply. But they are not staggering in view of today's production, marketing, and consumption possibilities in the major categories that constitute food.

This chapter has surveyed the present problems in transforming agriculture in light of the promise of technology. Discussion of related concrete policy proposals is left to Chapters 7, 8, and 9. What is abundantly clear is that the technology already exists to overcome problems of production, marketing, and consumption. Future technologies are even more promising.

In the accumulation of resources as well as their allocation the chief problem that emerges is that of socioeconomic priorities. It is clear that on the basis of present technology, production could be transformed, marketing improved, and the nature of demand partially refashioned. That is, the questions of what to produce, how, and for whom, can be answered in more technically efficient ways. As the persistence of poverty and hunger attest, they are not being answered adequately today. Why not? One of the reasons is power.

Markets respond to effective demand, not simply needs. Effective demand is an issue that rests primarily on socioeconomic power. The production, marketing, and consumption promise of technology has not been realized in today's food and agricultural system primarily because there has been no effective economic, political, or moral incentive to do so.

There can be no comprehensive analysis of poverty and hunger without an analysis of power. This is not to deny relative resource scarcity or relative problems in the genesis, adaption, absorption, or diffusion of technology, but rather to say that the resolution of both of those problems is bottle-necked precisely by the dynamics of power.

REFERENCES

Bell, Frederick U. 1978. *Food Farming the Sea: The Economics and Politics of Ocean Fishing.* Boulder, Col.: Westview Press.

Berg, Alan. 1972. *The Nutrition Factor.* Washington, D.C.: The Brookings Institution.

Brown, E. Evan. 1977. *World Fish Farming, Cultivation, and Economics.* Westpark, Conn.: Avi Publishing Company.

Buttel, Frederick H., Martin Kenney, and Jack Kloppenburg, Jr. 1985. "From Green Revolution to Bio-Revolution: Some Observations on the Changing Technological Bases of the Third World." *Economic Development and Cultural Change* 34, no. 1 (October): 31–35.

Conference Board, The. 1977. *Partners in Agroeconomic Development.* New York: The Conference Board.

Coombs, Philip H. 1974. *Attacking Rural Poverty: How Nonformal Education Can Help.* Baltimore: The Johns Hopkins University Press.

De Boer, A. J., and H. A. Fitzhugh, eds. 1983. *Sheep and Goats in Developing Countries: Their Present and Potential Role.* World Bank Technical Paper. Washington, D.C.: Winrock International.

Evenson, J. P., and A. J. De Boer. 1978. "Role of Root and Tuber Crops in Food Production Strategy for Semi-subsistence Agriculture." *Agricultural Systems* 13, no. 3: 76–84.

Feder, Gershon, Richard Just, and David Zilberman. 1982. "On Exports and Economic Growth." World Bank Reprint Series No. 254. Washington, D.C.: World Bank.

Fitzhugh, H. A., H. J. Hodgson, O. J. Scoville, T. D. Nguyen, and T. C. Byerly. 1978. *The Role of Ruminants in Support of Man.* Morrilton, Ark.: Winrock International.

Food and Agriculture Organization (FAO). 1977. *Fourth World Food Survey.* Rome, Italy: Food and Agriculture Organization.

_____. 1979. *Training for Rural Development.* Rome, Italy: Food and Agriculture Organization.

_____. 1985. *The State of Food and Agriculture*. Rome, Italy: Food and Agriculture Organization.

_____. 1986. *Fifth World Food Survey*. Rome, Italy: Food and Agriculture Organization.

Goering, T. James. 1979. *Tropical Root Crops and Rural Development*. World Bank, Staff Working Paper No. 324. Washington, D.C.: World Bank.

Goldberg, Raymond. 1968. *The Concept of Agribusiness*. Cambridge, Mass.: Harvard University Press.

Grigg, D.B. 1974. *Agricultural Systems of the World: An Evolutionary Approach*. London: Cambridge University Press.

"How Genetics May Multiply the Bounty of the Sea." 1985. *Business Week*, December 16, 94–99.

Johnston, Bruce F., and W.C. Clark. 1982. *Redesigning Rural Development: A Strategic Perspective*. Baltimore: The Johns Hopkins University Press.

Kenney, Martin, and Frederick Buttel. 1985. "Biotechnology: Prospects and Dilemmas for the Third World." *Development and Change* 16, no. 1: 61–91.

Lappe, Frances Moore, and Joseph Collins. 1978. *Food First*. 2d ed. New York: Ballantine.

Lebech, Warren W. 1979. "Futures Trading and Hedging." *Food Policy* 3, no. 1: 29–35.

Mayer, Jean, and Johanna Dwyer, eds. 1979. *Food and Nutrition Policy in a Changing World*. New York: Oxford University Press.

National Academy of Sciences. 1977a. *World Food and Nutrition Study*. Washington, D.C.: National Academy of Sciences.

_____. 1977b. *World Food and Nutrition Study*. Supporting Papers. Washington, D.C.: National Academy of Sciences.

Norman, D.W., ed. 1982. *Farming Systems on the Nigerian Savanna: Research and Strategies for Development*. Boulder, Colo.: Westview Press.

Riedijk, W., ed. 1982. *Appropriate Technology for Developing Countries*. Delft, Netherlands: Delft University Press.

Simmons, Dick, and Leland Fryer. 1977. *Food Power from the Sea*. New York: Mason/Charter.

Singh, Inderjit, Lyn Squire, and John Strauss. 1985. "Agricultural Household Models: A Survey of Recent Findings and Their Policy Implications." Economic Growth Center Discussion Paper No. 479. New Haven: Yale University.

Tewels, Richard J., Charles V. Harlow, and Herbert L. Stone. 1974. *The Commodity Futures Game*. New York: McGraw Hill.

Timmer, C. Peter, Walter P. Falcon, and Scott R. Pearson. 1983. *Food Policy Analysis*. Baltimore: The Johns Hopkins University Press.

Toulmin, C. 1983. *Herders and Farmers or Farmer–Herders or Herder–Farmers?* London: Overseas Development Institute.

United Nations Conference on Trade and Development. 1983. *Working Paper on Finance and the World Monetary System*. Geneva: United Nations.

U.S. Congress, Office of Technology Assessment. 1983. "Innovative Biological Technologies for Lesser Developed Countries." *Workshop Proceedings of U.S. AID, 1980 Conference*. Washington, D.C.: Government Printing Office.

_____. 1984. *Commercial Biotechnology: An International Analysis*. Washington, D.C.: Government Printing Office.

_____. 1986. *Technology, Public Policy and the Changing Structure of American Agriculture*. Washington, D.C.: Government Printing Office.

U.S. Department of Agriculture. 1972. *Improving Marketing Systems in Developing Countries*. Economic Research Service Report No. 93.

_____. 1986. *World Fertilizer Situation and Outlook*. Economics Statistics Service No. 93.

Waterston, Albert. 1979. *Lessons in Development Planning*. Baltimore: The Johns Hopkins University Press.

World Bank. 1986. *Poverty and Hunger*. Washington, D.C.: World Bank.

5 POWER AND SOCIAL ORGANIZATION

Most established development economists in the first world have been wary of discussing power. They either circumscribe it by assumptions that power is irrelevant, that it remains unchanged over the period of analysis, or that one must "realistically" accept it. Market theory, in fact, presupposes that the problem of power has been handled. When the realities of power are faced, it is usually under the sobriquet of "market imperfections," which call for fine tuning. The evidence is that one cannot be so sanguine. The fact is that there are very few, if any, competitive free markets. The imperfections of oligopoly and monopoly dominate the scene and seem likely to continue. Scarcity of final goods and services, as well as of natural resources and other production factors, is a real issue, but it is largely relative to the realities of power and the social organization of political economic life.

POWER, SOCIAL "VOICE," AND PARTICIPATION

Power represents the capacity to control, manipulate, or otherwise influence the social rules of the game and behavior of others so that they comply with one's desired patterns of action and behavior (Wrong 1978; Galbraith 1983). But there are various sources and forms of power, just as there are various motives for compliance (cf. Figure 5–1).

Figure 5-1. Aspects of Power in Development.

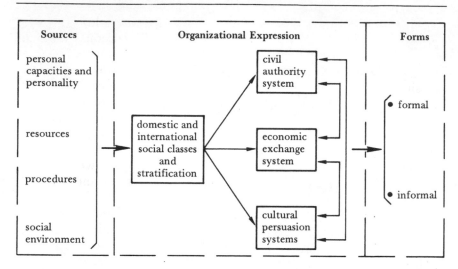

Power may be exercised in formal or informal ways, and in each case it may be legitimate or illegitimate. Formal power is attached to publicly known social rules, offices, or functions. For example, a property owner, the president of a corporation, the head of a department, a judge, or a police officer all hold formal power that is defined within the limits of socially recognized rules, offices, and functions. In democratic societies, power is considered legitimate when it is held with the consent of those who are subject to it. If one considers the example of the ruling parties of various countries today, all can be said to hold formal power. But not all do so legitimately for many have usurped that power and maintain it by coercion. The same holds with property rights.

Important as formal power is, it nonetheless does not represent all there is to real power. Informal power is far more intricate and difficult to analyze precisely because it is not official in the public sense specified above. In social organizations it is exercised in three principal ways: by extension, brokerage, and sanctions.

Informal power by extension refers to cases where people exercise real social power because they have strong personal relationships with those who hold formal power. One of the more celebrated examples of this phenomenon in recent times is Jiang Jing, the wife of Mao Dz-dong. Mao, of course, held power formally as chairman of the party. His wife had no formal position, but during the cultural revolution and its aftermath (1966–76) she exercised tremendous power in China. Within a month of Mao's death, however, she was arrested and jailed.

Brokered informal power is exercised by those who are in key positions or who have special expertise. Specialized consultants and bureaucrats furnish examples of this type of power. Bureaucrats, for example, can delay official approval of projects or obstruct the processing of important papers until they get certain favors. They use their position to negotiate benefits for themselves. Similarly, consultants may broker their expertise in committee work or project analysis to steer policy in a preferred direction; in this way expertise is parlayed into power.

Finally, those in positions of formal or informal power can make use of a wide variety of social and economic rewards and sanctions. They are capable of manipulating the performance of inferiors or of organizing coalitions against colleagues and superiors.

One also may speak of both legitimate and illegitimate informal power although the criteria of legitimacy are much more difficult to define. It may be commonly accepted, for example, that bureaucrats receive some under-the-table remuneration in exchange for approval of various forms. At the same time, there is frequently a social sense of acceptable limits, when such a person has succumbed to greed and overstepped the bounds of informal power.

Compliance with the social rules of the game and the dictates of those in power is very much tied to legitimacy. Legitimation will be treated more extensively in the following chapter. Here I focus primarily on internally motivated assent to the rules of the game, social roles, and strata that a power configuration embodies (see Chapter 2). Note here that when power is considered legitimate in this sense, compliance on the part of those conforming is more positively motivated. The rules of behavior and social roles are internalized. It seems right and good to comply, for the exercise of power is deemed to be just. In such a case there will be more public order and stability. When conformity is motivated by external considerations, such as fear of punishment, and when power is considered illegitimate, then public order depends upon sanctions and coercion and is much more destabilized.

Finally, in the realm of public policy it is worthwhile to consider how power is to be exercised. Direct power, where those in power simply give orders, is not always most effective. In fact it may breed resentment and lead to passive resistance and a loss of efficiency. The communist parties in eastern Europe frequently have had to learn this lesson. Indirect exercise of power is often more effective in building positive motivation and a desire to follow the policy line.

There are many sources of power. The principal ones are (1) personality; (2) control of property, information, and other resources; (3) efficient organization within social systems and control of procedures; and (4) control of public opinion and the social environment. Obviously these overlap. There are also many constellations of power in any social system. The metaphors of "free market," "class struggle," and "center/periphery" all characterize and implicitly evaluate constellations of social power. Such symbols describe power in a social system. Frequently, however, they are used in superficial ways and cover over the continually shifting configurations of social bonds and the patterns of power they embody.

The above has been presented by way of a general definition of power within social organizations. In a social system, however, there are always inequalities in degrees of power as well as different levels of participation. Some people have a dominant voice in society while others have practically no voice. Some participate in leading roles and have major responsibilities, while others are primarily passive and manipulated. All of these considerations are very important when we turn to analyze poverty and hunger.

THE PROBLEM OF EMPOWERING THE POOR

The discussion of population, resources, technology, and even economic method in the preceding chapters must be recast in terms of power. In many ways the antonym of poverty is not wealth but power. The ranks of the poor are primarily the rural landless, urban unemployed, and dependent women and children. These people are powerless in several respects. The first aspect of their powerlessness is found in the lack of development of their human capacities and resources. This type of absolute poverty was amply discussed in Chapter 1. Related to this (and tying in to the notion of relative poverty) are three other areas of powerlessness. These are the lack of impact in shaping the social environment, marginalization in social procedures, and the lack of resources.

How can the poor become empowered? If the poor wear the chains of oppression, they are also a part of their own problems. What is called for is actualization of their own capacities. This has proven to be a very difficult obstacle. Many who would speak for the poor are often dumbfounded by the resignation, caution, and distrust of their clients, who cling to the old ways and beliefs and who find the cure of social engineering worse than the malady. A wide variety of authors from Frantz Fanon (1965) to Mao Dz-dong (1958) and Paulo Freire (1970), have grappled with the problem of the lack of revolutionary consciousness among the poor. Local solutions to the marginalization of the poor are elusive and global solutions seemingly beyond reach.

The key point upon which people such as Freire focus is not simply speaking for the poor, as so-called vanguard parties attempt to do, but on "being-with" the poor. The notion pervades both some forms of socialist thought as well as Christian liberation theology (Gutierrez 1973). As expressed by Freire, "being-with the poor" involves "conscientization" of the poor as well as an identification with them. The aim is that the voice of the poor be heard and that they become self-actualized and active shapers of the social environment.

Conscientization first attacks the entrapment of the poor in poverty and unjust structures by addressing the cultural underpinnings of those structures and by transforming the values and ideology of the poor. It aims to make the poor have hope, desire change, and be agents of reform. In theory, conscientization differs from propagandizing the poor because it derives from a pedagogy that urges the poor to analyze their own experience in their own terms. It is a form of collective self-awareness. Needless to say, such a process of education is slow and painstaking, and follows no easy blueprint. The wreckage of utopian schemes of social engineering founded upon idealistic visions of the peasantry is everywhere to be seen. Some such process, however, is at the basis of any social participation in development and the exercise of social voice by those who are worst off.

Conscientization, the transformation of values and ideology, is a necessary task in overcoming poverty because it de-legitimates the status quo. But there is a concomitant necessity to gain accurate knowledge of modern social systems and to understand their structures and strategies of participation. The complexity of something like the world food system can be quite baffling, leading to useless gestures, frustration, and anger rather than to meaningful action. The basic problem is grasping the dynamic nature of the present social system and using that understanding to effect change. To become capable of functioning in the social system, a major emphasis must be given to practical issues of health, nutrition, and education in order to improve the quality of human capital for development. Only through practical programs can illiteracy, lack of educational opportunity, discrimination, and lack of effective organization be overcome.

A second part of the problem of empowering the poor is that for most people in society the poor count for little. Frequently, they do not matter to politicians and executives in the system, for they exercise little political or market clout. It is necessary to bring about a change of public opinion about poverty. Such a change can be motivated by a variety of reasons, ranging from justice and human dignity to the threats of political instability and the loss of markets that the poor represent.

A third aspect of empowerment of the poor involves resources. The four groups of poor mentioned above lack either the resources to produce food or purchase it. If private property (ownership of resources) is to be considered a social right, it is a right to be enjoyed by all. The right of private property thus provides an argument for land reform. Resource ownership is a very profound question that not only concerns land but the sharing of the ocean's resources, space, and technology. If poverty is to be seriously confronted, the issue of equitable resource distribution must be met. This applies not only to natural resources but also to intellectual property such as biorevolution technologies, which are largely in the hands of private corporations.

What has been said above can be drawn together in terms of building up participatory institutions. As is shown in Chapter 2, there are three basic types of systems that are of fundamental importance: an authority system (such as a government, with its legislative, judicial, and administrative functions and bureaucratic arms), an exchange system (such as a planning apparatus or a market), and persuasion systems (which are not identified with the authority or exchange system in a society, but which function within them: for example, schools, churches, media, artists, or interest groups). It is instructive to consider the powerlessness of the poor in all three.

I am convinced that the contemporary authority system is the linchpin of all development prospects. When government is reasonably enlightened, honest, benevolent, and efficient, then the prospects for development are fairly bright. These qualities cannot be presupposed. When they are lacking, it is very difficult to move ahead. There are two key functions that a civil authority system is responsible for: public order and safety, and public welfare. These functions are carried out in terms of legal and fiscal organizations and policies. They are crucial to the empowerment of the poor with regard to resources, procedures, and relevance to the social environment.

In the concrete area of development, then, it is crucial to begin by examining two key issues: the political legal environment and the budgetary base and processes. These are the bread-and-butter issues that provide the basis for a wide variety of infrastructure and planning measures. Frequently, the poor have practically no voice at all in these matters. Furthermore, all public administration and planning in any area is in the hands of bureaucratic organization and management. This makes it very difficult to incorporate the poor into the system. Prospects for change in social systems cannot be understood without a grasp of bureaucratic organizational politics. The issue is fundamental, and I return to it in the following section.

In the exchange system there are immediate power issues involved, e.g., patterns of ownership and manipulation of prices. Ownership patterns and prices frame the question of power in the marketplace, whether it is monopolistic or oligopolistic. These variables have already been seen in discussing the case of hunger. The market distribution mechanism does not work satisfactorily for the resolution of hunger, since the indigent poor own few resources, have little to exchange in the marketplace, and lack the purchasing power to buy many goods and services. A market is based on the notion of the power of ownership and the ability to accumulate a surplus for purposes of exchange. In bringing something to a market everyone expects to gain. Thus, a market involves command of resources, access, and a fair environment of exchange. All involve power.

Participants in the market hope to leave with as much, if not more, satisfaction from commodities, services, or money than that with which they entered. If the market system is to help solve the hunger problem, power conflicts must be resolved and markets made free of power abuse. Furthermore, markets do not work without profit. Therefore, any market solution to the hunger problem is necessarily based on mutual profit but not a zero-sum game. Moreover, a development project to combat hunger must not only be profitable, but as profitable to producers as alternative investments of capital or labor in the exchange world. No business concern will ever enter the food-hunger arena unless the rate of return at least matches the market rate of interest and compares favorably with the expected rate of return on alternative investments.

For reasons of power and profiteering, many socialists would like to banish private enterprise. The market system possesses great potential to help resolve the hunger problem. But power abuses cannot be ignored. It will always be necessary to take measures to assure fair competition and just prices and profits.

Finally, there are power problems in persuasion systems. The efforts of lobbyists and interest groups and numerous types of informal power are exerted upon those in the marketplace, those in the political arena, and the body politic at large. Universities, labor groups, consumer groups, environmentalists, churches, minority liberation groups, and old-boy networks all participate in shaping the market and authority systems. Such groups refuse to be either by-standers or to be bought off by the favors of the more powerful. The social role of those private voluntary organizations in the persuasion system is to uncover neglected issues, get at the truth, and to make it known. Their chief mode of action is the diffusion of information, dialogue, and public demonstration. Such activity is vital to the legitimacy of social systems. The problem of the poor is a compound one: they themselves are voiceless and few people or groups speak effectively on their behalf.

Perhaps no thinker has stimulated more thought on poverty and power than Marx. I have already distinguished my approach from neoclassical economics. I now distinguish it from neo-Marxist thought. In contrast to economics, the sociology of development has been fairly dominated by neo-Marxist analysis (dependency theory, the necessity of social relations emanating from capitalist modes of production, and the historical role of the working classes [Amin 1977; Baran and Sweezy 1968]). Those who criticize modernization models of development in terms of dependency theory have raised a number of good questions. I quite agree with David Booth, however, that contemporary development sociology has reached an impasse (Booth 1985). The impasse derives not so much from the questions asked (although there are some lacunae here) but in dogmatic deductions of the *necessity* of observed patterns of social relations from *theories* of capitalist exchange. The result is a procrustean bed where facts are fitted to theory.

As Booth points out there is a torrid debate among sociologists, economists, and political scientists over dependency theory. This criticism comes from the left as well as from the right. Szymanski, for example, takes Bornschier (1978) apart on the grounds of ortho-dox Marxist thought (Szymanski 1981). Dependency theory is criti-cized for being little more than tautology, for faulty deductions from weak theoretical postulates, and for weak empirical work (Booth 1985). The latter has been especially damaging as work done by Jackman (1982) and Muller (1984) show.

Why is the dependency metaphor attractive? There are a number of reasons. First, there is the legacy of the Monroe doctrine. There is ample evidence that this doctrine is still alive. It had led to the very unfortunate conclusion that the United States and Western Europe play a deceptive game with talk of democracy and markets. Their domestic institutions of politics and markets are very different than their international practice of supporting established oligarchies that are economically exploitive and politically authoritarian. Add to this the disillusionment with what passed for "development." The

Mexican and Brazilian growth "miracles" of the '70s were highly dualistic. Whatever "development" was, it did not reach the masses of the poor. Perhaps more than anything, *growth with poverty* caused the rejection of the modernization model and concomitant hostility towards the transnationals and the capitalist world.

Dependency theory has been wide and varied. There are a number of operative hypotheses that recur. These are:

1. The nature and quality of third-world political and economic institutions is a by-product of past and continuing relations between the core (OECD) capitalist countries and the peripheral client states (dominated by local elites who are in league with first-world leaders). This argument presents a variant of international class struggle. There is no self-sustaining growth in LDCs, and the terms of trade and international finance as well as resource control disproportionately benefit the elite classes.

2. A second thesis is more precise and focuses on deteriorating income distribution (Bornschier et al. 1978), social marginalization, and authoritarian politics that results from the rules of trade and finance, the role of TNC's, and the transfer of inappropriate technology and/or cultural alienation.

3. A third thesis rests upon the type of exploitive social relations (of the masses by the elite) that *necessarily* follow from capitalist modes of production and exchange.

In third-world circles a hybrid "common-sense dependency theory" has come to dominate highly ideological models. The common-sense view rests on basic questions that any well-informed person can ask:

1. Where does the third world find its primary market opportunities?
2. Who primarily controls GATT (and market barriers, etc.)?
3. What counts as foreign exchange?
4. Who primarily controls the IMF?
5. Who primarily imposes conditions on foreign investment and aid?
6. Who primarily controls present technology as well as R&D capacity?
7. Who provides support for "X" to stay in power?
8. What are the primary sources of information as well as of cultural commodities (programming, music, style)?

The principal answer to all of the above are OECD governments and/or OECD-based corporations. This has led dependency theorists to primarily view their plight in terms of external factors, although the various links are difficult to measure precisely (Gereffi 1984).

Dependency proponents can be criticized for a number of weaknesses. First, they generally neglect a solid critique of internal factors. If U.S. interference and strong TNC presence spell the formula for poverty, why is Canada not as poorly off as Mexico? Why is it that Taiwan and South Korea have done significantly better regarding poverty and income distribution than Mexico and Brazil (with no less authoritarian regimes) (Jackman 1982; Muller 1984)?

Secondly, Marxist literature on the poor reminds one of Rousseau's noble savage. It is supposed that none of the capitalist vices afflict them. Most ingenuously of all, solidarity among the poor is presupposed. There is too much evidence that the poor of one caste, ethnic group, or religion have little solidarity with poor of other origins. It is true that in Marxism one finds a *logical* explanation in terms of false consciousness and enemies of the people. But such dogmatic assertions stand upon flimsy historical evidence and have little explanatory power. They derive from a dogmatic belief in theory.

Thirdly, the Marxist analysis of power remains flawed. Not that it has failed to uncover exploitive social relations, but the vanguard party model (based as it is on an erroneous vision of the noble poor) has never historically led to anything but bureaucratic and coercive statism. I am not arguing this as some new law of history! But I am suggesting that the nature of bureaucratic power has not been understood.

Fourthly, the meaning and role of culture in development has not been understood in a positive way. Too often it is understood as false consciousness, an opiate to keep the masses in line. (This view, by the way, is particularly evident in the Ministries of Culture in contemporary socialist states.) The positive liberating and creative force of culture remains unexplored.

Lastly, the Marxist approach to social change is too narrowly confined to class conflict and is not clearly related to other mechanisms and agents of change. Third-world dependency on a capitalist first world leaves unexplained such things as patterns of dependency on a socialist second world (as in the case of Viet Nam, Mongolia, and Cuba), differences among third-world states (e.g., Taiwan, Kenya, Mexico), and why third-world countries have developed so little meaningful interdependence among themselves (removing trade restrictions, collaborating in research, and common currency agreements).

To conclude, a great debt is owed to Marx and the neo-Marxist traditions. But their value resides more in their method of inquiry than in their theoretical responses. The main contribution of dependency theory is its demand that power in development models be examined.

The dynamic processes of policy and the actions of participants in development can best be understood within a framework of social organization and power. In this context, the seeming resource scarcity and unequal diffusion of technology noted in previous chapters can be seen to represent problems of distribution and of social systems. I now discuss power in international development under three general rubrics: resources, procedures, and the social environment.

THE CRISIS OF RESOURCES IN INTERNATIONAL DEVELOPMENT

There can be no substitute for an in-depth study of each third-world country to get a clear picture of its resource endowment and to grasp its potential for development. Surprisingly, many countries to date have no such profile of their resources and growth potential. The general resource conditions of poor people was presented in Chapter 1. What follows here is more macro in nature and sketches some broad outlines of problems that many countries share in varying degrees. The basis of analysis will be power structures as they affect the fundamental factors of production (management and institutional factors are left to the next section). I discuss in turn plentiful resources and scarce resources.

As noted in Chapters 3 and 4, the plentiful resources for most countries are the goods of nature (land, climate, water) and labor. Agriculturally, for instance, most countries possess both the natural and human resources to be self-sufficient in food. Productivity is often very low, however, because the quality of natural and human resources is low and complementary inputs (such as tools and fertilizers) are lacking. The improvement of the quality of the relatively plentiful resources is constrained by the problem of scarce resources, namely, capital, management, and technology. The main problem is that financial capital, which is needed to purchase resources (such as machinery, technology and management skills) is in very short supply. This means that developing countries face severe constraints in building up physical capital. Financial capital accumulation and investment is the indispensable key to economic growth. For only such investment can lead to new productive capacity and, in so doing, create jobs for workers, as well as generate the production of goods and services to meet the needs of the population. The most serious problem facing developing countries today is to amass an investible surplus of financial capital. This is partially because the existing power structures are an obstacle to capital accumulation.

How can today's developing countries get their hands on capital for investment? There are three main ways: (1) earn it and save it, (2) borrow it, or (3) be given it. Each way has a price and raises issues of power. An investible surplus can derive from saving some of the revenue one has rather than spending it on nonproductive consumer goods and services. A country can earn revenue from either domestic or international markets. But when we think of that country saving some revenue in order to buy capital goods, management skills, new technology, or necessary resources (such as petroleum), there is a new twist. Most of those items are purchased with foreign exchange currency (unless a certain trade agreement allows barter in kind or the use of the country's own currency). This means that a country must not only save but must save hard currencies (first world currencies) or else pay in gold or on the basis of its position with the IMF (in terms of its holding of special drawing rights (SDRs) or its credit position). What are the prospects for poor countries to finance development?

Regarding domestic sources of savings, poor countries have bleak prospects. When a large part of the population lives at the subsistence level, they do not save, do not constitute a strong market for domestic goods, cannot pay much in taxes, and surely do not make up a market for financial instruments such as stocks and bonds. Furthermore, growing levels of population tend to consume whatever growth takes place so that no surplus builds up (the so-called vicious circle) (Todaro 1981).

Because the domestic markets hold so little potential (due in part to poor domestic policy), most countries depend on the international economy to accumulate their savings for investment. There they confront four main sources: private foreign investment, aid from foreign governments, earnings from their own trade exports, and borrowing on international financial markets. In the world economy today there are problems with all of these sources. (See Figure 5-2 and Tables 5-1 through 5-3).

Private foreign investment introduces the difficulty of dealing with the transnational corporations. In theory, the investment made by transnationals could be harmonized with local development plans and serve the mutual interests of both parties. Often enough in practice this is not the case, as the transnationals seek their own set of

Figure 5-2.   The Global Research and Development Budget.

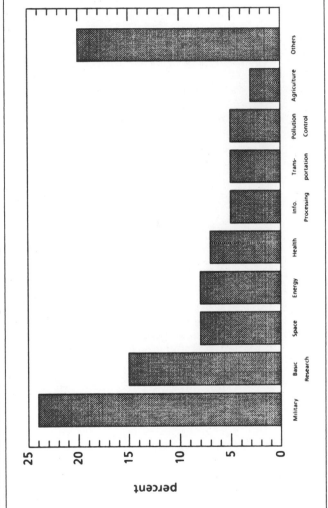

Source: Derived from Norman (1979: 6).

Table 5-1.   Terms of Trade and Purchasing Power of Selected Developing
Countries, 1970–1983.

Country	Terms of Trade (1980 = 100)			Purchasing Power of Exports (1980 = 100)		
	1970	1979	1983	1970	1979	1983
Low-income Africa						
Benin	177	116	75	193	88	57
Burundi	—	—	—	—	—	—
Central African Rep.	106	100	97	86	77	101
Ethiopia	156	139	86	132	133	101
Ghana	110	137	63	162	104	43
Guinea	—	—	—	—	—	—
Kenya	99	108	89	125	113	66
Madagascar	113	104	93	172	134	77
Malawi	138	112	126	74	97	89
Mozambique	112	104	96	197	94	39
Rwanda	79	89	66	114	177	117
Sierra Leone	146	122	94	202	131	64
Tanzania	108	106	91	214	129	79
Togo	73	109	107	60	77	63
Uganda	92	103	79	276	141	101
Zaire	198	114	92	191	100	37
Low-income Asia						
Bangladesh	140	99	107	256	105	115
India	177	119	98	122	130	108
Sri Lanka	132	128	98	159	129	123
Middle-income oil importers						
Brazil	169	114	92	73	106	115
Chile	284	115	90	132	115	89
Colombia	82	91	90	60	94	87
Guatemala	126	92	83	82	105	84
Jordan	112	103	101	26	90	112
Ivory Coast	110	120	102	65	106	71
Korea, Rep. of	142	128	100	22	117	152
Liberia	189	122	104	161	121	79
Mauritania	178	103	102	165	92	179
Morocco	97	115	99	84	105	100
Philippines	207	112	117	102	108	92
Senegal	101	111	88	134	146	124
Zambia	263	119	82	299	74	84

Table 5-1.   continued

Country	Terms of Trade (1980 = 100)			Purchasing Power of Exports (1980 = 100)		
	1970	1979	1983	1970	1979	1983
Middle-income oil exporters						
Algeria	18	65	102	20	70	93
Egypt	98	97	105	102	74	123
Indonesia	26	74	103	18	84	109
Mexico	56	78	105	29	66	153
Nigeria	19	68	94	15	74	48
Peru	155	100	109	112	114	85
Syria	23	74	105	38	94	104
High-income oil exporters						
Libya	17	67	98	36	84	57

Source: World Bank (1986: Tables B-4, B-5, pp. 61–62).

priorities and introduce unfavorable patterns of resource use, which in the long run damage the overall pattern of development (Turner 1976; B. Dinham and C. Hines 1984).

This point bears more consideration. Take the example of resource allocation. There is currently a profound dualism between international commercial agriculture and local subsistence agriculture. Indeed, the two are often seemingly on a collison course regarding the distribution of technology and the allocation of scarce resources (Kotzsch 1985; Danaher 1985). The term "cash crops" (for export rather than staple food crops for domestic consumption) is frequently used in a way that is rather imprecise. Nonetheless, as a body of literature has grown up on the subject, it is worthwhile clarifying the terms. In this context, food crops refer to crops grown to meet the nutritional needs of the locality or region under consideration. In this sense, they would be better termed basic domestic need food crops. Cash crops are all those agricultural products produced for the (primarily export) commercial market; the dynamics of production decisions in this case are concerned with profitable market exchange rather than giving explicit attention or priority to local subsistences needs. Cash crops may be industrial crops such as tobacco, cotton, and jute, or they may be food crops intended for affluent interna-

Table 5–2a. Debt of Developing Countries, 1984.

Region	Debt $ Billion	Ratio of Debt to GNP (%)	Ratio of Debt to Exports (%)	Debt Service Ratio (%)	Ratio of Interest Service to GNP (%)	Private Debt as Percentage of Total
All Developing Countries	686	33.8	135.4	19.7	2.8	65.0
Low Income Asia	53	9.7	100.0	8.4	0.3	16.7
Low Income Africa	27	54.5	278.1	19.9	2.1	18.4
Major Exporters of Manufactures	267	37.6	109.1	16.0	3.6	76.9
Other Middle Income Oil Importers	108	53.0	183.9	24.9	3.9	49.3
Middle Income Oil Exporters	232	43.8	164.2	28.1	4.0	75.1

Source: World Bank (1985: 24).

Table 5–2b.   Estimates of Net Capital Flight in Selected Developing Countries, 1976–1985, and Nonbank Residents' Deposits in Foreign Banks, 1985.

	Net Direct Investment Inflows	Change in Gross External Debt	Current Account Balance[a]	Change in Selected Gross Foreign Assets[b]	Capital Flight[c]			Nonbank Residents' Deposits		
					Total	1976–82	1983–85	Total in All Foreign Banks[a]	Banks in U.S.[b]	Other in Foreign Banks
Argentina	4	42	-15	-4	-26	-27	1	8.2	4.1	4.1
Bolivia	0	3	-2	-0	-1	-1	0	0.4	n.a.	n.a.
Brazil	20	80	-77	-13	-10	-3	-7	8.5	1.7	6.8
Chile	2	16	-16	-3	1	0	1	2.2	1.6	0.6
Colombia	2	10	-11	-2	0	0	0	1.6	1.8	0.8
Ecuador	1	7	-5	-1	-2	-1	-1	1.3	0.7	0.6
Mexico	11	75	-29	-3	-53	-36	-17	15.3	11.1	4.2
Peru	0	8	-6	-2	-0	1	-1	1.5	1.0	0.5
Uruguay	1	4	-3	-1	-1	-1	-0	2.0	1.2	0.8
Venezuela	-0	26	10	-5	-30	-25	-6	12.6	7.1	5.5
Subtotal	40	270	-154	-33	-123	-93	-30	54.6	30.3	24.3
India	0	22	-8	-5	-10	-6	-4	1.7	0.1	1.6
Indonesia	2	27	-15	-9	-5	-6	1	0.7	0.2	0.5
Korea	0	40	-22	-6	-12	-6	-6	0.4	0.1	0.3
Malaysia	9	19	-12	-4	-12	-8	-4	1.0	0.0	1.0
Nigeria	2	18	-15	4	-10	-7	-3	1.4	n.a.	n.a.
Philippines	1	23	-16	1	-9	-7	-2	1.1	0.7	0.4
South Africa	-2	16	2	2	-17	-13	-4	1.3	0.0	1.3
Thailand	2	17	-17	-1	-0	1	-1	0.4	0.2	0.2
Subtotal	14	181	-102	-18	-75	-52	-23	8.0	1.3	6.7
Total for 18 countries	54	451	-256	-51	-198	-145	-53	62.6	31.6	31.0

a. Minus sign indicates a deficit.
b. Minus sign indicates an increase in *foreign* assets by official monetary authorities and commercial banks.
c. Includes nonbank and private activity in capital flight.
Source: Morgan Guaranty Trust (1986: Tables 10, 11, pp. 13–15).

Table 5 – 3.   Power in Procedures: Access to and Participation in Social Structures.

1. *Enabling formation: Development of personal capacities*
    - education
    - health/nutrition

2. *Due legal process*
    - effective domestic and international law
    - eradication of corruption and special privilege

3. *Strategies for operating in bureaucracies*
    - lobbying and special interests
    - developing effective voice: organization and coalitions

4. *Rules of the game in international bodies*
    - UN Bodies
    - IMF and international capital
    - GATT, Lome, and trade conventions
    - Intellectual Property and Technology Transfers

5. *Intergovernmental relations*
    - Bilateral and Multi-lateral accords
    - Building effective international law/codes of conduct
    - geopolitical concerns

6. *Private investment*
    - establishing a favorable "Business Climate"
    - repatriation of profits
    - licenses, patents, technology transfers
    - joint ventures and wholly owned subsidiaries
    - bribery and corruption

tional markets such as strawberries, coffee, cocoa, avocados, bananas, and other fruits and vegetables that may be grown in warm southern regions for winter markets in cold and temperate areas. The key issues in the debate are priorities in the allocation of scarce resources: The question is not only what to produce and how but for whom? For example, is land and fertilizer to be given over to tobacco or rice, or to strawberries or maize, to meet the wants of the rich or the needs of the poor? This is not only an economic problem but a moral problem of just distribution.

Numerous examples can be multiplied regarding the dilemma between subsistence needs and the international commercial market. But taken together they emphatically underline the priority of meeting human needs in the political economy and public policy. The projections of per capita food commodity consumption, the implied "food deficit," and shortages predicted in contemporary literature precisely presuppose the continuation of present trends. That may be "practical," but it doesn't address the most fundamental issues: The market responds to power and profits, not a person's needs. It is in light of such historical conditions that some have been prompted to ask whether the market ought not to be moderated by a more equitable allocation system. In my opinion, planning is not the only alternative. Rather, much can be done to improve the quality of markets.

Intergovernmental aid is disputed almost as much as private investment. Bilateral aid from the richer countries often comes with little or no economic costs and would for that reason seem to be attractive. But the political costs, both in terms of international loyalties as well as domestic interference, can be and often are quite exacting. There is no reason in theory why intergovernmental aid could not work favorably. The point is, that very frequently it does not, either because of outright abusive power or because of diverging geopolitical or economic interests (Lappe et al., 1981).

There are problems both with private investment and aid. This leaves the local country with earnings or borrowing as the preferred means to accumulate an investible surplus. It is these two latter issues that dominated the agenda for UNCTAD VI.

Export earnings are blocked on two levels (Table 5-1). Firstly, many countries export raw materials. But the prices they receive for those exports tend to be low and unstable. They are low both in the sense that they do not generate much income and with reference to the prices of capital goods that developing countries want to import from the first world. That is, their terms of trade (the ratio of prices they receive to the prices they pay) and the purchasing power of their exports are deteriorating for most developing countries— recently even for OPEC countries.

Many developing countries have seen that they could realize a greater capital surplus from trade as well as create jobs if, instead of exporting raw materials, they exported processed and manufactured goods, e.g., export lumber instead of timber or shoes instead of leather. The problem is that they want to export these goods primarily to the first and second worlds, where they increasingly find protectionist trade barriers. So this otherwise theoretically attractive way to increase both domestic and foreign earnings is blocked to a considerable degree.

Countries that turn to borrowing do not necessarily find brighter prospects (Table 5-2a). Semi-public sector funds, such as the World

Bank, various regional development banks, and OPEC and EEC funds, in reality have very little money to give out. These sources of funds are attractive for they generally bear a low rate of interest, and they are also relatively free of the political pressures of bilateral aid. But they depend on the affluent countries for their loanable funds, and those nations generally prefer bilateral deals that increase their own leverage and benefits. Third-world debt is almost $700 billion and should continue to grow. The World Bank has less than $20 billion to give out each year. It is clear that borrowing is and will increasingly be in the hands of the multinational banks of the private sector (Table 5-2, column 7).

Private banks are willing to lend money but only on "market terms"; that is, with a high rate of interest and strong collateral. Recent figures confirm that only fifteen resource-rich countries receive about 75 percent of all private sector loans. For the private sector, the poor fifth-world countries (the forty-four "most seriously affected" countries listed in Chapter 1) do not represent an interesting market. The private debt of low-income Africa and Asia is less than 20 percent. Even so, all is not well for the countries that do receive loans because many of them face crushing debt burdens and can barely even cover the interest payments. In developing countries the average debt service ratio is 20 percent.

The ins and outs of the international economic system are obviously complex. Yet it is not too difficult to grasp the main outlines of the problem. The growth and development of poor countries is above all blocked by the lack of financial capital that is needed to make investments necessary for economic growth. The main issue is power. Power to accumulate economic resources; power to produce something with them; power of access to markets; power to accumulate an investible surplus of capital.

For most countries, there are grave problems with both domestic as well as international sources of such an investible surplus. In this regard one of the more astonishing facts to come to light is the flight of capital from debt-ridden third-world countries (Table 5-2b). The Morgan Guaranty Trust Company has attempted to measure the magnitude of the problem (1986). Since capital flight cannot be measured directly, the method used in this study was to add the first four columns of Table 5-2b. Morgan Trust admits problems of methodology but is nonetheless convinced that the magnitude of capital flight remains understated, in a few cases by as much as half.

During the decade 1976-85 the eighteen countries listed in the table accumulated some additional $450 billion in foreign debt, while losing nearly $200 billion in capital flight. The impact of capital flight on debt is considerable. Without capital flight Argentina would have a debt of $1 billion rather than $50 billion; Mexico $12 billion rather than $97 billion; Malaysia $4 billion rather than $20 billion; Nigeria $7 billion rather than $19 billion; the Philippines $15 billion rather than $27 billion; Brazil $92 billion rather than $106 billion; and Venezuela a surplus of $12 billion rather than a debt of $31 billion.

As shown in columns 8, 9 and 10 of Table 5-2b, private deposits in first-world banks from developing countries total $62.6 billion; 87 percent of that is from Latin America. Nearly half the funds are held in the United States.

Some capital flight is legal. That is, people are exporting capital that they honestly earned and doing so in accordance with the applicable laws. Some is illegal, even though people are exporting what they have honestly earned. Corruption may take place even when transactions are legal—the laws are corrupt. Most often corruption involves circumventing laws and stealing funds. This is done in a number of ways: misreporting of invoices and currency valuation effects, using shell corporations, getting unsecured loans, manipulating export and import prices, siphoning off foreign aid, and draining the central bank.

What emerges from all this is that capital flight is a significant part of the debt problem. It revolves essentially around the power of local elites.

Capital accumulation is a very difficult problem to sort out. There are clear problems of power. At the same time poverty itself is one of the main reasons why it is difficult to produce a domestic surplus; a subsistence economy has little scope for savings. On the international scene today, private investment, aid, export earnings, and borrowing are all circumscribed by grave problems, all of which combine to lead to the same result: a crippling insufficiency of funds.

Even if a country manages to accumulate funds from either domestic or international sources, its troubles are not over. It must deal with the complex and fluctuating markets of foreign reserves. A country's foreign reserve position is its holdings of foreign exchange, gold, special drawing rights (SDRs), and line of credit with the IMF. Even if a country could scrape together some domestic savings, it has to jump into the foreign reserve market in order to gain some international purchasing power. There are a number of problems involved in this area also, the most important being fluctuations in the price of gold and in currency exchange rates (themselves influenced by inflation). Most countries try to build up a diversified portfolio of foreign reserves that will at least maintain a stable value if not increase. Needless to say, such portfolio management is a crucial factor and represents another difficulty in the crisis of resources. There has been considerable talk on this point of the need for stability in reserves either by returning to fixed exchange rates or by basing trade and reserves on a basket of currencies such as Special Drawing Rights (the "SDRs" of the IMF). The problem is compounded when a country's own currency is beleaguered by inflation, for then its purchasing power in the foreign reserve market is eroded day by day.

A third major resource/power problem is found in the area of research and technology (R&D). The question here is not appropriate technology but control and transfer of technology. In the seventies, developing countries possessed only about 13 percent of world R&D capacity, measured in terms of the number of scientists and engineers. At the same time they had less than 3 percent of funding. In each case Asia (excluding Japan) accounted for about 60 percent of third-world capacity. The OECD countries had about 55 percent of world scientists and 60 percent of funding, while COMECON had about 30 percent of each. Except for Asia and Brazil, the developing world has little research capacity.

In OECD countries industry accounts for about 66 percent of R&D. In Chapter 4 it has already been pointed out that private industry is the leader in the development, control, and transfer of the new biotechnologies. There are clear issues of power here and the legal problems surrounding intellectual property are formidable. But if developing countries are to tap into the new technologies, they will have to come to terms with private industry. In many cases the R&D capacity of a major corporation exceeds that of a developing country.

In addition, there are issues of research priorities. As shown in Figure 5-2, military research accounts for more than a quarter of R&D. Figures are difficult to come by and many research categories overlap. Nonetheless, there is a significant contrast with funds devoted to agriculture, especially tropical agriculture. In the first world, research in agricultural technology is less urgent because most developed countries are awash with agricultural surpluses. At the same time, there seems to be little incentive to devote resources to third-world agriculture. The main issue would seem to be not a mere technology transfer but the development of third-world research capacity. (I discuss this more in Chapter 9.)

REALITY PRINCIPLES: POWER IN PROCEDURES

What are the reality principles governing international economics and development today? In asking this question I seek to uncover patterns of behavior, the so-called rules of the game, the realities of formal and informal power in procedures. For it is these rules of the game that "realists" appeal to in their problemsolving and pragmatic approaches, as if any possible alternative set of rules amounted to a chimerical utopia (see Table 5-3).

Firstly, the market. The rules of the marketplace are summed up under the rubric of profits—the bottom line. This is very important because any market solution to contemporary problems must be based on profits. And not just any profits but a level of profit that is commensurate with other alternative uses of available resources. Profits derive from two sources: economic efficiency and power. As was seen in Chapter 4, economic efficiency is defined, firstly, in terms of input-output ratios (where one maximizes output for a given set of inputs) and, secondly, in terms of cost management (where one maximizes revenues or minimizes costs). The power source of profits is seen in the case of market imperfections, and in oligopolies and monopolies, where one can manipulate either supply, demand, costs, or prices in a way to dictate the terms of trade and thereby increase profit. World markets today tend to be characterized by market imperfections and noncompetitive practices. The rules of the market represent not just efficiency but power in the marketplace.

Secondly, there are the rules of politics and governments. In this area the international rules of the game are dictated by the notion of *realpolitik*. Developing countries can expect little from the first or second world unless they come through with political favors such as support for the politics of the dominant country, the granting of military facilities, and other privileges. One of the main themes of UNCTAD since its inception in 1964 has been the interaction between countries of the center with those of the periphery; that is the dependency theory. Although of limited explanatory value, dependency theory does at least highlight gross inequalities in the distribution of powers.

The center/periphery dependency theory owes much of its origins to Raul Prebisch (Prebisch 1964; Gurrieri 1983). In many ways it has become an oversimplified metaphor used by some as a fully explanatory account of political economic injustice. I think there is more to injustice than international class relations. But I do believe that class structure is an essential explanatory variable. The theory is especially applicable to Latin America (which still has not emerged from the umbrella of the Monroe Doctrine) and to Africa (where the colonial heritage is still strong). It also applies to IMF and GATT rules.

Very few countries have been able to escape the hard necessity of somehow aligning themselves (either officially or not) with one of the superpower camps. Furthermore, disloyalty to either OECD or COMECON interests tends to be met with by interference in the domestic affairs of the developing nation in question. International democracy and true international law remain elusive. The political rules of the game are primarily played out in terms of national interest and bilateral treaties and in terms of the dominant monetary (IMF) and trade structures (GATT) that in their organizational apparatus clearly favor the first world.

The rules of the game in political economic circles emerge as dualistic. Ideally, their proponents seek a basis in economic efficiency in the marketplace and democratic self-determination in the political arena. But the hard reality in both the marketplace and the political arena is power, whether formal or informal. Furthermore, these hierarchies are reinforced by a set of political and economic sanctions. There are rewards for those who play by the rules and punishments for those who do not, which has led some developing countries to try to play the first world off against the second world (Indira Gandhi's celebrated phrase of milking two cows at once). But that is a risky business and few succeed in the long run.

If international political economic relations are dominated by power exercised by the nation-states, transnational corporations, and coalitions of both, the same can be said of the domestic scenario; local elites commonly exploit their own people and cast in their lot with international political and economic elites. The center-periphery dependency then reproduces itself on the domestic scene in terms of dominant classes and marginalized masses.

International financial power rests with the developed world. Private international banking, which occupies a position of key importance, is firmly in the hands of first-world multinational banks. The primary political institutions, the IMF and GATT, are likewise clearly dominated by first-world governments. In international trade and finance, the reality of power is that the first and second worlds (the north) dominate the third world (the south).

Where can developing countries turn? All such power is not absolute but is rather vulnerable and relative. For instance, the power of Europe and Japan is greatly limited by the fact that they are essentially commercial economies and depend greatly on imports. Local elites must continually exert themselves to maintain the coalitions upon which they depend. The fact that power is in some way limited suggests its instability and the possibility of change.

The main issues in international economics and development are not just technical. In fact, few people would argue that there are no means to solve the problem. The main problem is that the political will to resolve the outstanding issues is lacking. This lack of political will is a problem of power in both national and international structures and institutions.

The question of where developing countries can turn is one of organization and management. There is no shortage of imaginative solutions to the problems of international economics, ranging from schemes of international law to taxation of the production and sales of armaments. But there is a distinct shortage of solutions that would actually work. There are many reasons for this. I discuss them in terms of bureaucratic power and organizational politics.

THE CRISIS OF ORGANIZATION
AND MANAGEMENT

One of the most outstanding features of contemporary international political economy is that it is organized into large political and economic bureaucracies that are administered by managerial elites. In both governments and in economic processes it is an age of large complex organizations. It is not always simple to determine how goals are set nor it is easy to clarify the motivations of different people and groups in adhering to them. Furthermore, the lines of responsibility and processes of cooperation and change are not easy to schematize. No one has been able to pinpoint all the relevant dynamics of organizational politics on the international scene.

The first problem is amassing adequate information on the issues of global poverty and international trade, finance, and development. One would not suspect that in the modern age of scientific data collection and processing, there would be so many gaps in information as well as continuous production of disinformation. One example from the area of development is revealing: the distribution of income in a country. Only very recently has this data even been collected or published; in its place the misleading indicator of growth in per capita income (which tells nothing of distribution) is presented as a sign of increased welfare. Tied to a highly skewed distribution of income domestically, one finds local corruption and the amassing and export of large amounts of capital by local elites. Obviously, neither they nor the international banks that offer the protection of secret accounts are very forthcoming with any information. But it is known that many poor countries—selling raw materials, for instance—channel their funds through holding companies in Switzerland where they are protected by secrecy (Table 5–2b). This was the case that the IMF uncovered with Mobutu in Zaire. What is not clear is how much of the new income, credit, and aid destined for poor countries ever reaches those countries or is used for anything else than aggrandizing the positions of those in power.

What is lacking is both a government and corporate information process that renders a fairly accurate picture of what is happening and circumvents the systematic dissemination of disinformation. It is not uncommon for "official sources" to attribute the causes of poverty primarily to the impending catastrophe of the population explosion and to defend the trickle-down theory of increasing welfare implied in aggregate per capita income measures. Disinformation is crucial to the functioning of the status quo for it anesthetizes those who feel unrest.

That being said, there are both political and economic bureaucracies involved in a solution of the present crisis. Both of these systems, of course, interact. International credit is increasingly in the hands of the private banks that make their decisions according to market criteria. Furthermore, the private banking sector cannot plan and carry out its activities without taking close account of the political and legal environment. Needless to say, if these two managerial elites form a coalition to serve their own personal interests, the effects upon development and welfare would be devastating. The problem is that no effective system of international accountability is in place, while many potential loopholes remain.

Enforcing the private sector's accountability in international economics and development will apparently not be easy. People continue to speak of the necessity of some codes of conduct and, even more, of intergovernmental agreements in the face of the lack of any really effective international law. In all the discussion, a greater awareness of the issues has emerged, but next to nothing in terms of viable measures. The situation is one where, firstly, information is not furnished (regarding, for example, capital transfers) and, secondly, when knowledge of what is happening is acquired, there is not an effective system of accountability. Without honest home governments that can also effectively integrate the corporate sector's own profit interests with the chosen strategy of development, there is little hope of a solution. The problem facing developing countries is just how to integrate the foreign private sector into its development plans and international economic policy. In theory, such an integration is not impossible. It depends, however, almost totally on the quality of local governments as well as on international accords between governments.

These processes of establishing accords between governments represent the second major process in the organization and management of the international economy. Presently, the two most important agencies are the IMF and GATT, which grew up in the aftermath of the Bretton Woods meeting and the attempt to reconstruct the world economy after World War II (McBean and Snowden 1981: ch. 5). These are powerful organizations because their rules and agreements carry some teeth. But in their structures of voting and lending they decidedly favor the first world. At the same time, one finds numerous commodity agreements (e.g., sugar), as well as commodity and trade programs such as the "Stabex" Program of the Common Market countries that govern trade with the developing countries. Most of the above agreements represent multilateral structures that nonetheless tilt toward the first world. They do succeed in channeling some monetary and trade advantages to the developing countries, but the transfers are meager when compared with the needs. For years the OECD countries have pledged to devote 0.7 percent of their GNP in aid to developing countries, yet few of them have ever done so or even come close (Weiss and Jennings 1983). These multilateral mechanisms have historically brought only limited benefits to developing countries.

These inequalities have prompted the developing countries to call for a "new international economic order." They have met with little success and have since turned to develop other fora such as UNCTAD, ILO, UNESCO in the United Nations' organization, and the Group of Seventy-seven that represents the so-called nonaligned movement. These organizations have little real power to set terms of trade or to affect the world of credit; they serve primarily as fora for discussion and the dissemination of information, necessary but not sufficient measures.

There is a paralysis in international economic organization and management. Third-world debt is nearly $700 billion. Developing countries are spending an average of 20 percent of every dollar earned by exports just for debt servicing (repayment of principal with interest). But most Latin American countries are beyond this and can barely manage debt servicing. Brazil, for example, is borrowing heavily, and 80 percent of what it has been borrowing in the mid-1980s went to debt servicing alone. The result of such realities is that there is not much left for investment or for needed imports. The long-term effect is a potential decline of exports that will also affect the first world. For example, in 1984 the United States lost more than $6 billion in exports to Mexico alone because Mexico could no longer afford to buy.

The IMF, for its part, has a plan to help developing countries. Firstly, it grants emergency loans to stave off an immediate crisis (however, most of this goes right back to the banks in terms of debt servicing). Secondly, it is involved in rescheduling debts, for no one would gain if a country went bankrupt. Thirdly, the IMF leadership wants to raise the amount a country can licitly borrow from the IMF based on its quota. Fourthly, it is trying to persuade first-world countries to bring down interest rates, thus making the cost of loans cheaper. But most first-world governments have chronic deficits and are borrowing heavily. This may drive interest rates up again and reduce fixed investment. To cure the deficits, first-world government spending (which averages 43 percent of gross domestic product) would have to be reduced. This would mean trimming spending for social services, a politically risky proposition. Finally, the IMF is insisting on domestic austerity measures (high conditionality) in developing countries before granting a loan.

This final point deserves more attention. It is called belt tightening. But the question is, whose belt is being tightened? The IMF committees generally call for cutting social expenditures (e.g., health, education, pensions, and price subsidies). They want low wages (even abolishing minimum wages). They also call for eliminating government deficits that are said to derive from social spending. The government is to control inflation by slashing its own deficits and keeping a tight reign on the money supply (done by setting higher interest rates, which have the effect of decreasing investment). Price subsidies and controls should be abolished and market forces should rule. Exchange rates should not be overvalued. Businessmen should be allowed to make good profits and taxes on capital gains should be low in order to stimulate investment, which would also create jobs. There is a hard economic logic to all of this. But there is also a lag of three to five years before any good results are produced. In the meantime it is the voiceless poor and disadvantaged who bear most of the burden. I know of few IMF conditions linked to sharply reducing military expenditures or to blocking the flight of capital. It is important to examine who bears the burden of what might otherwise be sensible economic policies. The rich are considered untouchable, either because they are manipulating discussions on their own behalf or because of "political realism." If some of the above measures are necessary, as they seem to be, then a more equitable way of sharing the costs must be found. The above proposals are not simply cutting the fat out of budgets. They are cutting the poor and weak. Those more capable of bearing the burden, the rich within the country and the first-world countries, are not asked to move to a new level of social responsibility and accountability. Perhaps that is unrealistic, but there are limits to both individual and national self-interest. If budget cuts are necessary, it might be better to begin with armaments rather than food and medicine; if more taxes are needed, it might be better to begin with those who have the ability to pay rather than squeezing them out of the poor. The lessons of fallen despots should be heeded: Abject poverty of the masses (especially in the face of the wanton luxury of local elites) breeds revolution. The authoritarian regimes of South Korea and Taiwan have at least had the good sense to gear development policies to help the poor economically in a direct way.

There is no doubt that the way to more justice and peace in international economic and development relations is a long and winding road. There are no great leaps forward; there are also setbacks and reversals. But the journey cannot be renounced because of "realism." There will be many more international meetings before the IMF and GATT are transformed and more significant international solidarity is forged. This leads to a larger question: public opinion and the manipulation of the social environment.

DEVELOPMENT, POWER, AND SHAPING THE SOCIAL ENVIRONMENT

The first-world countries are just emerging from various stages of economic stagnation and inflation. They grapple with mounting unemployment and inflation, often facing trade and general budget deficits. These problems are at least of the magnitude to make the governments of those countries worry about their own survival. The plight of the developing countries, unless they are of geopolitical importance or have a domestic constituency in the first world arguing their cases, tends to be ignored. If something is done, it must almost necessarily manifest the objectives of national self-interest and it tends to be structured in bilateral terms to assure that self-interest — treaties of friendship and similar alliances. The crisis is not that present organizations and structures cannot work but that they more and more respond to narrow interest groups and what is euphemistically called mutual self-interest. There is a particular power associated with shaping public opinion and creating a favorable environment for one's priorities.

No one has developed a formula for galvanizing political will around a set of social priorities. It is a very complex process of technical and human factors. How is it possible to set priorities that correspond to people's needs and aspirations in a fair way and actually move to achieve them? Recently, increasing attention has been given to modes of *popular participation in development* as well as to a certain degree of self-reliance in the context of global interdependence. Above, the role of the local government with reference to other nation-states and private economic interests was stressed as a matter of absolute importance. The same government is no less important in the domestic economy in creating a fair legal climate and an efficient infrastructure of public administration, financial structures, education, health, general welfare, and housing where people can function effectively.

As indicated in Figure 5-3, politicians and government bureaucrats possess powerful tools to influence both business and private voluntary organizations in shaping the social environment. Foremost among these tools are provisions for taxation, budget allocations, and regulatory legislation. Yet these same people are susceptible to great pressures from both business and other special interest groups. Business interests generally prove to have more clout by far. But the Islamic movement as well as Christian social activism suggest that the dynamics of "political will" can be far more complex. Both governments and business exert great efforts to manipulate public opinion and private voluntary organizations. The two main tools for doing this are media control and financial support extended for various reasons, including co-option. Coercive measures and force also figure, but not as preferred instruments. Overcoming poverty and hunger presents a very complex international case, because political will must be galvanized in rich and poor countries alike.

There is a sharp contrast between available modes of participation in the first world countries and in most third-world countries. The key difference is in the quality of the legal system which protects procedures of public process. First-world reforms of the economy are overwhelmingly public policy oriented. As such, they take a legislative and regulatory form. Economic solutions based on voluntary choice and market dynamics are not excluded. Historically, however, they have not been sufficient. For example, food policy (both domestic and international) emerges from a public policy process featuring intense lobbying involving (1) on farm production groups, (2) consumer organizations, (3) agribusiness firms engaged in farm input and post-farm activities, and (4) other interest groups (for example ecologists), (5) public officials and civil servants, and (6) legislators.

Figure 5-3.   Power and the Shaping of the Social Environment.

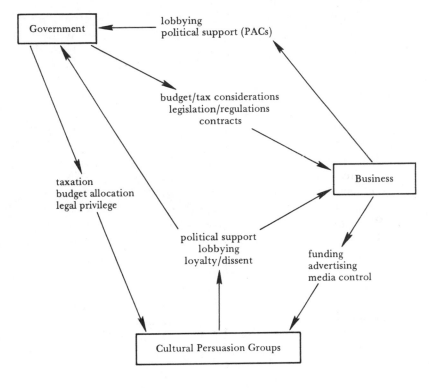

Due to the nature of the participants, food policy emphasizes mutual self-interest and generally has something for everyone. Thus, a food aid program (such as food stamps) pleases farmers (who sell more), agribusiness (which processes food products), consumer groups (which can specify target groups and nutritional levels), humanitarian groups (which are satisfied that the poor have something to eat), and the politician (who hopes to satisfy all and remain in office).

The policymaking process is circumscribed by a variety of interest groups that seek to exercise some sort of voice in the policy formulation process. Nonetheless, the poor and hungry themselves are often ignorant, distrustful, or otherwise marginalized in the policymaking and general political process. As such, they do not represent political power in proportion to their numbers.

In developing countries, the public policy process is often markedly different. One of the priorities is such a case is to improve system access and integrate people into the policymaking process. In the face of governmental processes the main problem is that the local elites often control the levers of power and manage "development" in their own interests. For example, Richard Grabowski has shown a complex interrelation exists between technical innovation and the institutional structure of society (Grabowski 1982). Powerful local elites act as gatekeepers. The Green Revolution has much to offer. Yet it has been frequently objected that the *type* of research underlying Green Revolution technologies has tended to reinforce existing structures and generally failed to help the very small farmer (let alone the landless) or bring about equitable rural development (Crist 1983). Technology is not neutral regarding agrarian structures. It is to be expected that the powerful jealously guard their position in the face of innovations; this affects diffusion of technological information, implementation, and participation (Freeman and Azadi 1983; Waseem 1982).

There are many points in modern organizations and management that need to be reformed. The first is to work for the development of both domestic and international forms of accountability (that is, a fair legal system). The second is to train people so that they can function effectively in a modern international economy. Thirdly, bureaucracies must be streamlined and coordinated so as to increase both the level of competence and efficiency. Fourthly, emphasis should be placed on subsidiarity and modes of organization that favor popular participation in economic decisions and development processes. International economics and development should reflect, to as great an extent as possible, a participatory society rather than the fiefdom of managerial elites and political and economic oligarchies, whether local or international.

CONCLUSION

Power is frequently ignored in North Atlantic development discourse. This is a mistake, for power and social class possess considerable explanatory relevance in the context of poverty, hunger, and development.

On the international level "interdependence" takes on a different hue when interpreted in terms of domination of the periphery by the center. And so does the "development" that emerges from those relations, for it is a mode of development that systematically produces poverty and hunger. As has been seen, scarcity of the goods and services necessary to satisfy basic needs may result from population pressures as well as from the lack of technological development. But it is also produced by abuses of power, which directly affect both the distribution of resources and access to technology. To improve the quality of interdependence one must address the structures of power on both international and national levels.

It is difficult to interrelate the population/resources, technology, and power questions. One does not find the same configurations in all places; nor are the causes of scarcity always ranked in the same order. In this sense, I part company with more dogmatic neo-Marxist analyses of power structures and abuse. Nonetheless, speaking in a general way of the third world, I think that both national and international corruption and national self-interest are the primary causes of the maldistribution of the goods and services necessary to meet basic needs and of the resources necessary to produce those goods and services. I would rank underlying causes of poverty and hunger in the following order of importance: corruption and power abuse, lack of technology, and population pressure.

Power, furthermore, must be grasped in terms of subtleties of social organization and interaction. On this score, I find practically all United Nations and official government documentation very limited because there is hardly ever a competent analysis of the power of the civil authority system undertaken. It is *assumed* to be both legitimate and benevolent. Blame for persistent problems is then uncritically unloaded on population problems or the activities of the multinationals. The multinationals, in turn, strenuously exonerate themselves from any responsibility for persistent poverty and hunger. Further, persuasion groups (such as churches) also generally fail to recognize their own compromises and complicity in abusive power structures. All such partial approaches are clearly inadequate. They are face-saving and fail to grasp the realities of power in the interrelatedness of contemporary political economic social systems.

My approach views development as a process of social change. Therefore, it means changing configurations of power as expressed in social organization. Development is rooted in the unfolding of human capacities, command of resources, meaningful participation in public processes and procedures, and shaping of the social environment so as to galvanize the political will necessary for development.

REFERENCES

Amin, Samir. 1977. *Unequal Development. An Essay on the Social Formations of Peripheral Capitalism.* New York: Monthly Review Press.

Baran, Paul A., and Paul M. Sweezy. 1968. *Monopoly Capital.* New York: Monthly Review Press.

Booth, David. 1985. "Marxism and Development Sociology: Interpreting the Impasse." *World Development* 13, no. 7: 761–87.

Bornschier, Volker, Christopher Chase-Dunn, and Richard Rubinson. 1978. "Cross-National Evidence of the Effects of Foreign Investment and Aid on Economic Growth and Inequality: A Survey of Findings and a Reanalysis." *American Journal of Sociology* 84 (Novembr): 651–71, 678–79, 682–83.

Crist, Raymond E. 1983. "Land for the People—A Vital Need Everywhere." *American Journal of Economics and Sociology* 42, no. 3: 275–90.

Danaher, Kevin. 1985. "How the U.S. and Europe Caused Africa's Famine." *UTNE Reader*, August–September, 101–103.

Dinham, Barbara, and Colin Hines. 1984. *Agribusiness in Africa.* Trenton, N.J.: Africa World Press.

Fanon, Frantz. 1965. *The Wretched of the Earth.* Trans. Constance Farrington. New York: Grove Press.

Freeman, D. M., and M. Azadi. 1983. "Education, Power Distribution and Adoption of Improved Farm Practices." *Community Development Journal* 18, no. 1: 60–67.

Freire, Paulo. 1970. *The Pedagogy of the Oppressed.* New York: Continuum.

Galbraith, John K. 1983. *The Anatomy of Power.* Boston: Houghton Mifflin Co.

Gereffi, Gary. 1984. "Power and Dependency in an Interdependent World: A Guide to Understanding the Contemporary Global Crisis." *International Journal of Comparative Sociology* 25, nos. 1 and 2: 91–108.

Grabowski, Richard. 1982. "Peasantry, Technical Change and Rural Poverty." *Peasant Studies* 9, no. 3: 197–204.

Gurrieri, Adolfo. 1983. "Technical Progress and Its Fruits—The Idea of Development in the Works of Paul Prebisch." *Journal of Economic Issues* 17, no. 2: 389–96.

Gutierrez, Gustavo. 1973. *The Theology of Liberation.* New York: Orbis.

Jackman, Robert W. 1982. "Dependence on Foreign Investment and Economic Growth." *World Politics* 34 (January): 175–97.

Kotzsch, Ronald. 1985. "How Our Food Choices Affect the World." *UTNE Reader*, August–September, 94–101.

Lappe, Francis M., et al. 1981. *Aid As an Obstacle.* San Francisco: Institute for Food and Development Policy.

McBean, A. I., and P. N. Snowden. 1981. *International Institutions in Trade and Finance.* London: George Allen and Unwin.

Mao Dz-dong. 1958. *On the Correct Manner of Handling Contributions Among the People.* Beijing: Foreign Language Press.

Morgan Guaranty Trust. 1986. *World Financial Markets*. New York: Morgan Guaranty Trust. March.

Muller, Edward N. 1984. "Financial Dependence in the Capitalist World Economy and the Distribution of Income Within Nations." In *The Gap Between Rich and Poor — Contending Perspectives on the Political Economy of Development*, 9th ed., ed. Michael Seligson, 256–82. Boulder, Colo.: Westview Press.

Prebisch, Raul. 1964. *Towards a New Trade Policy for Development*. Report by the Secretary General of UNCTAD. New York: United Nations.

Szymanski, Albert. 1981. *The Logic of Imperialism*. New York: Praeger.

Todaro, Michael P. 1981. *Economic Development in the Third World*. 2d ed. New York: Longmans and Todd.

Turner, Louis. 1976. *Multinational Companies and the Third World*. New York: Hill and Wang.

Waseem, M. 1982. "Local Power Structures and the Relevance of Rural Development Strategies: A Case Study of Pakistan." *Community Development Journal* 17, no. 3: 225–33.

Weiss, Thomas G., and Anthony Jennings. 1983. "What Are the Least Developed Countries and What Benefits May Result from the Paris Conference?" *World Development* 2, no. 11: 337–58.

World Bank. 1985. *World Development Report*. Washington, D.C.: World Bank.

_____ . 1986. *Poverty and Hunger*. Washington, D.C.: World Bank.

Wrong, Dennis. 1979. *Power: Its Forms, Bases, and Uses*. New York: Harper & Row.

6 CULTURAL PARADIGMS
Values and Preferences

The complex interrelations between culture and development have not received sufficient attention in the economics literature. Although there are a number of cultural anthropological studies of the modernization of traditional societies, the fruit of these studies has only rarely been introduced into discussions of economic development. To my knowledge, the most significant attempt to integrate socio–cultural and political factors into economic development models has been the work of Irma Adelman and Cynthia Morris (1973). Yet it seems to lean toward affirming the necessity of inculcating modern (Western) attitudes and values (Adelman and Morris: 37), which affect dynamics of social participation and the qualities of institutions. The common assumption until very recently has been that the traditional cultures were backward and inhospitable to progress. Such an assumption proves to be both gratuitous and simplistic. It has also rendered many development plans ineffective (Timmer 1982).

In this chapter, I will concentrate on two key social dynamics of culture in development. The first is that of social legitimacy, whereby cultural worldviews, values, and paradigms are brought to bear upon the political economic "rules of the game" in a manner either to bless them or denounce them.

The second is the pivotal role that cultural preferences and customs have to play in the design of development strategies. I argue that, rather than simply being ignored as backward, such dynamics have a positive and indispensable role to play in processes of development. This is easier said than done. While sociocultural dynamics need to be fully integrated into development planning, the requirements of efficient use of economic resources cannot be set aside. They are not alternatives. Along these lines Dirk Kohnert (1982) criticizes the narrow sociocultural approach and argues for measures to specify more adequately the target groups in the rural population and to give precedence in planning to the actual development interests of these target groups so as to elicit their participation and support.

The word *development* carries a bit of semantic confusion (Arndt 1981). One sense is more economic: It means to productively exploit resources (e.g., to build an hydroeclectric power system) or to institute a new line or mode of production in the economy (e.g., to begin a steel industry). This first usage is linked to economic growth. A second usage of the term is more institutional and linked to broader discourse of progress and modernization. Modernization, as it has historically occurred in the West, is a complex social syndrome that includes (1) self-sustaining economic growth, (2) democratic political participation, (3) diffusion of secular values, (4) a high degree of geographical and social mobility, and (5) personality transformation (suitable to the efficient functioning of modern institutions).

Development in this context is usually associated not only with a scientific technical mentality but also with the virtues of democratic social and legal institutions and with the individualist spirit, hard work, and thrift that are necessary for the accumulation of an economic surplus. Most economic development work seems to presuppose the necessity of changes in economic values and attitudes towards modern Western patterns.

This second use of the term grounds the prevailing Western ideology of development that challenges the basic structures of traditional societies. Thus, by way of reaction in the third world today, one finds increasing questioning of the *quality* of development. It is helpful to keep two distinctions in mind. The first is tradition versus modernization; the second is cultural identity versus Westernization. Many third-world developing peoples are searching for forms of modernization that do not destroy core cultural identity. Because of the nature of contemporary patterns of socialization, political economic life is increasingly international and interdependent. Isolation is no longer a real possibility; cultures cannot remain static. Yet it would be a mistake to make the easy identification of modernization with Westernization.

The prime instruments of modernization have been rational thought, science, and technology. As these are introduced into and diffused throughout traditional cultures, they act as catalysts and mechanisms of change. Such change will almost certainly transform local cultures, but need not destroy local core cultural identity. In fact, new forms of cultural modernization can be evolved to embrace both the old and the new. Perhaps the best historical example of such development to date is Japan. When all is said and done, however, the modernization of Europe, North America, and Japan are illustrative examples for other cultures rather than normative models for the developing world to imitate. They underscore the dynamics of modernization rather than provide a blueprint. Yet clearly, traditional cultures should neither simply jettison their past nor look upon it as some sort of paradise lost. They must creatively transform themselves. It remains for traditional societies to chart their own course of overall social development on the basis of their own sociocultural dynamics.

THE LEGITIMACY CRISIS: SECULAR
AND TRANSCENDENTAL MODELS
OF DEVELOPMENT

The preceding chapters have sketched the outlines of the present system of international economics and development. When one discusses the legitimacy of this system, one calls into question the guiding vision of human development and the sense of ultimate reality that underpin actual patterns and models of development. Cultural analysis must be brought to bear upon actual patterns as well as theoretical models of development.

Cultural analysis is to be reduced neither to the internal subjective states of individuals nor simply to social structures. Culture consists of socially established structures of *meaning* (Geertz 1973: 12). Cultural analysis is precisely an attempt to interpret the meaning of the "symbolic-expressive" aspect of behavior, whether that behavior is oriented primarily toward the discussion of values or the rational-purposive manipulation of the material world (R. Wuthnow et al., 1984: 255ff). In all of this there is a view of the human person involved: the person is a symbolic actor; symbolic meaning is public not private. Cultures express a people's collective self-conscious and self-constituting nature.

In cultural analysis there are a number of relevant points of investigation: worldview and definitions of absolute reality, group identity, the growing penetration of the state into the individual realm, and the internal legitimation of established patterns of social relations (social structures). In a sense these issues interpenetrate each other. My main interest in this section, however, is the legitimation of actual patterns of social relations embedded in contemporary forms of economic development. I use legitimation here in the sense of social patterns and rules being *internally assented to* (on the basis of values, worldview and symbolizations of meaning) rather than being adhered to out of external motivations based on sanctions or incentives (which may not be grounded in the same way). Social order and patterns exist only insofar as there are symbolic boundaries demarcating what, after all, is meaningful. "Society's forms are culture's substance" (Geertz 1973: 28), for social structures and rules *institutionalize* values and meaning.

The dialogue over cultural meaning will never end. It is fundamental to the human family's search for wisdom so that it might grow in grace. That is, it is fundamental to human development. The task at hand is to examine patterns of human reproduction (Polgar 1971), use and distribution of natural resources, diffusion of technology, and structures of social power against the backdrop of ultimate reality and meaning that a particular culture represents (United Nations Education and Social Committee 1981; World Development 1980). This endeavor is clearly normative because it seeks to know not only what is happening but what should happen to people in the processes of political economic relations.

Today such discussions of the legitimacy of the actual world economic and development systems are polarized around the two dominant modern paradigms of the political economy: capitalism and socialism. And each is discussed on two levels: (1) the ideal level, which presents a vision of human development, and (2) the pragmatic level, which argues that the status quo represents the best of all realistically possible worlds. The point to note is that each level of discourse aims at the acceptance of a certain system as legitimate and, in fact, good.

As was noted in Chapter 1, the pervading capitalist and socialist models of development are both secular in nature: The one because of hierarchical and privatized views of religious psychology, the other because of avowed atheism. It is not surprising that the greatest challenges to development patterns and models today are coming from the major religious traditions. This point is nothing new in itself. Indeed, nineteenth century social scientists were well aware of the conflict, but they assumed that the religious traditions would die off as so many fetishes, totems, and taboos held over from the dark ages. What has happened instead is a modernization of religious traditions themselves. With the exception of Protestant Christianity, the major religious groupings have had a very difficult time adjusting to "modernization." In addition, they have frequently clung to the status quo. This posture has been rooted in a number of perceptions of the world: the struggle of the human condition, a belief in an hierarchical world order, and a demeaning attitude toward secular concerns.

There is considerable evidence that this is changing as most major religious groups struggle to come to terms with modernization. This is evident in the Catholic Church in the Second Vatican Council, in contemporary Islam, and in Buddhism. All of these traditions are focusing on development. While sharply criticizing the modernist model, however, they have not yet discovered their own.

The point of conflict for these religious groups emanates from the contradiction between their transcendental ideals and the reality of secular development policies. Their new active posture marks a profound change from their former posture of passive resignation.

Anyone at all familiar with Buddhism, Christianity, or Islam is well aware that there are countless schools of thought within each. It is not my purpose to resolve those issues. My objective is to highlight the types of questions such groups pose for development. In this and the following section I do not pretend to speak for one group or the other. Rather, my intent is to propose a general typology of development issues rooted in transcendental concerns. The aim in doing so is to highlight the relevance of culture to development and to suggest the outlines of post–modernist development.

In my approach I rely upon ecumenical Christian thinking on social issues (Steidlmeier 1984; Goulet 1983; Bennett 1958), the work of Godfrey Gunnatilleke (1983) and colleagues in questioning development on the basis of Buddhism, and Masudul Choudhury (1983) in presenting the outlines of Islamic economic ethics. Edward Zipperstein (1983) has also presented an outline of business ethics in the Jewish tradition that has proved useful. And Guy Standing (1980), in a more philosophical vein, has set forth the primacy of nonmaterialist basic needs.

From this literature I have distilled a general typology of points of contrast. I first discuss these in general. In the following section I develop their ethical implications and relevance for development policy.

In Figure 6–1 the main points to consider are set forth in terms of general worldview and approaches to development.

The discussion of a grounding view of reality is complex indeed. Such a worldview proposes a model for human conduct. As such, it articulates a view of ultimate reality and meaning. One cannot deny the fact that in the world today there is considerable pluralism over

Figure 6–1. Secular and Transcendental Models of Development.

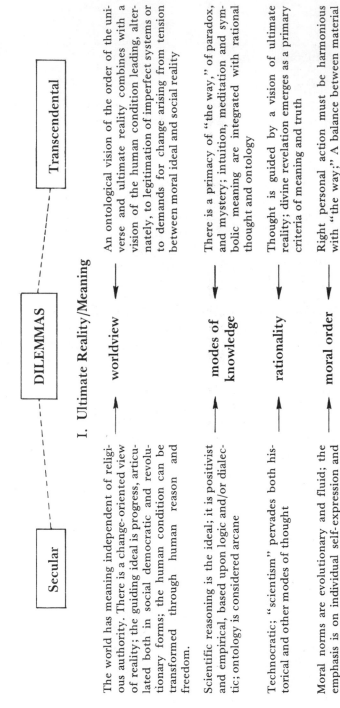

I. Ultimate Reality/Meaning

	Secular		Transcendental
worldview	The world has meaning independent of religious authority. There is a change-oriented view of reality; the guiding ideal is progress, articulated both in social democratic and revolutionary forms; the human condition can be transformed through human reason and freedom.		An ontological vision of the order of the universe and ultimate reality combines with a vision of the human condition leading, alternately, to legitimation of imperfect systems or to demands for change arising from tension between moral ideal and social reality
modes of knowledge	Scientific reasoning is the ideal; it is positivist and empirical, based upon logic and/or dialectic; ontology is considered arcane		There is a primacy of "the way," of paradox, and mystery; intuition, meditation and symbolic meaning are integrated with rational thought and ontology
rationality	Technocratic; "scientism" pervades both historical and other modes of thought		Thought is guided by a vision of ultimate reality; divine revelation emerges as a primary criteria of meaning and truth
moral order	Moral norms are evolutionary and fluid; the emphasis is on individual self-expression and utilitarian results in the context of a social contract; there is an emphasis on functionalism and a separation of religion from social reality		Right personal action must be harmonious with "the way;" A balance between material and spiritual well-being is sought
personal goals	Primary goals are self-realization and maximization of material well being; the emphasis is on this world and people having liberty and		Goals of achievement, family, and career are seen within a context of eternal life, calling, and spiritual well-being

II. Development Patterns and Models

Goals are set as priorities over time; the primary emphasis is upon growth in an utilitarian sense; trade-offs with other goals are seen as necessary	**goals**	Growth must meet the demands of a good moral life, articulated by social justice, community, equity, and participation
There is a pragmatic choice of strategies to produce growth; trade-offs are a practical necessity, leaving policy open for other goals to be realized later; policy is change-oriented in light of immediate goals	**strategies**	There is a simultaneous pursuit of the total goal cluster; pragmatic trade-offs between growth and primary values are rejected; strategy is order oriented in terms of equitable sharing of benefits and costs in light of transcendental order
The means employed are pragmatic in terms of technoeconomic efficiency; the emphasis is upon the economic bottom line and providing economic incentives based on self-interest and mutual self-interest	**instruments**	The means employed must be in harmony with ultimate ends; expedient choices of efficiency over primary goals are rejected; equity in bearing social costs and sharing benefits is called for
The majority rules, whether in institutions of democratic choice or by the masses seen as under the tutelage of a vanguard party; there is no direct role for religious authority as such	**nature of social choice**	Choice is guided by religious authority and those who speak for "ultimate concerns;" human reason and individual choice are limited by religious authority and divine law

worldview. Policy formulation (insofar as it implies something about human fulfillment) will, therefore, always ultimately be characterized by dialogue over the meaning of reality in general and of the human person in particular.

This discussion becomes very concrete once people ask how a culture or a religion views poverty and hunger, how it views human reproduction and the quality of life in this world, how it views inequalities of power and resource control. This level of discussion fundamentally explores whether people generally accept a system or not. To the point, Marx's critique of religion as the opium of the people underscored his view that religion is a proponent of a false consciousness, lulling its adherents into passivity and submission.

Transcendental and secular models of development imply very different worldviews. They also embody different approaches to rationality: the one related to transcendental goals, the other technocratic and instrumental. In addition, they employ different methodologies, the one emphasizing mystery that remains ineffable, the other stressing problems that can be solved.

These different orientations and modes of proceeding lead to different assessments of development patterns and models. Gunnatilleke addresses the issues of values in terms of three clusters: growth, equity, and participation. I treat this in greater detail in the next section. Suffice it to note that values set the stage for articulating and working toward personal and social goals as well as clarifying the requisites of a moral order, which would truly be an expression of integral human development.

Even if values and social goals could be clarified, the issue of social responsibility remains very complex. It must be anticipated that in collective social action various groups of people may be seeking quite different ends and priorities, each employing different means leading to diverse consequences. In considering the relation of values to ends and means, the discussion is transformed into an evaluation of social conscience, which itself is in a constant state of development. Social conscience represents a people's collective ethical judgment on values, ends, and means and the acceptability of consequences. In examining the dynamics of social conscience, one comes face to face with collective assent, that is, the process of internally legitimating a development model and its social structures, institutions, and outcomes.

To recall, legitimacy is expressed in two ways: (1) values and ideologies that attempt to present the rationality of the dominant paradigms or ideal types and (2) symbols and stories (narrative) that tend to fill out the broader meaning of social patterns by concretely presenting a model for society in terms of political and economic heroes. In these ways, the actual patterns of social relations in political economic systems are legitimated as contributing to overall human development.

These points are clearly illustrated in the cases of secular models of capitalism and socialism that currently dominate development discourse. The democratic market-oriented model of development has its roots in the modernist spirit and in the philosophical heritage of Hobbes, Rousseau, Locke, Bentham, Smith, and Mill. It is not atheist, but presents a very restricted view of the relevance of economic events to religious living. One finds refined and elaborate theories of democracy, the social contract, and the free enterprise of individuals. All of these notions coalesce in the theory of the marketplace. Once the theoretical presuppositions and preconditions of a free market are granted, these theories have considerable explanatory power. They possess an internal logic and consistency regarding the accumulation and allocation of economic resources.

But theory is not all; in fact the more persuasive elements in the model have been the stories of self-made men and women, who by reason of hard work, thrift, and ingenuity pulled themselves up by their own bootstraps. These stories of manifest destiny and the white man's burden, of new frontiers to be conquered, of the land of the free and the home of the brave, of God's blessing from sea to shining sea, all tend to legitimate certain social structures and patterns. These stories are, of course, told from a point of view: that of the victors. Native Americans, blacks, and other oppressed groups have other stories to tell. In fact, it is on the basis of different stories and histories that contemporary appeals for a new economic order rest.

In the socialist view, the democratic market-oriented model of society foundered on the shoals of power—not the theory of power but the brutal reality of exploitation. In his theory of dialectical materialism, class struggle, and communal solidarity, Marx reexamined production forces and production relations and forged the new all-embracing paradigm of "scientific socialism." This model also possesses a powerful internal coherence and logic once the presuppositions and preconditions are granted. Again, though, it is the socialist narrative of the victory of the oppressed that is the most powerful, with its stories of class struggle and solidarity, long marches and victory, visions of community free of domination, and identification of selfless and efficient planning with the satisfaction of human needs.

The paradigms that dominate international development discourse today are both profoundly Western in origin. They appear to be secular (in the sense that legitimacy derives from human reason rather than from religious authority) yet they have a clear basis in religious and philosophical visions of the human person, society, and the meaning of life. They are not simply models of economic development but of overall human development. People espousing these models need not reject God or religious living. The point to note is that, as secular models, their main elements are not based on any religious faith. In fact, development is seen as devoid of religious content and character. Thus, religious considerations should be strictly separated from development discourse.

It should not be surprising that when these models are transported to nonwestern developing countries or religious-based cultures, they encounter more than simply technical problems. This cultural disjunction has become increasingly evident in Latin America (liberation theology), in Islamic countries, and in Africa (where folk religions are especially important) as peoples confront the complexities of developing new notions of development itself.

Such an endeavor is clearly normative for it raises the issue of values and overall human development. Policy debates take place, however, within what ethicists call the limits of social conscience, which cannot be assumed to be free of bias.

The distinction between values and conscience is absolutely fundamental. If social conscience represents the de facto or actual guiding vision of society, the discussion of values represents an attempt to continually push beyond the frontiers of present paradigms to more adequate and comprehensive models of human development and responsibility. This probing takes place in evaluative questioning of the components of social conscience: intention or the ends sought, constraints upon freedom or liberty of action, the means employed, and the adequacy of the consequences that ensue. These pose very practical questions for any development plan: What is the morality of the objectives of development, of the means employed, and of the results? To what extent can political will be galvanized into effective freedom?

The distinction between ultimate values and actual social conscience evokes another basic distinction: that between the essential freedom of the human person and effective freedom. Essential freedom affirms that the very nature of the human person possesses the capacity for free choice. Yet this choice is often limited and may even be considered to be effectively determined by psychological, social, historical, and natural resource factors. This means that a group may in reality be unable to realize its intrinsic values. This is especially the case in the realm of public policy, where freedom is exercised collectively and calls for cooperation and trade-offs with others.

To conclude this section, the legitimacy of development patterns and models evokes a social ethical component in the discussion of development policy. Such discourse probes the adequacy of social paradigms or models-for social relations. As such it is distinct from positivist efforts to sketch out "value-free" models-of such relations. "Models-of" development are descriptive of actual patterns of behavior and related probabilities. Models-for development are normative and discuss (1) values and conscience, on the basis of which it then (2) evaluates ends, means, and consequences of social policy, and (3) assesses the prospects and patterns of accountability and responsibility in collective social choice and freedom.

With this general background on the structure of the problem, I now turn to discuss some ethical themes that are being debated in development policy.

POVERTY AND THE ETHICS OF DEVELOPMENT POLICIES

Discussion of poverty and hunger today is dominated by two schools of thought. The first school bases itself on the "scarcity" aspects of food availability and food production resources. The second focuses on problems of distribution. Each analysis yields different ethical priorities.

In the food question, the first moral problem for the scarcity school is related to the use of resources. The ecosystem may possess food production capacity that is still untapped or is being used for purposes other than food production. Nonetheless, it is limited and there are limits to growth. To disregard these limits or to contribute to the deterioration of the ecosystem, it is argued, is an unjust and a nonresponsible way of behaving toward others (Ehrlich 1976; Hardin 1973). Secondly, one should not lay claim to more than "one's share" of the earth's resources. Concepts of fair share or just distribution necessitate an acceptable philosophical compromise (or contract) upon which members of a given society might agree (In fact, the issue seems often to be decided by the balance of power, which is then called "just.") The first moral issue, then, is to ask to whom the earth is given and what the moral requirements of stewardship are (Jegen and Manno 1979).

A second major issue is that of population. Here there are a number of points to consider (Aiken and LaFollette 1977; Lucas and Ogletree 1976). The first argument focuses on available resources and the birth rate. It is argued that if people contribute to the overcrowding of the universe and are unable to care adequately for their progeny, it is irresponsible and unjust, both with respect to the progeny and with respect to other members of society. Responsible parenthood is, therefore, not just a personal issue but a social one as well. There is more to this argument than simply having enough resources to survive. There is a desire to attain a certain standard of living and quality of life. It is argued that uncontrolled births will only further depress the quality of life for all. That, too, may be unjust. Moreover, those who act irresponsibly when the means are at hand to control fertility forfeit any justifiable claim upon other members of society to command a further share of society's resources. At issue is the nature of personal and social moral obligation to maintain a certain standard of living by finding means to control population.

These basic moral problems of the "scarcity school" in the hunger debate pose several analytical dilemmas. They must be resolved in terms of moral norms and values. This means that in discussion one must make explicit one's worldview (including one's ontological worldview and philosophical anthropology) and methods of moral reasoning. In addition, one must carry out a thorough empirical investigation and try to be free from loyalties or bias in observation.

Can the hunger problem be correctly described in terms of a "lifeboat" or "triage"? The types of problems suggested in these images focus upon moral choice under conditions of supposed scarcity. The first point is empirical. Many observers of the world food complex do not think that scarcity is the main issue. Rather, they concentrate upon distribution as the central moral problem. Accordingly, a different set of moral questions is emphasized: Does the world economic system structurally produce poverty?

The facts of scarcity and distribution are basically empirical. But the answers to the "scarcity" and "distributional" moral questions will be framed by one's ontological worldview and philosophical anthropology in addition to empirical assumptions regarding the availability of resources. Within the context of the preceding chapters, I now present my own approach based on an ecumenical tradition of Christian humanism (see Figure 6-2).

Religious social teaching represents both a testimony of conscience in the search for ultimate values and a testimony to grace, which brings forth ever greater freedom in social action. The religious traditions of which I speak do not fully accept either the liberal or the collectivist scenario as legitimate in terms of overall human development. The reason for this is that they propose a communitarian social ethic that is distinct from both individualism and collectivism

Figure 6-2. Development Models in the Context of Cultural Worldview and Values.

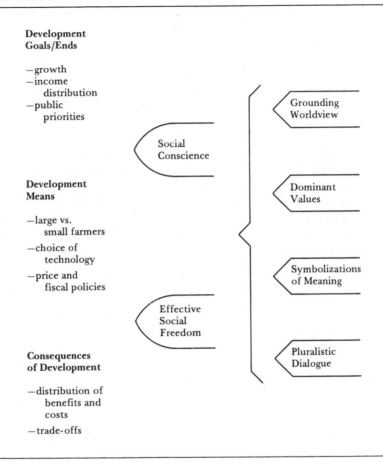

**Development
Goals/Ends**

—growth
—income
    distribution
—public
    priorities

Social
Conscience

Grounding
Worldview

**Development
Means**

—large vs.
    small farmers
—choice of
    technology
—price and
    fiscal policies

Dominant
Values

Effective
Social
Freedom

Symbolizations
of Meaning

**Consequences
of Development**

—distribution of
    benefits and
    costs
—trade-offs

Pluralistic
Dialogue

in terms of both the meaning of ultimate reality and of the human person. This communitarian ethic is easily misunderstood as the work of Peter Bauer (which criticizes the Catholic tradition) so clearly shows (Bauer 1984: ch. 5). Bauer's work is clearly argued and he correctly notes points on which he is at variance with official Catholic teaching. Yet he fails to portray the grounding positions correctly and ends up presenting an unconvincing attack against equality of distribution. His position is inadequate because it assumes the legitimacy of the "initial position" of "legal" patterns of resource control and mechanisms of distribution.

Bauer's analysis lacks a distinctive vision of human community, founded upon the dynamic unity of the love of God and the love of neighbor. On the level of social relations this expresses itself in terms of solidarity. There is no question but that social relations are inherently religious in character. What is happening to one's neighbor in the economic system is a religious issue. There are two general overarching principles to note: (1) the obligation to do no harm (nonmaleficence) and (2) the obligation to do good (beneficence). These two points are insisted upon because they are fundamental prerequisites of community; human community cannot exist without them. They clearly impose limits on individualist or utilitarian rules that would harm others in the process of the pursuit of self-interest. They also limit collectivist tendencies that would repress legitimate individual rights in favor of the perceived will of the group. Secondly, these principles suggest that in the face of evil or the need of one's neighbor, those who have an ability to solve a problem of injustice have an obligation to do so, even though they may not have caused it in the first place. It is clear that these principles differ from both the ideal types of liberalism and collectivism as well as from their pragmatic interpretations.

In the general typology I am developing, these two fundamental orientation principles have been fleshed out in terms of three other general social principles: the dignity of the person, the universal destiny of all the goods of creation, and the notion of a common good.

The dignity of the person derives from the fact that all people are created to live in harmony with God and be children of God. Thus, there is a fundamental dignity of human nature, a sacredness in just being a person itself. This principle does not deny human weakness and a propensity for egoistic sinfulness but integrates these dynamics into human development and a call to salvation. It also affirms in the present development debate that each person enjoys inalienable natural rights and that these have political, economic, and cultural components. At the very least they imply that any system that does not protect those rights or prevents people from meeting their fundamental needs would not be legitimate.

The universal destiny of all the goods of creation fiercely conditions the right to appropriate any goods of creation as one's private property. It neither forbids private property nor differences in wealth; rather it sets conditions of acceptable limits for both (on the basis of fundamental prerequisites of community noted above). God created the earth and it is good; he gave the earth and everything in it to the whole human family. While it may be licit to socially distribute the goods of the earth to individuals, families, and even states, those rights are conditioned by the imperative that everyone receive a fair share. This principle has far-reaching consequences when one speaks of the distribution of economic resources and the rights to international migration.

The principle of the common good is distinct from the liberal view of society that is based upon an aggregate of individual self-interests as expressed in a social contract or upon simple utilitarian criteria. It also places value upon the dignity of individuals and their development and is thus distinct from the anonymous collective that exalts the dictatorship of the group. Ideally, the notion of the common good tends to hold in check an excessive form of individual self-interest, which would fail to recognize the duty to contribute to the common welfare; that is, there are just limits to individual liberty. At the same time, it rejects an excessive collectivist tendency that would centralize activities and expressions that properly belong to free associations and individuals as part of their human development. There is thus an attempt to integrate individual with social rights and duties, and liberty with responsibility, in a notion of universal solidarity.

In defining the common good, it is not enough to set if off from sheer individualism or collectivism. Rather, it suggests a profoundly positive vision of the social nature of the human person. The increasing degree of social relations in modern times is seen as both a positive and necessary component of human development, whereby people give creative expression to human solidarity.

In the world today, these principles have a striking relevance to the political economic scene. Their relevance has been discussed in terms of (1) mutual rights and duties between equivalent moral agents, (2) the rights and duties of the lesser units in society to the greater, the parts to the whole, and (3) the rights and duties of the greater units toward the lesser, the whole to the parts. With reference to our theme, what is at stake is the sketching of political economic rights and duties both within nations and between nations.

There is here an underlying question of general social equality and the legitimacy of differences: Do all persons and peoples deserve the same social consideration and treatment? This point comes into focus in terms of five themes found in the general typology I have sketched and in contemporary international economic and development literature: dependency, marginalization, deprivation, apathy, and sanctions. The positive content of the common good can be made more specific in terms of these themes. Each point poses a different question of general social equality.

Firstly, liberty versus dependence: Are all persons and peoples to enjoy the same degree of liberty and self-determination? In terms of its communitarian ethic, Christian thought affirms the rights of states and of individuals and groups within states to self-determination. In this case, the freedom of the oppressed and the dependent takes priority over the license and liberty of the powerful.

Secondly, equality of opportunity: Are all persons and peoples to enjoy the same rights to participate in social structures? Marginalization is a phenomenon in which individuals, groups, and states are denied the right to participate fully in political, economic, and social life. Pushed to the edges of these social structures and institutions, the marginalized must endure all the duties and strictures of society without receiving a proportionate share of the benefits. Affirming the right of the poor and marginalized to meaningful participation in social structures has clear ramifications in the context of IMF and GATT rules as well as for local resource control and social privileges.

Thirdly, deprivation versus equality of distribution: Should all persons and people receive the same amount of resources, goods, and services and of the power attached to social offices? Deprivation underlines the cases of those who live in poverty and cannot even meet their needs on either an individual or national level. This affront to human dignity is exacerbated by the excessive wealth of the privileged who are driven by materialist consumption and possessiveness. Regarding distribution of resources, goods, and services, I would affirm the priority of the needs of the poor over the mere wants of the rich. In distribution, four criteria are advanced. The priority is given to needs and then to effort (those who work more) within a context of equal opportunity. Claims based upon meritocracy and privilege also are recognized but are conditioned by the common good and the moral obligation to do good. The priorities in Christian thought are ranked in this order: needs, effort, merit, and privilege. This does not preclude differences but conditions them.

Fourthly, apathy and egoism versus contribution: Should all persons and peoples be required to make the same effort to contribute to society's well-being? The plight of the poor is often met with apathy and unconcern on the part of those who are well-off. I would stress the duty of all members to make a contribution to society according to their abilities and find the refusal to do so, whether deriving from egoism or apathy, an unacceptable position. There is a social duty to be responsive to other's needs and to contribute according to one's ability.

Finally, dissent and due process versus coercion: Should all persons and people enjoy the same degree of due process in social structures? Economic and political sanctions can only be considered just if the rules of the game are themselves just. Coercive sanctions that treat individuals, groups, and nations like things, as instruments for either personal or group or national self-interest, are unacceptable. Furthermore, in the face of unjust rules of the game (such as unfair property laws), dissent is a social duty.

As may be seen from the brief sketch presented above, the religious-based questioning of development proposes a vision of the human person and of ultimate reality that provides a guiding vision for political and economic development in the world today. Many may disagree with it. In that case I call for dialogue. But the five questions noted above are indispensable in assessing actual development patterns as well as models. They directly confront the four sources of the powerlessness of the poor: lack of development of human capacities, little control over resources, lack of access to and participation in social procedures, and little voice in shaping the social environment.

The communitarian social ethic that has been sketched presents no concrete blueprint. While clearly normative, it is inherently open-ended as to concrete prescriptions and realizations. It does not automatically lead either to political or market conclusions. Indeed, it is anticipated that in different cultural settings and historical circumstances a wide number of different but suitable paths to justice may be creatively imagined and given concrete shape.

The main point of this whole discussion is to underline the pivotal role of culture (including religion) in determining the legitimacy of development patterns and models in larger terms of overall human development. Many in the field of development economics would rather not bother with such considerations, either because they think they are impractical or that economics is somehow value-free. They are mistaken. Policy analysts will never grasp what is underway in Latin America, Africa, the Middle East, and Asia unless they come to terms with normative discourse.

CULTURAL PREFERENCES

The preceding discussion has focused on how a cultural vision of ultimate meaning and reality grounds social values. These factors are of pivotal importance in either legitimating social systems and development patterns and models or denouncing them. I now turn to how cultural preferences interact with the various development issues raised in the preceding chapters. For purposes of discussion, I distinguish values from preferences in the sense that I consider preferences as various constellations of behavior patterns that represent alternative paths to the realization of values.

It is instructive to reflect on a simple example: What is food? Food is more than food in the obvious functional sense. To begin with the physiological part of the definition, any substance taken into and assimilated by a person to keep one alive and enable one to grow is human "food." But as noted by the National Academy of Science Study Team (National Academy of Sciences 1977: vol. IV, 16ff, 75ff), there is much more to human food; it enters into and is in part defined by the whole process of human existence. Thus, the definition of food includes cultural dimensions and social definitions of what is edible, as well as psychic motivations underlying why people eat what they do and why diets change. Food is generally eaten in a socio-cultural context and is shared with others; it must taste, look, and smell "good." Behavior towards food is influenced by a wide variety of physical, psychic, and sociocultural factors. As the above cited report continued (National Academy of Sciences 1977: vol. IV, 77-78):

> Food alone does not mean growth and health. There are societies in which the calories consumed are at or below minimum standards and yet where people are vigorous and healthy, even into very old age. . . . Conversely, infants may stop growing physically when deprived of love and human contact, even if they receive "adequate" nutrition. . . . In effect, we do not know, except for basal metabolism, how many calories are needed for people to live their daily lives. There is not yet any satisfactory way to specify the characteristics of good nutrition for people within a social setting, much less to quantify the full meaning of this objective.

The above example underlines the critical function of traditions and social preferences, which represent a cultural framework for alternative paths to realization. In what follows, I discuss social preferences regarding (1) general social structures, (2) outlooks towards change, and (3) some particular economic attitudes (cf. Figure 6-3).

General Social Structures

In this section, I am speaking of culture primarily in terms of a persuasion system (in distinction to civil authority and economic exchange systems). The point is to discover how this persuasion system interacts with other persuasion systems and with the realities of civil authority, on the one hand, and economic exchange, on the other. In speaking of society I am speaking of shared social relations: Social experience amounts to more than a mere aggregate of individuals. It connotes shared consciousness, shared meaning, and shared behavior. As was pointed out in the preceding section on legitimacy, it is the cultural worldview that confers cohesion upon social experi-

Figure 6–3. The Economic Person in a Cultural Key.

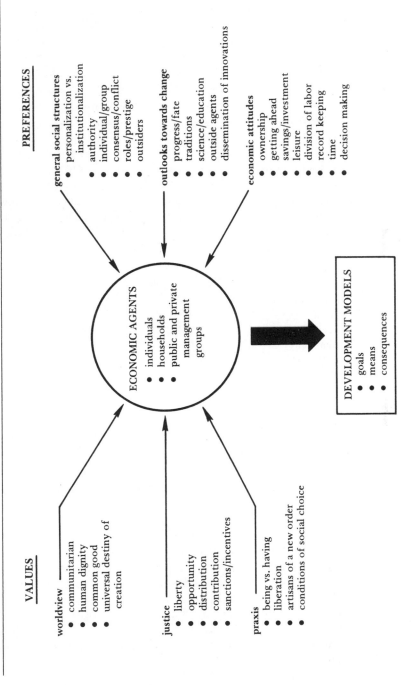

ence and effectively integrates patterns of social relations into a sense of ultimate meaning and reality.

A primary question in most developing countries is the extent to which the social order is effectively institutionalized or dependent upon the personality system. In China, for example, there is considerable evidence that the informal personality system plays a leading role in social cohesion (Oksenberg 1982a, 1982b; Steidlmeier 1982). Chinese leadership takes place in a complex social policy milieu. There are four systems of formal organization that act upon policy formulation and implementation: the organizational apparatus that has control over public personnel; the economic apparatus, which is in charge of accumulation and allocation of productive resources; the propaganda apparatus that covers the activities of the information system; and the coercive apparatus of military planning and public order and discipline. In present-day China Deng Xiao-ping's faction is important in all four apparatuses but must contend with other factions in each.

These four apparatuses of power are formally linked by bureaucratic ties and informally linked by what Chinese call *guanxi* (loosely translated as the personal relations network based upon family, geographic origin, school companions, place of work, patronage, and friendships). What puzzles observers of contemporary China is the nature of the shifting constellations of these variables in the arena of contemporary policy. The role of *guanxi* is of fundamental importance in commanding people's loyalties and cannot be overemphasized in the exercise of power. But this means that policy tends to be highly personalized rather than institutionalized and is subject to volatile swings following a change in leading personalities. Deng Xiao-ping's faction has been ruling by coalition. Higher level officials have close *guanxi* with Deng. Lower level officials have close *guanxi* with their own higher officials (who themselves are allied with Deng) or with Deng's own immediate allies. A leader's policy is accepted not necessarily because *it* is the best but because of *guanxi, he* offers the best situation possible.

The above discussion is very important for policy when one places it in the context of social authority. The personality system of family, kinship, and friends will often be more authoritative than political economic institutions and impersonal structures. In the case of a conflict between the two, it is more likely in such societies that the personality system would prevail. The rules and procedures of more anonymous social structures and plans emerge as secondary matters. In fact, one would be inclined to bend the rules to meet the needs and expectations of primary relationships.

Authority is enmeshed in the broad web of personal relations and also in the traditions of a group, that is, social authority not only derives from persons but from tradition. The modern Western mentality emphasizes freedom from external and unexamined authority. It frequently regards tradition as a collection of superstitions, totems, and taboos. The wisdom of the elders is to be scrutinized by reason and scientific knowledge; their decisions are to be discussed and evaluated in a democratic spirit. This modern mentality runs counter to the practices I observed in many parts of Asia and Africa, where, for example, rationality is related to transcendent goals and the thinking of tribal elders and chiefs is accepted as normative (because of the relations at stake). Their decisions are to be followed, even when one disagrees (Daphne 1982).

In such a context, a spirit of individualism is not considered a virtue. This does not mean that individuals do not seek to develop their capacities; rather self-development itself is understood within a process of socialization into the primary group. One internalizes the group's identity, customs, and values as one grows to maturity. Attitudes of aggressiveness, competition, drive, and meritocracy, which are virtues in an individualist, institution-oriented society, are not primary values in a more communal personalist-oriented society. For in such societies, the common good is not a mere aggregate of individual self-interests, but expresses the realization of the goals of the primary group and emphasizes a spirit of solidarity and communal well-being. This point is very important, when for example, one considers officials in a bureaucracy. In a communal personality-oriented system it would be unthinkable for them simply to pursue their own careers; they must concern themselves with furthering their fellows and bringing benefits to the entire primary group, even if this means bending the rules of organizations or altering the directives of plans (Waterston 1976).

Within the primary group, consensus is frequently valued above conflict, even when consensus amounts to being less efficient in the accumulation and use of resources. Conflict within the group breaks up the solidarity of relationships and threatens the continued well-being of the traditional structures, institutions, and relations that are the prime carriers of meaning. Ideas of democratic "loyal opposition" are very foreign indeed in such a setting. When conflict must be subordinated to consensus, it means that projected changes must often be long delayed until the traditional leaders who oppose innovations or changes either change their minds or pass away.

At the same time, while consensus is sought within the group, those who stand outside the network of a particular set of group relations often merit little or no consideration. For example, I have observed that in parts of Africa conflict with other tribes, or in China conflict with other factions, or in India conflict with other castes or untouchables, is acceptable to the degree that it serves the interests of the primary groups in question. In this sense, ideas of equal rights and opportunities for all, including those who stand outside primary groups, is often considered a strange notion that has very little chance of being realized in practice.

Furthermore, in the context of traditions and customs of various peoples, one finds that certain roles carry social prestige while others are considered quite menial. In many parts of Asia and Africa, physical work with one's hands is not highly esteemed. This is especially true of agriculture in the developing world. In many parts of the developing world, the life of a farmer or herdsman is considered very low class. It is the last thing that any young person would want to do. There are also many tribes that devote themselves to specific roles such as herding to the exclusion of farming and vice versa.

Many farming tasks within tribes are traditionally correlated with sex roles (Wilson 1985). There are certain tasks for men to perform and others for women; men will remain idle rather than perform those that women should do. Sexual roles in development have recently been receiving far more attention. The disruption of the traditional roles of women in the rural economy by the ill-considered introduction of innovations and by negative governmental policies toward women have combined to weaken food production (Muntemba 1982). Sex-differentiated roles in production, resource control, and noneconomic opportunities and well-being make it an imperative of development planning to give explicit attention to the traditional and evolving roles of women in the political economy (Black and Cottrell, 1981; Blumberg 1981).

Outlooks Toward Change

Related to all the preceding characteristics of general social structure is the perspective a group takes on social structure itself in the context of time and history. As noted, the eighteenth and nineteenth century ideas of progress undergird the modern notion of economic development. The notion of time and history underlying such development is linear and dynamic. It also emphasizes an idea of progress that is cumulative, evolutionary, and self-correcting. History forms part of the human destiny in the sense that people are to mold and shape it through the exercise of their reason and freedom. The material world in modern thought is seen as secular and as a matter both of fundamental importance and of human responsibility. Such a vision contrasts with a fatalistic view of history, where poverty and hunger are interpreted in terms of inexplicable destiny, or cyclic views of history, where suffering in this life is related to the sins of one's ancestors or even one's own sins in a previous life. In this latter context, social structure emerges as something to be endured and submitted to rather than reacted against and shaped by human reason and freedom.

Economic development, as it is commonly conceived, means thoroughgoing social change. As such it often threatens the existence of traditional customs and roles. Perhaps the most striking example of a nonWestern nation that has developed into a modern economic giant is Japan. Modernization was not an easy process in Japan, although the policies begun under the Meiji Restoration in 1868 were extraordinarily enlightened for the time and quite effective. In China during the same period there was considerable discussion of and resistance to the Westernization that modernization implied. Today, the same struggle is visible in the Islamic world, where there is spreading alarm over the weakening of Islamic culture as development takes place. In Africa, ethnic traditions already have been considerably weakened during the process of colonialization and its aftermath.

Resistance to the cultural change that development implies is not surprising. In early development literature in the West, other traditions were considered backward and an obstacle to progress. As noted in Chapter 2, the contemporary idea of progress is profoundly Western in origin and in spirit. The question that many developing countries are rightly asking is how is it possible to develop and modernize their own traditions and heritage rather than jettison them. It is a valid question. It will not be adequately handled, however, by those who fiercely protect their heritage in order to recover a pristine past. Nor by those who simply discard their tradition. What is needed instead is balanced, constructive attention to the dynamic aspects of heritage and tradition. Culturally based development means modernization in terms of science and technology and requires the transformation of traditional values, institutions, and structures, but it does not have to mean imitation of the West. The biggest challenge to developing countries stems from the scientific mentality, precisely because it questions the grounds of truth, meaning of tradition, and foundations of authority. But such a mentality need not be feared when the various peoples who are undergoing development are themselves participants in development processes, the subjects and architects of their own development rather than passive objects. It is not surprising that many traditional cultures maintain attitudes of fear and hostility toward scientific innovations, for they necessarily imply a transformation of their traditions and the evolution of new cultural forms. Such transformations, however, can be an artistic expression of creative growth within a tradition rather than an annihilation of it.

To the point, attention is increasingly being given to "participatory research" (Fals–Borda 1982). This research is based on the presumption that local groups possess their own unique forms of rationality, knowledge, production, and diffusion. The idea is for developmentalists to become deeply immersed in a particular culture, grasp its inner dynamics, and build off of traditional philosophies and practices to bring about social development and changes. To this end many experiments have been conducted using popular theater as a catalyst to change in developing countries (Eskamp 1984).

The modern scientific approach to education suggests that all truth is based upon experience and knowledge and is meaningful only when it has concrete applications to everyday life. But modern science has tended to be one-sidedly empirical and rationalistic. Broader categories of meaning, as found in narrative, presentational, and symbolic artistic forms, as well as philosophical and ontological questions, have tended to be ignored. Myth for example, has come to be equated with falsity. Such a position is erroneous.

A key aspect of whether traditional cultures can adapt to change is whether they can integrate their literature, history, and traditions with the study of science in creative new forms of humanistic education. The result will lead to the transformation of both science and tradition on the basis of nonWestern humanism. This is what has taken place in Japan and is also underway in China, India, and other parts of Asia and Africa. In the Americas, the local cultures have already to a great extent been vanquished in the process of modernization, with the result that the dominant cultures of both North and South America are largely derivative of European culture.

The key point under consideration here is whether a culture in transition is open to the dynamic development of its own cultural forms. A new humanistic approach to education involves a new pedagogy that leads to the refashioning of both science and of tradition. At the same time, it will raise questions about social organization—social roles, prestige, and social mobility. At issue is whether a society is capable of dealing with outside agents of change and evolving new forms of leadership that social innovation and mobility imply. Science brings with it not merely new knowledge but new structures inherent in and deriving from scientific method itself. Science rewards questioners and innovators; it suggests a shift away from the personality system to more neutral institutions and structures based upon the participation and consent of those involved. Thus one principal challenge of development is the opening of social organization to become truly participative.

There is no easy blueprint to follow regarding such culturally based patterns of modernization. Yet a key point upon which many observers focus is the importance of beginning with indigenous patterns of leadership (Go 1983; Rogers 1982; Samanta and Reddy 1983). Only when such participation is guaranteed is there a realistic hope of developing the motivations and institutions (e.g., of information and cooperation) that community-based efforts to overcome poverty call for.

Hardly any area has received more attention in the economic literature than the adoption of new technology by traditional farmers. Not surprisingly, economic analysis frequently ignores cultural factors. A recent World Bank study (Feder, Just, and Zilberman 1981) proposed an extensive model covering cash reserves, information, experience, risk, scale, fixed costs, and timing but failed to address culture. It is strange indeed not to explicitly relate economic technology to the social system and the ecosystem. That it is not sensible either (1) to assume that these factors are irrelevant or (2) held constant is copiously attested in the literature of recent years on African Pastoralists (Dyson–Hudson 1982), in studies of irrigation (Coward 1980; Merrey 1979), ploughing (Webster 1982), natural resources practices (West 1983), the Green Revolution (Leaf 1983), or birth control (Warwick 1982).

It is safe to say that most of the information produced by rural sociologists and anthropologists has not been incorporated into the economics literature nor into the planning of rural projects (Alao 1982). Obviously there are no hard and fast laws of adoption of technological innovations. The economic variables mentioned by Feder and colleagues are surely important, but they must be understood together with sociological and anthropological variables: kinship, socioeconomic status, leadership, literacy, extension contact, equity issues, property rights, factions in the community, the role of community organizing, and social learning (Arokoyo 1981; Carlson and Dillman 1983; Forestier–Walker 1982; Mwaniki 1980; Voh 1982; West 1983).

The interaction of all these variables is in many ways culturally specific. In each case there is a process of initiation of innovations followed by their possible transformation and reworking, legitimation, and finally implementation. It remains difficult to assess the role of local social and economic organizations and outside factors such as central government bureaucracy. Yet any sensible planning must include them on a checklist of project evaluation.

The widely disparate assessments of the Green Revolution reflect the current differences in methodological techniques. In his study of a Punjab village, Murray Leaf (1981) centers upon the interaction between six cultural subsystems; ecology, division of labor, economy, kinship, religion, and political party. Significant changes in any of these variables would lead to widely differing assessments of the Green Revolution. The point that I am underscoring here is that the development implied by the Green Revolution has to do with much more than either economics or technology; it necessarily has a sociocultural and historical base.

These remarks on general social structure and cultural outlooks toward change are of fundamental importance for development planning. Plans that do not take them into account have little hope for success. The next step is to examine the variety of economic attitudes manifested by traditional cultural groups.

Some Particular Economic Attitudes

The Western economic model of development idealizes individual genius, initiative, effort, aggressiveness, and competitiveness (McClelland 1963; Inkles and Smith 1974). It is this vision of human motivation and perfection that underlies the notion of the entrepreneur and free market as socially beneficial. Western models of development seem to imply that it is desirable and even necessary to inculcate an individualist, entrepreneurial spirit. As noted above, however, such an individualist, spirit is often at cross-purposes with more communal feelings of solidarity native to many cultures. In the latter case, the individual is not to go forward unless the primary group also goes forward. It is often not socially acceptable within the group to distinguish oneself or strive to get ahead. In this case, decisions regarding innovations must be arrived at by consensus and implemented communally. Entrepreneurship takes a more social form. Increasingly, discussion turns to the entrepreneurial potential of traditional grassroots peasant organizations (Cernea 1981).

A second notion of fundamental economic importance is that the means of production, especially land, are often considered a communal patrimony. Thus, individual ownership and even management of land and other resources as well as individual profit poses considerable social difficulties. In Africa, user rights rather than ownership rights predominate. Management is itself subject to the wisdom of the elders and to traditions regarding both what is produced, when and how it is done, and for whom. Often there are subsidiary users such as herdsmen. In such systems it is very difficult for an individual to emerge as the catalyst of development either in terms of just working for him or herself or in terms of leading the group in resource development and entrepreneurial activities. When one does not possess a traditional leadership role, or when one acts for individualist rather than communal goals, there will be resistance to proposed development measures.

Such attitudes greatly complicate the process of capital accumulation for investment. First of all, traditional values often do not place an emphasis on accumulating a surplus for investment. Economic aspirations frequently do not proceed beyond the satisfaction of immediate needs. Indeed, when there is a surplus, it is often devoted to increased consumption by the family or to social purposes (such as a marriage dowry). Furthermore, it is difficult for individuals to save in the context of communal personality-oriented structures. One's fellows can always make a claim upon one's surplus.

If development policies are to prove durable, the accumulation and management of resources must be rethought in terms of communal structures. Considerable attention is now being devoted to traditional financial group markets in many parts of Africa (Miracle et al. 1980; Obioma 1983; Tapsoba 1981). These structures give evidence of being efficient means of saving and they possess considerable potential for rural development. There is frequently an inability (e.g., because of illiteracy) or a general reluctance (e.g., because of lack of trust) for peasants to organize and participate in formal social organizations (Mabry 1979). Traditional organizations have the potential to develop into workable alternatives.

Attitudes toward work and leisure are also of great importance. These attitudes are obviously connected with thrift and the accumulation of a surplus. In many traditional societies the work ethic is not a primary virtue. Leisure and social activities have a higher priority and are seen as more conducive to overall human development. They represent time to enjoy the pleasures of family and friendship. Work is entered into in order to meet the needs of primary groups but is not seen as the factor that gives most value to life partially because "getting ahead" of others is not a primary social value.

A further matter of considerable importance are attitudes toward information and record keeping. Part of the difficulty with keeping accurate statistics and records can be blamed on illiteracy, which practically renders the accumulation and processing of information impossible. But many traditional societies also display a casual attitude toward numbers and quantitative methods. This posture not only involves cultural paradigms but political and social apprehension: since it is the government that generally seeks to compile adequate records, local groups perceive that it is not in their interest to

turn over to such outsiders demographic data or information on production, income, and consumption. Thus, information and records
are primarily seen in a sociopolitical sense than in an economic sense.

All of this, of course, complicates planning. The lack of concern
for records has important ramifications for economic efficiency. This
is not to say that traditional farmers cannot be efficient; in fact, they
are often very efficient in an intuitive sense. But it does mean that
the approach to optimizing input–output and profit–cost relations
remains intuitive and bound by tradition. In terms of decisionmaking, the farmer will often tend to view comparative economic
advantage through the prism of historical experience and risk avoidance. Comparative advantage is not analyzed simply in terms of economic potential but in terms of family security. This means that
innovations must not only be presented as potentially profitable but
also as secure. Numerous studies attest that traditional farmers are
not unresponsive to higher prices and new methods as such but that
security and risk avoidance are more important motivational factors.

It is important to give some consideration to how traditional farmers view time in an economic sense. The economic vision of time is
primarily shaped by traditional periods of planting and harvesting.
Meeting schedules and being punctual is not seen as greatly important. Frequently enough, punctuality and saving time are often not
important for traditional agriculture. When this attitude is carried
over to development, problems ensue.

One of the main irritants of Western people in third-world countries is wasting time—whether in clearing customs, processing forms,
waiting for transportation, or beginning business. In modern societies, timing is obviously important in an economic sense. In processes of industrialization, timing is crucial. In coordinating the economic activities of various enterprises in the modern world, it is of
the essence. It is also important for modern agriculture. For example,
in getting fertilizer cleared through the port, transported to farmers,
and applied to crops at the critical periods or in getting parts and re-
pairing machines so that they will actually work when needed during
planting and harvests. Without careful attention to timing and coordination, development planning ends in shambles.

CONCLUSION: PROGRESS REVISITED

I have examined part of the relevance of culture for development.
My conclusion is that development needs to be rethought in cul-
tural terms. The facile identification of modern development with
Westernization has proven to be an obstacle to development itself.

What will be the shape of modern nonWestern development? It is an open field. Japan provides an interesting case study, yet no convincing generalizations can be drawn for other regions of the world. If development planning is to be effective, it must root itself in and build off of the dynamic positive elements of local cultures. It cannot simply ape Western modernization. Development cannot be imported from abroad nor will it come simply from the top down.

The process of development is circumscribed by patterns of resource control, social meanings and symbols attributed to it, and subjective perceptions of social change (Attir et al., 1981: 54-58). Up to now, sociology of knowledge has been preoccupied with ideology. What is more at issue here is the structure, distribution, and interaction of knowledge-related social functions, on the one hand, and cultural norms, values, and preferences, on the other.

Development processes are a form of social change. This change encompasses demographics and ecologically sound resource use, technological innovations, and social power. It also means profound cultural change. The modern development in third-world countries need not ape the West. Social attitudes and behavior will both change. How, it is not clear, but there would appear to be a reciprocal interaction between innovations in one area and changes in the other. That is, changes in attitudes can precede changes in behavior, though the contrary is also true in some cases (James and Gutkind 1985).

My assessment of the reality of poverty is that population pressure, resource scarcity, and the lack of technology are real problems, but they are relative to the larger social system. In principle they can be resolved, but they will not be resolved soon unless the dynamics of that larger social system are also addressed. That means development models must formally address power and culture. These sociological factors are the major problems in development today.

REFERENCES

Adelman, Irma, and Cynthia Taft Morris. 1973. *Economic Growth and Social Equity in Developing Countries.* Stanford, Calif.: Stanford University Press.

Aiken, William, and Hugh LaFollette. 1977. *World Hunger and Moral Obligation.* Englewood Cliffs, N.J.: Prentice Hall.

Alao, J.A. 1982. "Understanding Small Farmer Adoption Behavior: The Nigerian Experience." *Inaugural Lecture Series.* No. 44: 30. Ife, Nigeria: University of Ife.

Arndt, H.W.H. 1981. "Economic Development: A Semantic History." *Economic Development and Cultural Change* 29, no. 3 (April): 457-66.

Arokoyo, J.O. 1981. "The Diffusion and Adoption of Recommended Agricultural Practices Among Farmers in the Northern States of Nigeria." Ph.D. dissertation, University of Wisconsin–Madison.

Attir, Mustafa, Burkart Holzner, and Suda Zdenek. 1981. *Directions of Change, Modernization Research and Reality.* Boulder, Colo.: Westview Press.

Bauer, Peter. 1984. *Reality and Rhetoric.* Cambridge, Mass.: Harvard University Press.

Bennett, John. 1958. *Christians and the State.* New York: Scribners.

Black, N., and A.B. Cottrell, eds. 1981. *Women and World Change: Equity Issues in Development.* Beverly Hills, Calif.: Sage Publications.

Blumberg, R.L. 1981. "Rural Women in Development." In *Women and World Change: Equity Issues in Development*, ed. N. Black and A.B. Cottrell, 32–56. Beverly Hills, Calif.: Sage Publications.

Carlson, J.E., and D.A. Dillman. 1983. "Influence of Kinship Arrangements on Farmer Innovativeness." *Rural Sociology* 48, no. 2: 183–200.

Cernea, M. 1981. *Modernization and Development Potential of Traditional Grass Roots Peasant Organizations.* In *Directions of Change: Modernization Theory, Research and Reality*, ed. Mustafa Attil, Burkart Holzner, and Sdenek Suda, 121–39. Boulder, Colo.: Westview Press.

Choudhury, Masudul Alsm. 1983. "Principles of Islamic Ethics." *Middle Eastern Studies* 19, no. 1: 93–103.

Coward, E. Walter, ed. 1980. *Irrigation and Agricultural Development in Asia, Perspectives from the Social Sciences.* Ithaca, N.Y.: Cornell University Press.

Daphne, P. 1982. *Tribal Authority and Community Organization.* Occasional Papers, No. 3. University of Zululand: Center for Research and Documentation.

Dyson–Hudson, Neville, and Rada. 1982. "The Structure of East African Herds and the Future of East African Herders." *Development and Change* 13, no. 3: 213–38.

Ehrlich, Paul. 1976. *The Population Bomb.* New York: Ballantine.

Eskamp, Kees. 1984. "Going 'Popular' with Culture: Theatre As a Small-Scale Medium in Developing Countries." *Development and Change* 15, no. 1 (January): 43–65.

Fals–Borda, O. 1982. "Participatory Research and Rural Social Change." *Journal of Rural Cooperation* 10, no. 1: 25–40.

Feder, Gershon, Richard E. Just, and David Zilberman. 1981. *Adoption of Agricultural Innovation in Developing Countries.* World Bank, Staff Working Paper No. 542. Washington, D.C.: World Bank.

Forestier–Walker, C.O. 1982. "Integrated Technology Projects for Rural Communities." *Science and Public Policy* no. 5: 226–35.

Geertz, Clifford. 1973. *The Interpretation of Cultures.* New York: Basic Books.

Go, A.S. 1983. "Determining Leadership Indicators and Communication Tasks of Sociometrically Chosen Farmers in Eastern Visayas." *VICARP News* 4, no. 2: 1–13.

Goulet, Denis. 1983. "Obstacles to World Development: An Ethical Reflection." *World Development* 11, no. 7: 608–24.

Gunnatilleke, Godfrey, N. Tiruchelvam, and R. Coomaraswamy. 1983. *Ethical Dilemmas of Development in Asia.* Lexington, Mass.: Lexington Books.

Hardin, Garrett. 1973. *Exploring New Ethics for Survival: The Voyage of Spaceship Beagle*. New York: Penguin.

Inkles, Alex, and David M. Smith. 1974. *Becoming Modern: Individual Change in Six Developing Countries*. Cambridge, Mass.: Harvard University Press.

James, Jeffrey, and Efraim Gutkind. 1985. "Attitude Change Revisited: Cognitive Dissonance Theory and Development Policy." *World Development* 13, no. 10/11: 1139-49.

Jegen, Mary Evelyn, and Bruno Manno. 1979. *The Earth Is the Lord's: Essays on Stewardship*. New York: Paulist Press.

Kohnert, Dirk. 1982. "A Critique of the Sociocultural Approach to Development Planning." *Intereconomics* 17, no. 6: 296-99.

Leaf, Murray J. 1983. "The Green Revolution and Cultural Change in a Punjab Village." *Economic Development and Cultural Change* 31, no. 2: 227-70.

Lucas, George R., Jr., and Thomas E. Ogletree, eds. 1976. *Lifeboat Ethics*. New York: Harper & Row.

Mabry, Bewars D. 1979. "Peasant Economic Behavior in Thailand." *Journal of Southeast Asian Studies* 10, no. 2: 400-19.

McClelland, David. 1963. "The Achievement Motive in Economic Growth." In *Industrialization and Society*, ed. Bert F. Hoselitz and William F. Moule, 74-95. Paris: UNESCO.

Merrey, D.I. 1979. "Irrigation and Honor: Cultural Impediments to the Improvement of Local Level Water Management in Punjab, Pakistan." Water Management Research Project, Engineering Research Center, Technical Report No. 53. Fort Collins, Colo.: Colorado State University.

Miracle, Marvin P., Diane S. Miracle, and Laurie Cohen. 1980. "Informal Savings Mobilization in Africa." *Economic Development and Cultural Change* 28, no. 4 (July): 701-24.

Muntemba, S. 1982. "Women as Food Producers and Suppliers in the Twentieth Century. The Case of Zambia." *Development Dialogue* 1, no. 2: 29-50.

Mwaniki, N. 1980. *Pastoral Societies and Resistance to Change: A Revaluation*. Bloomington: University of Indiana.

National Academy of Sciences. 1977. *World Food and Nutrition Study, Supporting Papers*. Vol. 4. Washington, D.C.: National Academy of Sciences.

Obioma, Bennett. 1983. "Traditional Financial Group Markets—Lessons from the Nigerian Experience." Ph.D. diss., Pontifical Gregorian University, Rome, Italy.

Oksenberg, Michael. 1982a. "Economic Policy-Making in China: Summer 1981." *China Quarterly* 90 (June): 165-82.

_____. 1982b. "China's Economic Bureaucracy." *The China Business Review* (May-June): 22-28.

Polgar, Stephen, ed. 1971. *Culture and Population: A Collection of Current Studies*. Chapel Hill: North Carolina Population Center.

"Religious Values and Development." 1980. *World Development* (July, August): entire issue.

Rogers, M.L. 1982. "Patterns of Change in a Rural Malay Community: Sungai Raya Revisited." *Asian Survey* 22, no. 8: 757-78.

Samanta, R.K., and M.N. Reddy. 1983. "Farm Leadership Among Koya Tribes of Andhra Pradesh." *Man in India* 63, no. 2: 174–79.

Standing, Guy. 1980. "Basic Needs and the Division of Labor." *Pakistan Development Review* 19, no. 3: 211–35.

Steidlmeier, Paul. 1982. "Management and Policy Issues in China's Rural Development." *Intereconomics* 17, no. 6 (November/December): 302–307.

_____ . 1984. *Social Justice Ministry: Foundations and Concerns.* New York: Le Jacq Publishing Co.

Tapsoba, E.K. 1981. "An Economic and Institutional Analysis of Formal and Informal Credit in Eastern Upper Volta: Empirical Evidence and Policy Implications." Ph.D. diss., Michigan State University.

Timmer, W.J. 1982. *The Human Side of Agriculture: Theory and Practice of Agricultural Extension.* New York: Vantage Press.

United Nations Education and Social Committee (UNESCO). 1981. "Technology and Cultural Values." *International Social Science Journal* 33, no. 3: entire issue.

Voh, J.P. 1982. "A Study of Factors Associated with the Adoption of Recommended Farm Practices in a Nigerian Village." *Agricultural Administration* 9, no. 1: 17–27.

Warwick, Donald P. 1982. *Bitter Pills: Population Policies and Their Implementation in Eight Developing Countries.* New York: Cambridge University Press.

Waterston, J. 1976. *Development Planning: Lessons from Experience.* Baltimore: The Johns Hopkins Press.

Webster, Peter. 1982. "To Plough or Not to Plough? A Nevar Dilemma." *Pacific Viewpoint* 22, no. 2: 99–135.

West, P.C. 1983. "Collective Adoption of Natural Resource Practices in Developing Nations." *Rural Sociology* 48, no. 1: 44–59.

Wilson, Fiona. 1985. "Women and Agricultural Change in Latin America: Some Concepts Guiding Research." *World Development* 13, no. 9: 1017–35.

Wuthnow, Robert, James Davison Hunter, Albert Bergesen, and Edith Kurzwell. 1984. *Cultural Analysis.* Boston: Routledge and Kegan Paul.

Zipperstein, Edward. 1983. *Jewish Business Ethics.* New York: KTAV Publishing Co.

III DEVELOPMENT AS SOCIAL CHANGE
Policy Alternatives

7 DEVELOPMENT POLICY AND MODELS OF SOCIAL CHANGE

At the core of today's development crisis is the fact that over the past forty years the number of poor and hungry has continued to grow in absolute terms despite ambitious development plans and strategies. In some areas of the world, the poor have become poorer while the rich have gotten richer. At the same time a growing awareness exists that, at least in a theoretical sense, the technical capacity is at hand to solve the problem of poverty.

As noted in Chapter 2 on method, the crisis goes to the heart of the social sciences themselves. In the past years there has been a considerable rethinking of development (Bruton 1985). The present divisions and methods of the social sciences are seen to be inadequate for they do not lead to a comprehensive and integrated analysis of *social* facts nor do they lead to realistic planning. The proliferation of technical economic problemsolving approaches and projects may be a necessary part of development policy, but, in and of themselves, such piecemeal efforts are not sufficient. Such endeavors must be integrated into an overall strategy of social change.

In this chapter I first discuss the development framework in terms of agents, ends, and means. Secondly, I evaluate current approaches to development on the basis of models of social change. This is followed by a discussion of techniques of modelling policy alternatives. I conclude with reflections on the requirements of comprehensive and effective policy in the context of a social market economy.

199

Table 7-1. Some Leading Dilemmas in the World Food Complex.

A. *Production of Food*

1. Allocation of production factors and economic opportunity in a way that does not benefit the poor.
2. Welfare distorting power/profit interests, whether local elites, international business, or former colonial masters.
3. Obstacles to accumulating factors of production both nationally and for the small farmer (especially credit).
4. Agricultural dualism, both national and international, market orientations are pitted against basic needs.
5. Patterns of mechanization that displace labor and cause unemployment.
6. Resource exhaustion and destruction of the ecosystem.
7. High resource consumption levels, especially with energy-intensive agricultural technology.
8. Poor nutritional quality of product (from chemicals, etc.).
9. Inappropriate technology and lack of adequate research and development in soils, new seed uses, pests, climate control, and so forth.
10. Lack of extension services and management training.
11. Unavailability of new technology (to the poor) and general lack of complementary infrastructure.

B. *Consumption of Food*

12. Adequate nutrition is too much correlated with high income.
13. Good quality food is too high priced.
14. Consumption patterns of the affluent world drain away food resources (notably for feed).
15. In processing, consumer value may be sacrificed to profit.
16. The consumer, as price taker, has all costs passed on.
17. Inadequate international reserves in times of crisis.
18. Ignorance regarding nutrition.
19. Population growth (demand) outstrips production supply.

C. *Distribution of Food Products*

20. Poor people who are hungry do not have enough income to enter the market.
21. Food aid in terms of rationing, price controls or an income supplement is necessary.
22. Food has become an instrument of power for personal and national interests.
23. Waste because of poor storage, processing, pests, etc.
24. Patterns of industrialization and urbanization often do not mesh with supply patterns.
25. Lack of market information, transport, and other related services.

Table 7-1. continued

D. *Attitudes and Value of Orientations*

26. The grounding of moral values; especially the split between communitarian and individualist orientations.
27. Narrow nationalism and conflicts with international food policy goals.
28. The self-interest of business and government managerial elites.
29. Ignorance of the cultural base of hunger (e.g., the role of religion or philosophy, whether positive or negative).
30. False images of nutrition and hunger in symbolic media.

THE DEVELOPMENT FRAMEWORK: AGENTS, ENDS, AND MEANS

What are the problems development policy must resolve, and who are the agents to solve them? How are they to do it? Development policy must be devoted to attacking a wide number of targets simultaneously in an integrated way that anticipates the interaction between specific problems and areas. In Table 7-1, I present a summary outline of the main dilemmas encountered in the poverty and development equation in terms of the economic dynamics of production, consumption, and marketing in the context of the sociocultural background. The problems listed are referred to in a global aggregate sense. Needless to say, the reality of poverty differs greatly from place to place; accordingly, these factors will assume varying degrees of importance from region to region. Nonetheless, good development policy must simultaneously address some such array of problems.

What sort of policy is called for to adequately address these issues? A convenient approach (to which I have frequently referred) has been suggested by Martin Rein (1976). Development policy should be empirically comprehensive, value-critical, technologically feasible, and systems manageable. These points formed the basis of Chapters 3 to 6 in which I analyzed development in terms of the resource base, the technology set, power, and culture. If this development framework is basically correct, then policy must articulate a concrete strategy of social change which effectively addresses it.

Most literature in development economics has not made the final step of scrutinizing research findings in the light of a broader social science context, which includes power and culture. Since the mid-seventies there has been growing dissatisfaction with narrow neoclassical analysis and a reassertion of an historical structuralist perspective (in the older tradition of political economy) has taken place. The question is how ideas about development can be translated into effective programs of social change. It is not possible here to present a plan for a local area, a region, a nation, or the world. But it is possible to analyze the framework that such plans imply. Development aims to bring about social change. The agents are those individuals and groups I delineated in my discussion of social power. They include individuals acting in their various social roles, but most of all the agents of development are groups of people acting in a collective way. There are four possible points of focus for their actions.

The first strategy is a *person-to-person* approach, which attempts to persuade individuals to change their analytical frameworks, priorities, and values. It concentrates on influencing those in key roles. This strategy endeavors to recast individual behavior within social systems.

The second focus of action is social *prophecy*, which attempts to challenge and refashion the pervading models of analysis, cultural value systems, dominant social paradigms and ideologies, and prevalent social interpretations of reality. It does this through a variety of means ranging from discourse on values to innovative programs and forms of social conflict.

The third strategy is *politics*, which is here defined as the art of organizational participation so as to effect the common good. This strategy aims to transform the social system, not only in its individual roles, but also in its general rules, the formal legal system, its ideologies, its patterns of stratification, and its social control mechanisms. Politics in this sense is work on behalf of the common good. It represents a struggle over legitimate social authority and should not be narrowly identified with "government."

The final point of focus is *economic activity*, which involves the use of the market or exchange system to influence behavior. As such it may include strikes, boycotts, shareholder responsibility initiatives, cooperatives, the formation of free economic associations, and the use of economic incentives.

None of the above focal points of strategies is of itself superior, and the proper strategy mix depends upon the situation being addressed. The first two involve strategies that are primarily modes of persuasion. The third and fourth use civil authority systems and economic exchange systems, respectively, to change social behavior. Both are involved with groups and institutions as social agents more than they are with individuals.

What do agents of change seek? What is the ultimate purpose of development? These questions focus on the human values of development policy. I approach the ends of development in terms of (1) social participation, (2) growth, and (3) distribution. The pivotal element to underline in any social system is the right of all people to have access to and participate in the structures and offices of that system and of society. To be legitimate any civil society must guarantee participation. Such participation connotes (1) a level of individual liberty compatible with a like liberty for others as well as (2) equality of opportunity. Participation, based upon liberty and equality of opportunity, is the prerequisite of justice in civil society and governs the possibility of attaining a common good that truly represents the public interest rather than the despotic will of small elites. While participation guarantees the "subject character" of development patterns, it is not sufficient. Provision must be made for both growth (to meet demand stemming from both quantitative increments to population as well as affluence) and equitable distribution.

The first task of such a participative society in developing countries is to establish the nature and goals of these other aspects of development. This task is to be carried out through processes of dialogue characterized by fairness, due legal process, and cultural appropriateness. As noted in Chapter 6, the discussion of values and human development is inherently open-ended. In this sense, value questions and development goals will never be settled. In the meantime, however, plans are drawn up and implemented in terms of the knowledge, wisdom, and values that a society has accumulated to date. I hold that development goals should be established through participative processes that are culturally suitable. This in itself is a formidable problem, for many developing countries allow very little participation.

I have said that development should be based on culture if it is to be successful (see also Bruton 1985: 1100–1113). At the same time, it must be recognized that cultural forms can function negatively as well as positively with respect to social participation. A caste system, for example, is openly discriminatory. In such instances, economic development is the pushed back to a more fundamental stage: building participatory institutions. Participation can be considered as both a goal as well as a mechanism of development.

Questions of growth and distribution arise within the context of participation. These are areas of very concrete decisionmaking. To the point, the body politic (which is the subject of development) must come to terms with four further questions:

- What rate and composition of growth is desired and how is it to be achieved?

- What would amount to a fair pattern of distribution of offices, goods, and services in society?
- What is the duty of each member of society or group to render service to the public and contribute to the common good?
- What types of incentives for conformity as well as sanctions for nonconformity would be just?

These four questions as well as the two prerequisites for social participation noted above correspond to the main issues of social ethics of development discussed in the second section of Chapter 6. It goes without saying that any development policy implies such normative questions. When it gets down to the concrete, then, I advocate a certain qualitative orientation in development policy based on the following priorities: the liberty of the oppressed over the freedom of the more powerful, the social opportunity of the marginalized over their exclusion by certain elites, the needs of the poor over the mere wants of the wealthy, the duty to contribute to the common good according to ability rather than be apathetic or merely seek narrow self-interest, and the reinforcement of patterns of social justice through social incentives and sanctions rather than surrendering the determination of due process to mere group egoism or vindictiveness. Each of these goals is a value statement in the sense that it indicates priorities regarding what should happen. I am well aware that others may disagree. Nonetheless, the positions that any society takes with respect to any of these questions will directly determine the overall orientation of development as well as the policy instruments and strategies involved. My point is that these issues must be explicitly addressed. These notions then go together to provide a social ethical component to the assessment of economic efficiency, which provides the foundation of what I call a social market economy.

Such social efficiency includes more than economics. It is normative in a broad sense, and it is very difficult either to summarize or measure. It raises the question of the *quality* of markets and other economic institutions (including bureaucratic planning). The history of development itself attests that there is a need for more explicit attention to social justice in determining the orientation of the economy. In some versions of economics, such as under multiple assumptions of perfect competition, it is assumed that adequate levels of justice and human welfare follow as a corollary from technical and price efficiency. Yet in the day-to-day functioning of economic systems, dysfunctions occur that lead not only to economic inefficiency but social inefficiency as well. There is a social opportunity cost and inefficiency associated with unemployment as there is with the stifling of innovations through overcentralized bureaucracy.

The society-wide delineation of social efficiency, however, is difficult to specify in detail. Social efficiency implies some sort of public choice of priorities. That is, it implies a position of concrete goals regarding the above questions as well as an evaluation of how satisfactorily these social goals are being met. As such, the analysis of social efficiency entails a wide social assessment of benefits and costs. To take a microeconomic example, in agriculture social efficiency includes both the strict economic efficiency of farming operations as well as their effects on ecology and the environment, on farm safety, on levels of wages and employment, and on the nutritional quality of the product. It includes narrow economic efficiency but is more extensive. It can only be concretely assessed if society has reached some performance expectations regarding such broader issues.

Macro applications of the social efficiency notion come to the fore in terms of farm legislation, which provides income support to farmers, supplies food to needy persons, and monitors the areas of employment, ecology and the environment, farm safety, insurance, and product quality. Social efficiency is at least partially based upon ethical analysis and public priorities. It frequently calls for political action in addition to market dynamics, particularly in areas of structural change. Some institutional aspects that are frequently discussed: land tenure policy, extension services and cooperatives, and supportive infrastructure. There is a vast amount of literature on each of these topics. Many of the issues are functional rather than ideological. It is clear that without an economic infrastructure for irrigation, rural electrification, transport and feeder roads, and marketing and storage facilities, local agricultural production and markets will be severely hampered. This in turn will have an impact upon consumer welfare and the broader performance of other sectors of the economy. The point is that more restricted technical economic considerations, such as farm size and land use patterns, must be evaluated within their social setting with a view to adapting them both to higher productivity as well as other social goals.

Theoretically, there are many possible solutions to development problems. The role of management in both public and private spheres and on both micro and macro levels is absolutely pivotal. Both public and private management serves to integrate various social agents, foster the social articulation of goals or ends, and judge the suitability of means and ends as well as outcomes.

What are the means to the end? Even within the same set of social goals and priorities, a number of types of social organizations remain theoretically possible. There is no demonstrably unique path to socially just patterns of economic development. To take the example of agricultural organization, which is so important in overcoming poverty and hunger, the world today confronts a wide variety of agricultural subsystems. The immediate challenge for development is not simply to imagine a theoretical alternative but to figure out how one can go from the status quo to something that, in fact, would be better.

Assuming that the responsible agents in a country reach some consensus regarding general development orientation, what are the means to the end in terms of the economic questions that a country faces? Any economic system confronts three basic questions: What to produce? How to do it? And for whom? These questions provide a concrete framework for development in both its normative and technical components.

What to produce? It has been pointed out in the case of agriculture that myriad production possibilities exist. One must decide to produce final consumer or intermediate goods. If producing food, one must decide whether to produce grain or beef, export crops, or both. Countless farmers make these decisions in terms of their comparative advantage in production and markets. A society guides these decisions in terms of its social goals, in general, and on the basis of human consumption needs and the social environment of markets, in particular. Market demand is a shorthand way of indicating the personal consumption needs and preferences of people when they are effectively able to enter the market. Need and market demand, however, are not necessarily equivalent. One of the functions of public policy is to resolve such disparities.

How to produce? With this question a society touches, first of all, the general principles of organization of the economy; for example, is it to be socialist, market, or "mixed?" Secondly, individual farmers must decide on the composition of inputs and the level of technology employed in producing a certain set of commodities, determining whether the system will be more capital intensive or labor intensive. The social and individual decisions interact reciprocally.

Finally, for whom? Does one produce primarily for oneself or for a cash market? If for a cash market, does one produce luxury goods (for those who are better off) or goods to satisfy basic consumer needs or both? In this question, there is an implicit discussion of the principles of distribution in the political economy: Who is to receive what benefits and why? Again, social choice (in terms of budgets and fiscal policy, for example) reciprocally interacts with individual decisions.

It should be clear that there are many agents of development, ranging from individuals to groups in government, market, and other social circles. It is their task, first of all, to forge a social consensus on the purposes of development and to articulate at least a working definition of social economic efficiency for public policy purposes. There is no demonstrably unique end or goal nor a demonstrably unique set of means to the end. The choice of a particular strategy among alternatives represents a political economic process based upon assessment of probable outcomes of different scenarios and their acceptability. I now turn to examine such scenarios as embodied in development theory.

DEVELOPMENT THEORY IN A SOCIAL CHANGE FRAMEWORK

Most economic models of development have assumed a simplified theory of social change without examining its foundations. Such implicit models of change are often so heavily circumscribed by unrealistic assumptions and conditions that they rarely work out in practice according to the line of development indicated in the theory. It is very difficult indeed to achieve a realistic and integrated perspective on rural development and to identify effective mechanisms of change (Ruttan 1982).

Sociologists and political scientists have never succeeded in developing an adequate theory of social change. Neither "laws of the market" nor socialist "laws of history" are in fact laws. As noted in the discussion of method in Chapter 2, some recurrent elements in the process of social change have been identified. But there are no universal laws of social change nor is there some kind of blueprint by which economics can abide. Indeed, patterns of change seem to be specific to particular historical and sociocultural milieux. To discover what types of development policies may work in a certain region, it is advisable to master the history and culture of that place in order to understand how things evolve and are accomplished in that specific context. Historical and institutional analysis is the key to discovering the inherent dynamics of change in a particular milieu and that can provide the best hints regarding the most fruitful paths to follow in development policy.

In the literature on economic development one encounters many diverse and even conflicting theories. Most of the theories that have stood the test of time in the literature possess an internal logic;

Table 7-2. Development Typologies and Social Change.

| Development Typologies | Categories of Comparison | | |
	Primary Goal of Development	Criteria of Performance	Principle Instruments
Growth	• growth of GNP and GNP per capita	• market-rational growth • economic efficiency	• capital markets and investment • law to assure fairness in markets
Revolutionary	• growth in areas of social priority • radical redistribution of productive resources • egalitarian social relations	• plan-rational growth • economic efficiency	• planned investment • authority of party
Redistribution With Growth	• growth of GNP • incomes policy	• economic efficiency • basic income level for all • improved market quality	• markets/investment guided by income policy • budget/public policy
Basic Needs	• satisfaction of basic needs • growth and improvement of the quality of life	• needs met • growth in needs–meeting capacity	• planning of supply and demand • government authority over markets • limited markets within planned goals
Self-Reliance and Popular Participation	• participatory social relations • meet people–identified needs and goals in growth	• popular self-determination in development • needs met • growth in meeting peoples' goals	• decentralized: emphasis on grass-roots organization • new educational pedegogy • communal economic decisionmaking for investments, etc.
Integrated Rural Development in a Social Market Economy	• sociocultural defined quality of life • growth guided by social choices	• culturally appropriate self-determination • needs met in guided market • integration of resource, population and technology policy with culture and historical institutions	• decentralized grass-roots organizations • markets guided by communal decisions, public policy • monetary and fiscal policy are the main tool to guide markets

Table 7-2. continued

Categories of Comparison			
Key Mechanisms	Principal Agents	Dominant Values And Cultural Vision	Main Problems
• technical innovation • inculcation of modern mentality • social mobility • individual liberty of action	• entrepreneur • market agents	• liberty/political rights • individual self-interest • utilitarian social goals • meritocracy • due process and opportunity	• exploitive concentration of power • market failure • Western cultural bias
• conflict • thorough social organization • revolutionary consciousness	• vanguard party • proletariat • government bureaucracy	• communal life in an egalitarian society • social duty linked to ability • primacy of need in distribution • collective liberty of disenfranchised	• lack of popular participation • planning inefficiency • poor implementation
• technical innovation • reforms of public policy • appropriate technology	• market agents • public policy, institutions and participants	• individual liberty with utilitarian social goals • long-term mutual self-interest • basic equity and due process	• growth/distribution tradeoffs • inadequacy of income alone to meet needs
• diffusion of values of human dignity • public institutions • appropriate technology	• vanguard elites • poor people • government bureaucracy	• human dignity expressed in political and economic rights • solidarity • distribution in communal life based on needs	• government bureaucracy • "top-down" approach • implementation problems
• diffusion of communal values • popular participation • self-reliance • appropriate technology	• decentralized, self-reliant • grassroots agents • cooperation with outside agents and central government	• communal self-determination and participation • people as subjects • self-reliance • solidarity • equity	• integration of local with central governments and outside change agents • institutional innovation and transformation
• cumulative interaction of social system • value diffusion • public choice guides economy	• grassroots and traditional cultural leaders lead • central government and outside agents cooperate • primarily market	• priority of human development and cultural pluralism • balance between individual rights and communal self-determination • participation, equity solidarity in social rights and duties • "wholeness in life"	• overcoming negative aspects of culture • institutional innovation and transformation • integration among various participants

otherwise, they would have been dismissed long ago. The basis of diversity and even conflicting opinion is located more in the presuppositions of the various theories. In this light, I examine a number of theories against the backdrop of their implicit presuppositions regarding social change. I consider in turn theories of (1) growth plus trickle-down, (2) revolution, (3) redistribution with growth, (4) basic needs, (5) self-reliance and popular participation and, finally, (6) integrated rural development in a social market economy. These distinctions are not airtight and some overlapping is evident. Yet it is instructive to consider them as general typologies, which serve to provide development policy with a fundamental orientation in terms of agents, ends, and means. For each model, I discuss the goal of development, criteria of performance, principal instruments, key mechanisms, principal agents and institutions, dominant values and cultural vision, and principal problems (Table 7-2).

Growth Models

The dominant Western theory of economic development is a theory of growth. The framework of analysis is narrowly economic and focuses on input/output. The main goals of development are growth in gross national product and growth in GNP per capita. The primary question is how is it possible to stimulate the growth of a country's GNP. The answer is found in the accumulation of the factors of production and their allocation in an economically efficient manner.

In this theory, economic efficiency provides the criteria of performance of development policy. It is defined in a two-fold manner (see Chapter 4, section 2, pp. 129-30). The first component is technical efficiency. This refers to maximizing output from a given set of inputs. The second component of economic efficiency is variously called price efficiency or allocative efficiency. This refers to minimizing costs or maximizing profits from a given fixed output. Cost minimization and profit maximization are related but not equivalent goals.

Economic efficiency is predicated primarily of the allocation of the factors of production. In practice, efficient farm management is very complex. A farmer faces a number of questions that have to be decided in an atmosphere of risk and uncertainty: What to produce? How? When? Where? And for whom? Those decisions are made first of all on the basis of available resources: the goods of nature (land, water, and climate), labor, capital, management, and technology. They are also made in light of market information and sociopolitical constraints or opportunities.

What is the principal instrument of growth? Growth theorists have traditionally recognized that the many decisions between types of product to produce, what input set to use, and how to optimize the factor/product relations all present management difficulties. But they have concentrated on the inputs that are most difficult to accumulate, the lack of which presents the greatest obstacle to development.

The primary focus falls upon capital accumulation and investment. Capital is accumulated domestically—primarily through savings. The possibility of accumulating savings is, of course, tied to technically efficient and price efficient management, on the one hand, and witholding some income from consumption uses, on the other. Countries that go along on a subsistence level are caught in the poverty trap because they always consume all that they produce. Furthermore, when their population is growing, their production-consumption cycle may fall into a vicious circle of increasing poverty. There are two primary ways to accumulate savings: to increase output efficiency leading to higher profits and to decrease consumption, either through population policy or by abstaining from higher levels of consumption.

Capital accumulation catalyzes growth. The key mechanism is technical innovation that leads to the scientific transformation of the economy. Natural resources can be improved through irrigation and reclamation projects, the quality of labor can be raised through education, health, and nutrition programs, needed mechanical and biochemical technological inputs can be acquired, and by extension training programs the quality of management can be made more efficient. Improved factor accumulation, both in quantity and in quality, will generally lead to overall production increases and higher factor productivity. This process can be represented by an upward and expanding circle where growth produces more savings, which leads to further investment and more growth.

In such an expanding scenario, there is increasing demand for the factors of production. In the context of labor it is assumed (on the basis of the adoption of a certain technology set) that more and more jobs will be created. Entrepreneurial investments produce growth, which benefits workers in terms of increased jobs. They and their families will have more money to spend. Thus, effective demand in the marketplace will increase and entrepreneurs will respond with further increased investment. This theory does not really anticipate limits to growth: the process can theoretically continue in an ever-expanding way.

Growth theory presents a model of change primarily based on private economic agents acting rationally in free competitive markets. Government has a secondary role in maintaining the quality of markets through the legal system and monetary and fiscal policy.

Generally this theory either ignores broader normative discussions or assumes a satisfactory outcome (trickle down). Nonetheless, there is an implicit normative vision. In terms of the five normative questions I raised in Chapter 6, the emphasis falls upon individual liberty with general equality of opportunity guaranteed by due legal process. Distribution is articulated primarily in terms of meritocracy. Social duty is argued in utilitarian terms and is tightly linked to incentives and sanctions.

Within its presuppositions, the growth theory model is logically complete in charting the course of development and makes considerable sense regarding growth itself. Its weakest point is distribution. Why has trickle-down not worked? Those who support the model defend its inherent logic and cite the interference of governments, the political distortion of factor prices, overvalued exchange rates, and the poor success rate of birth control programs as the causes of failure. With the startling decrease in mortality rates (made possible by modern science and technology) population growth has soared, for birth rates have not come down to a satisfactory level. On the demand side, the trickle-down theory presupposes a demographic transition, if savings are to be made possible rather than being merely consumed by escalating population.

On the supply side, the trickle-down theory has been criticized for its theory of change based upon the entrepreneur. This theory has firm roots in the capitalist world, especially in neoclassical theory. It does not anticipate that the profits and surplus deriving from growth are more and more accumulated in the hands of the entrepreneurial class and that the real bulk of the fruits of growth are not passed on. Skilled managers and workers often benefit, but in the context of a large pool of surplus labor, wages in poor countries have tended to hover around subsistence. The anticipated general increase in consumer welfare in poor countries has frequently not materialized and demand has faltered. Developing countries found themselves in a vicious circle of another sort, which was caused by the concentration of economic power. This is particularly true of the economic scene today, where new investment may utilize a capital-intensive technology and thus entail the creation of very few jobs.

As an historical model, trickle-down has seemed to work in Europe and North America. But it did not do so without critical legislative changes throughout the past century. The socio-cultural institutional framework of the West, however, cannot be presupposed in most parts of the developing world today. In the theory of social change, which underlies the growth model of economic development, the positive functions of wider social factors (such as law, public investment, and social infrastructure) is assumed, rather than explicitly analyzed. This has proven to be improper, both on the production as well as the consumption side of the equation.

Revolutionary Models

The second theory of development that has proven to be of enduring historical importance is the Marxist revolutionary theory. The goal of development is not only growth but a radical redistribution of resources. Marx's analysis of poverty and underdevelopment focuses upon alienation in light of two considerations: production forces and production relations. The former refers to the economic input/output framework discussed above. The latter refers to the structural institutional framework and social relations between various classes. According to Marx, these relations are primarily based upon the control of production resources and the concomitant division of labor. Marx agreed that investment and more efficient management of resources would indeed produce economic growth and greater wealth. What he denied is that these benefits would trickle down to the workers and the poor.

The criteria of performance for Marx were not only aggregate growth but the elimination of poverty and achieving of equality in distribution. He saw the entrepreneurial class as denying the poor the surplus economic value that was produced by means of their labor. He also saw the population and poverty problem as derivative from the dominant social structures. Social structures, not overpopulation, produced scarcity and poverty.

The principal instrument of development for Marx was structural and institutional change: The social system of production relations is indicted for systematically producing underdevelopment, poverty, and misery. The way to development was to overthrow those structures. Marx did not deny that production forces themselves need to be continually transformed on the basis of science and technology. Nor was he against growth; he viewed capitalism as a necessary phase in historical change. His point was that economic development will not reach the poor without political change.

The Marxist model of social change basically centers on class conflict, and its dynamic progress is based on the vanguard party and the proletariat. The members of the party have the task of awakening and leading the oppressed classes in the seizure of power by revolutionary class struggle. After the struggle, there is a period of administration envisioned where the masses become reeducated and the enemies of the people are rooted out once and for all. The principal institutions are political planning and management of supply and demand processes.

The Marxist model presupposes rational and selfless human motivation by the liberated classes. The proletariat is described in terms reminiscent of Rousseau's noble savage. Socialist thought invariably highlights communal solidarity and equality of distribution. Social duty is articulated in terms of ability: one's abilities to contribute constitute a duty. Within this vision of human communal solidarity, individual liberty, due process, social opportunity, incentives, and sanctions emerge. There is a clear subordination of the individual and family to the "will of the people" as manifested in more collective forms of organization and enshrined in party directives and economic plans.

There are a number of problems with Marxist thought. He assumed both that all social evil was located in the oppressive capitalist class and its agents in religious, philosophical, and cultural spheres. Furthermore, he assumed that solidarity existed among all the oppressed people and between these people and the party. One of the main policy problems for radicals has been that the poor and dispossessed, whose cause they champion, are often unwilling clients. They are passive, distrustful, and fearful for themselves and their families. Marx blamed the passivity of the workers on the fact that they were mesmerized by the ideological superstructure and the opium-like hold that religion and other cultural forms had over them. The poor had first to develop a revolutionary consciousness.

Vanguard parties can and have done some good. In accepting Marxist theory, however, one must presuppose (in addition to the above considerations) that the party is in general enlightened, benevolent, honest, and efficient. Furthermore, one must presuppose that its program invites and encourages the participation of the workers and the oppressed. That is quite a bit to presuppose. Wherever Marxist theory has been implemented, the final stage of the revolution—the transformation from the dictatorship of the proletariat (exercised through the tutelage of the party), to democratic and scientific socialism—has never occurred. Marxists continually blame class enemies for this failure. One must ask whether there might not be a fundamental flaw in the theory, especially regarding social change and "laws of history."

I believe that flaw is found in the theory of power and the assumptions regarding social change, which is based on an oversimplified theory of conflict, the seizing of formal power as a solution, and the existence of effective solidarity among the poor. As important as seizing formal power may be, there is a lot more to social change.

Finally, the Marxist notion of planning is based upon an extremely rationalist view of the human person unencumbered by poor data or logistical problems. This is a fundamental miscalculation of both the agents of change (party members and proletariat) as well as of mechanisms and institutions (party rule and planning). More important, the historical economic results of planning models have been generally weak, particularly in agriculture. Historical facts do not completely bear out the theory, especially in growth and productivity. Distribution has been more successful.

Redistribution With Growth

The lack of success of development policies based on either growth or revolutionary models in the post-war era has led to further questioning of both in the sixties and seventies. One model that emerged—primarily in the circles of World Bank emphasis on poverty and income research—was characterized by the goal of redistribution with growth (Chenery 1974). This theory first emphasized the fact that mere growth models were not adequate to stem the increase in the numbers of the absolute poor in the world. Secondly, growth models ran into other economic problems, for the production growth that was taking place in developing countries was not matched by access to international markets or internal market development. Developing countries increasingly competed among themselves for the limited first-world markets for their raw materials, agricultural products, and light industrial products. The almost exclusive production growth emphasis failed to generate domestic markets for goods and services. Income did not trickle down to the poor, and thus, they could not constitute a market.

The criteria of performance in redistribution with growth theory are not only efficient growth but providing sufficient income to all persons so that they can participate in a market system.

The principal instruments of policy are capital accumulation and development explicitly geared to an income policy. Redistribution with growth is not a precise formula. In an economic sense it emphasizes the simultaneous development of production capacity, improving patterns of income distribution, and hence, the generation of domestic markets.

Insofar as social change goes, the redistribution with growth theory heavily relies upon the diffusion of technology as the main mechanism of change on both the production and consumption sides of the equation. But the technology adopted must be appropriate in terms of generating jobs and channelling adequate income into people's hands. Furthermore, in growth models the demand in the marketplace that did eventually materialize was very often for imported goods rather than domestic products. Domestic products were often of inferior quality and design. In addition, many of the goods and services produced domestically did not correspond to domestic demand. This point amounted to using public policy as a mechanism for restructuring the domestic product mix.

The agent of social change is not merely the entrepreneur acting in markets. The government enters in as a key element of change in basically guiding the investment policy, as well as instituting an explicit income policy. Nonetheless, the key economic institutions remain very much market institutions.

The value set in redistribution with growth models is similar to that in growth models. Primary emphasis falls upon individual liberty, equality of opportunity, and due legal process. But there is more emphasis on mutual self-interest (argued in utilitarian terms) than on mere individual self-interest. Also, while distribution is viewed primarily in utilitarian terms, there is also a notion of human dignity in terms of a basic quality of life that should be met. The main shift is in means: public economic policy is called for because the market has not and will not function adequately by itself. Ironically enough, Taiwan and South Korea, which are cited as redistribution with growth successes, are neoConfucian in spirit and authoritarian in practice. They are paternalistic and provide a strange contrast with the value set implied in the Western theory of redistribution with growth.

Redistribution with growth policies have been implemented with some success in Taiwan and South Korea. Growth rates remained high, domestic markets developed, and absolute poverty decreased. It is not clear, however, whether their success can be imitated. Both received something from their status as former Japanese colonies, both followed aggressive export policies, both had very strong and efficient governments (even if dictatorial) and both had Confucian and Buddhist cultural traditions. It has remained difficult to sort out which factors accounted more for the development success and how they related to each other.

What are some of the problems with this theory? It is argued by some that redistribution of income necessarily means less growth. For there would be less money for investment. Furthermore, whatever surplusses might accrue would be so dispersed throughout the country that they could not be marshalled for investment purposes. There has been, therefore, a considerable discussion in development circles over the trade-offs between growth and income redistribution. That there may be trade-offs is not denied, but it is questionable whether these trade-offs are one to one. Income in the hands of consumers can be transferred back to entrepreneurs in two ways: by means of market purchases and by means of savings. While talk of trade-offs tends to focus single-mindedly on production, in many ways it is more important that market structures have not developed and that savings institutions have not been in place to channel savings towards investors.

Basic Needs

As its name states, the goal of the basic needs theory is to ensure that all can, in fact, meet their basic human needs of food, clothing, shelter, health, and education. Redistribution with growth theory attracted wide attention in the seventies. At the same time, it was observed that in countries with different cultural traditions than East Asia basic needs have remained unsatisfied despite growth and even some income redistribution. In the redistribution with growth theory it is assumed that all basic needs can be satisfied in the marketplace: All that is needed is sufficient income to become a market partici-pant. The basic needs critique claims that incomes policy is a neces-sary but not a sufficient condition to achieve satisfactory levels of social welfare (Cole and Lucas 1982). One problem is that the in-comes of the poor generally remain too limited. Another is that pro-ducers have not been keying their investments on basic needs, but, instead, have been concentrating on other domestic and export areas, which have promised a more favorable financial return.

The criteria of a basic needs strategy are not all that clear. Often enough in the literature, "basic needs development" represents more a general orientation rather than a precise set of goals. Criteria of basic needs activities must be established. Richard Szal (1980) has attempted to do just that. He identifies eight criteria: (1) to increase the income of the (socially determined) target group, (2) to contrib-ute to a direct impact upon core needs of health, education, housing, water, and nutrition, (3) to increase the production of other (socially determined) goods and services, (4) to increase decentralization and self reliance, (5) to use simple equipment, (6) to use low skill tech-nology, (7) to use local material, and (8) to use small-scale labor intensive capital construction. These criteria are not exclusive, but they do provide a relevant series of questions for policy analysis.

The basic human needs and redistribution with growth approaches share many similarities. They both imply a "capacities approach" to absolute poverty and both recognize that the growth with trickle-down model is inherently flawed. Yet basic needs approaches go fur-ther in several respects (Weeks and Dore 1982).

What kinds of activities form part of a basic needs strategy? There is in theory almost an infinite variety of instruments. In addition to an agricultural development program to increase production they concentrate on investment in rural works (especially storage, transport, access to roads, and water supply), health and nutrition services, programs of adult literacy and extension, provision of housing and related services, and promotion of the informal sector.

The principal mechanisms of a basic needs strategy are, firstly, public articulation of what are basic needs. Secondly, public policy processes provide the integrative mechanism for all economic decisions.

The agents of change are the people themselves. There is a role for private entrepreneurs. More important, major intervention of the state is envisioned, not merely in income distribution but in production, in what is called "supply management." Development budget priorities are not geared merely to increasing GNP but also to providing public services necessary to meet human needs and build up infrastructure. It is primarily the government that does this. That there may be "trade-offs" with GNP growth rates is accepted. Basic needs approaches do not share the same commitment to growth as that enshrined in neoclassical theory; nor do they share the basic market orientation that redistribution with growth implies. To the extent that a market operates in basic human needs approaches, it is very much a politically guided market economy.

The value set places emphasis upon human dignity and the empowerment of people. This is conceived of first, in terms of a fair distribution of wealth and economic assets (e.g., land and credit). Secondly, basic community structures of political participation are stressed. Thirdly, the composition of what is produced (i.e., of growth) is clearly weighted against nonessential goods and services, which satisfy wants rather than needs.

Basic needs theory emphasizes equality in distribution as well as the duty of all in society to contribute to meeting the needs of all. A basic needs strategy calls for establishing a minimum quality of life. The meeting of fundamental and identifiable needs is the priority of government budgetary and fiscal policies. As such, it calls for increased direct investment in the provision of core needs: health services, education, clothing, housing, and nutrition (including supplies of clean water). This suggests a significant change in the output of goods and services.

Problems with basic needs are seen in areas of growth and bureaucratic administration. As this idea is relatively new, policies are only beginning to be formulated to make such a strategy operational. What would be the effects of a basic needs approach upon overall economic growth? There has been little time to empirically observe any countries that are trying to implement such a strategy. So far much of the discussion remains quite theoretical, but it is important, nonetheless, in raising questions of priorities for development. As to bureaucratic problems, one significant criticism is that the basic needs approach has emerged from government bureaucrats and academicians who tend to view bureaucracy benignly. Also, the theory tends to favor a view of social change that operates from the top down. It is more a program of doing things for people rather than people developing themselves. This reaction has fostered a popular participation variant.

Self-Reliance and Popular Participation

The primary goal of popular participation models is that people truly be subjects of their own development. Popular grass roots participation is necessary if development is to be humanistic and if development programs are to succeed. For only then can basic needs be identified, resources mobilized, and measures drawn up (all by the people themselves) to improve the distribution of goods and services. In such a strategy, there is a clear reaction against the authoritarian type regimes found in Taiwan and South Korea, which allegedly squelch the satisfaction of some nonmaterial basic needs. Participation models stress that it is crucial to satisfy the people's desire to participate and to be the active architects of their own destiny. The ordinary people must be responsibly involved in the design, implementation, and evaluation of projects and policies.

The criteria of performance stress popular self-determination through full participation. The basic needs approach is refashioned in terms of national and local self-reliance and the establishment of social structures and institutions that elicit and guarantee popular participation. In this context more specific criteria are discussed that include economic growth, income distribution, and material welfare as well as larger concerns of human development. Basic needs are expressed in terms of both a material and nonmaterial component. The latter recognizes human dignity in terms of self-reliance and participation.

It is not easy to identify the principal instruments of such an approach. The discussion of popular participation models is quite diverse. The general formula emphasizes self-help, local resources, initiative, and leadership; it stresses the effective impact of traditional ways and of rural village organization and insists on "development from below" ("The Power to Organize" 1982). One of the clearest expositions of an (ideal) participatory development project has been provided by Guy Gran (Gran 1983: 22, 145 ff). He lists eight characteristics:

1. A significant percentage of the specified group must participate in and control as many elements of project initiation, design, operation, and evaluation as is possible.
2. The project design must include clearly defined and operational participatory mechanisms to guide administrative, productive, and distributive elements of the project.
3. The institutional linkages of the project with the larger economic and political system must be functional for those at the bottom; the aid inflow and the productive gains must be protected. Thus the hostile development environment and prevailing confidence mechanisms must be explicitly dealt with in project design.
4. Technological and organizational aspects must be culturally feasible. If women are the farmers, it is counterproductive to train only male agricultural extension agents.
5. The project design must reach some reasonable standard of ecological soundness that reflects an empirically defensible analytical framework by the participants.
6. The project must show the potential for self-reliance; resources should serve a catalytic function, not a welfare function encouraging further dependency.
7. Comparable potential for self-sustainment must be evident; conventional aid activities often die when funding stops.
8. The project design must include enhancement of self-directed learning. Intellectual dependency, as much as political and economic dependency, saps creativity and productivity.

In addition to instruments of change seen in basic needs theory, popular participation theory gives considerable attention to pedagogy and to the conscientization of the poor. This pedagogy focuses upon human values, but it also focuses upon conflict as a mechanism of change as in revolutionary theory (although not necessarily violently). The instruments of change are similar to those in basic needs theory, but the spirit of self-reliance places particular emphasis upon local resources. Development is not to be imported from a foreign government or even from the national government but must be based upon and initiated with local resource endowments.

From the above, the key mechanisms of popular participation emerge. It is a program to empower people. This involves creating active citizens by overcoming the underdevelopment state of mind, emphasizing humanist economics in terms of the self-actualization of persons and peoples. On a more practical level, this program calls for small group organization and decisionmaking. This model also features the local selection and training of development catalysts and effective participation in project design.

The agents of change are clearly the local people. Specific roles and responsibilities emerge from processes of dialogue. Institutions tend to be decentralized and fluid. The task for the local people developing themselves is to identify their goals and to figure out what the next possible step for them is on the basis of their own resources. This point does not deny the need for national infrastructure or even for some outside inputs. It aims to overcome simply being passive recipients by becoming active subjects of development. It is also wary of the benefits of tutelage by vanguard parties.

Most of the popular participation models are articulated in close connection with basic needs theory and the leading role it assigns to governments. It should be recognized, however, that there is also a strong private enterprise/market strain of popular participation theory, which is analytically closer to growth and redistribution with growth models (Johnson 1984). The eventual outcome will be what people decide.

The value set in popular participation typologies emphasizes communal solidarity and more equal patterns of distribution of both resources and economic products. Individual rights and duties are placed within the context of communal solidarity; theoretically, at least, they remain intact through the normative criteria of participation (corresponding to equal opportunity).

The main problem with popular participation is its actual orchestration. The primary agent of change is seen as the poor themselves, and the problem of the "pedagogy of the oppressed" is not easily overcome. In the literature, one also finds an enlightened elite of intellectuals, religious figures, and community leaders who argue the case of the poor both in front of the entrepreneurial class and government bureaucracies as well as to the poor themselves. The identification of the agents of change bears similarity to the revolutionary theory, for it depends on people-based initiatives (as well as upon a vanguard elite).

Finally, the precise role of entrepreneurs and markets as well as the role of government remains unclear. The tendency to decentralize, however, would seem to favor markets and make government more of a facilitator that provides infrastructure and information and maintains public order in a way that effectively protects basic communities of the poor from the predatory instincts of the local elites.

Integrated Rural Development And
A Social Market Economy

In integrated rural development the goal of development includes not only economics but institutional development that is modern while remaining true to the spirit of a culture. Integrated development theory attempts to save the good features of growth models while securing adequate income, meeting basic needs and ensuring popular participation. In a sense it attempts to integrate previous theories. Economic development has come to involve much more than economics. The new element this theory introduces to economic development literature is found in the explicit attention paid to the role of culture and structures of power in processes of modernization and social change. The possibilities for social change are seen in a way that is historical and very much explicitly culture specific.

As far as criteria of performance go, integrated rural development seeks to simultaneously achieve growth while meeting basic needs and ensuring participation. At this point it remains rather theoretical. "Integration" as a criteria of performance has several different meanings (Fasbender 1982: 202):

- social integration, which aims to incorporate the impoverished population into the development process
- multisectoral integration, builing off of the linkages and complementarities between sectors
- regional integration, which aims to reduce regional disparities and to foster positive interdependencies
- institutional integration, which aims to achieve efficiency in organization and management by ensuring that they are suitable to local cultures and also that they provide avenues of true participation and codetermination bv all involved in the development process.

The principal instruments of integrated rural development are the diffusion of technical innovation coupled with the authentic transformation of traditional institutions (power configurations and cultural values and preferences). It combines agricultural development, institutional reform, redistribution of income, and the establishment of welfare services and a normative orientation toward justice. It aims to overcome intense urbanization by coordinating micro- and macro-level planning by intersectoral integration of the economy and by simultaneously changing the economic, physical, social, and organizational aspects of society. It targets and actively promotes the economically weaker groups in society in order to foster political and socioeconomic development. Agriculture retains primary importance for it possesses the potential to mobilize resources and place them at the disposal of the rural community.

As for mechanisms of change, the cumulative interaction between social subsystems is very much emphasized, such that narrow economic or political approaches are considered insufficient in and of themselves, however necessary they may be (Faenza 1981). The cultural mechanisms are many and diverse, including the arts and literature, education, and popular participation in social life. The principal economic mechanism can be summed up as a social market economy, that is, a market-oriented economy guided by public choice in areas of social priority.

The principal agents and institutions are those characterizing a democratic market-oriented economy. In addition to the cultural emphasis in integrated rural development, a social market economy possesses the following operational characteristics:

1. A democratically based political system including a fair legal system that serves to define and protect fairness, participation and due process in markets. Here there is great scope for individual agents as well as families and free associations. Criteria of social responsiveness (social duty) are progressively linked to the ability to contribute and an equitable bearing of social costs. The primary duty of government is to foster the common good of the body politic. This does not imply that the government controls all resources, initiatives, and activities in its own hands, but that it politically supports a legal, economic, and social environment that promotes the expression of all legitimate political, economic, and social rights.

2. A fundamentally market exchange system and subsidiarity in political economic activities. Subsidiarity means that no activity be centralized to higher collective levels than can be efficiently accomplished at lower levels. (Thus, for example, farming should be household based rather than state collectives.) There is tremendous scope here for intermediary private voluntary organizations based upon free association, local cultural values, and institutions.

3. The public role is concentrated on:

   - A leading position regarding public goods (particularly social infrastructure of research, transport, and human resource development).

   - A setting of social priorities through fiscal (budget) and monetary policies. There is reliance upon monetary and fiscal policy tools to achieve a market-rational economy, i.e., neither plan or market ideological but market guided by political choice. This position recognizes that private market decisions have profoundly public effects and, therefore, must be integrated into public choice and normative social criteria of justice.

- Erecting a legal framework providing public order, safety, and due process.

- Public policy includes a multilevel distribution policy that addresses both the fairness of the "initial position' of resource ownership and wealth in society (e.g., land tenure) and a formula of distribution linking in a prioritized manner (1) needs, (2) effort, (3) merit, and (4) social privilege.

In my articulation of the theory, the value set of such an approach corresponds to my own position, articulated in Chapter 6. The problem with such an approach is that its cultural component remains largely theoretical. While such a social market strategy has characterized the Western industrial democracies since 1945, it is not clear that it is transferable to other countries with different cultural traditions. These and other points will be discussed in more detail in Chapter 8.

MODELING POLICY ALTERNATIVES

The above six typologies of development are theories. As such, they are gross oversimplifications of reality. Yet each represents an attempt to synthesize in a concrete way each of the analytical elements presented in Chapters 3–6: population and resources, technology, power, and culture.

These typologies overlap in considerable detail. Yet some points of difference are worth underlining. Firstly, they give evidence of significantly different methodological approaches. Secondly, each model includes the four analytical variables, but they rank them in quite different orders of importance. The most significant differences emerge in the areas of power and culture.

Finally, theory presents no blueprint or easy answer to development. While the first two models have been the most tested, much of all the theories remains untried. The models remain very hypothetical. Yet they do serve to raise a series of important questions that it would be unwise for development practitioners to overlook.

How does a country go from goals to policies to programs that work? In the economic development literature considerable emphasis has been placed upon translating theories into models that would serve as a basis for estimating future performance of various policy scenarios. There are three main types of models, and I will briefly comment upon each: quantitative, futurist, and historical.

Quantitative models have proliferated in Western countries partially because the academic community, whose social science methods implicitly mimic the natural sciences, has come to associate quantitative models with rigorous analysis. I will not further discuss the methodological issues here as they have already been raised in Chapter 2.

Quantitative models generally concentrate upon estimates of global inputs and outputs. In the area of poverty and hunger they have attempted to simultaneously estimate local, regional, and international resource availability. Regarding resource availability, considerable accuracy is possible, as satellite systems aid in estimating the natural resource parameters and increasingly accurate world statistical systems make it possible to assemble a fairly precise profile of productive resource endowments. There are of course great inequalities in the ability to gather such information. For example, in addressing an international conference of UNIAPAC in the spring of 1980, the Kenyan Ambassador to France stated that his country is often at a disadvantage in dealing with transnational corporations because those corporations have a more complete profile of Kenya's resources than the government itself has (UNIAPAC Conference 1981).

Over the past years very sophisticated models have evolved for both global modeling of food and agriculture (Centre for World Food Studies 1980) as well as for sectoral and regional programming and assessment of risks in agricultural models. In addition there has been a long and detailed analysis of production functions and their proper specification (Kaneda 1982). It is not my intention here to examine the construction of such models and their inner logic, but to underscore their usefullness. As an *Economist* (1985) article put it, they are better than a blindfold and a pin. But great care must be exercised in their application to policy decisions. The care need be exercized primarily with respect to economic, social, cultural, and historical presuppositions and their conditions.

There are great difficulties in estimating the output from a given set of resources. Innumerable production possibility sets exist and it cannot be determined a priori how government administrators and local farm managers will choose to employ their resources. The answers that all the various decisionmakers in the system will make to the questions of: What to produce? How? When? Where? And for whom? cannot be known in advance. In a certain sense the past history of resource use can serve as a guide. But not completely so, for so much of decisionmaking is predicated upon prices and risk assessment. The best that quantitative models can do is to anticipate a number of diverse scenarios based upon variable conditions.

One of the most telling analyses of the usefulness of economic theory and models is provided by Andrew Kamarck (Kamarck 1983: chs. 7 and 8). He begins with a remark of Keynes to the effect that economics is a science of thinking in terms of models joined to the art of choosing models that are relevant to the contemporary world. The ability to choose good models is rare and beset with difficulties.

The main problem lies with the subject matter of economics itself that sets it off from the natural sciences. Economists study nonrecurring events that provide limited scope for experimentation and no shield from uncontrollable outside occurrences. The data are both peculiarly beset by the subjective bias of participants in the events under study and also represent a moving target, for economic reality is in constant flux. In addition, the conceptual foundations of economic motivation and behavior remain loose and imprecise.

The performance of econometric models has not been impressive. Their results are frequently undermined by the assumptions of a model that abstracts from political, historical, and cultural factors and assumes economic behavior based upon mechanistic "laws" rather than voluntary decisions and even caprice. Consumer theory and the theory of the firm are circumscribed by an extremely unrealistic set of assumptions, both with respect to the behavior of consumers as well as to the behavior of managers.

It is true that as the science of statistics has developed over the years it has been possible to identify key swing variables of economic decisionmaking and performance. Nonetheless, great care must be taken in interpreting the future outlined by quantitative models and their associated probabilities. The major methodological problem with quantitative models is how to assess qualitative data (including political, historical, psychological, and cultural factors), which bear upon decisionmaking and resource use. Qualitative problems are not very great in estimating such things as fertilizer production functions or in estimating optimal feed mixes through linear programming. But estimating human decisionmaking on either the production or consumption side of the equation is very difficult. Modern managers, for instance, are rarely profit maximizers as represented in theory (Kamarck 1983: ch. 8). Increasingly they are salaried professionals who hold relatively few shares and are not the primary legal owners. They are frequently responsible to themselves as members of the board, and their motivation is targeted on short-term performance and career advancement. These and other intrusions into the economic scene from the arenas of politics or culture cannot be realistically set aside. Geopolitical crisis and sensitivity to values such as seen in the Islamic Revolution have generally caught the proponents of quantitative models by surprise.

Two attempts have been made to handle these difficulties. The first, and the most reliable, is to depend upon past historical behavior within a certain social milieu. Such past behavior patterns can to a certain extent be quantified and taken as a rough proxy for qualitative issues. In this method, however, little indication will be provided for abrupt changes. A second method has been to use game theory, which incorporates prices as a proxy for quality and includes probability estimates of risk assessment. Game theory models are very elaborate both with respect to their formulas of interrelations and their presuppositions regarding human behavior and the selection of quantitative proxies for qualitative issues. They are more useful over the short term, when it is more logical to presuppose that qualitative issues remain more or less constant. But they often confuse statistical significance and rigor with either political or economic relevance. It is worth recalling here that such models were used with undesirable effects by the U.S. State and Defense Departments during the Vietnam War and the Iranian crisis.

It would be a mistake to think that because econometric models are beset by limitations they are useless. Indeed, considerable research is going into assessing model performance and reworking them to avoid some of the pitfalls noted above (Lakshmanan 1982; Hall and Thorbecke 1982). And they have already proven useful in a number of areas: (1) testing the consistency of theories and plans with data, (2) simulating alternative paths in "what if . . .?" type scenarios, (3) probing isolated Input–Output relations, (4) testing conditions for optimizing economic behavior, (5) discovering disruptive variables, and (6) monitoring short-term behavior.

A better example of how to employ quantitative models in decisionmaking is provided not by economic theory but by a comprehensive survey of decisionmaking by transnational corporations, where such estimates correspond to just one element in a lengthy deliberative process actively integrated into historical, psychological, political, and cultural factors.

Dissatisfaction with the reductive view of human interaction inherent in narrow quantitative models has led to an expansion of studies in what is now called futurology. Futurist studies tend in general to give much more emphasis to values and qualitative issues than the quantitative methods surveyed above (Masini 1981). Quantitative issues, such as natural resource limitations that inhibit growth, tend to be taken as data to be incorporated into futurist projections rather than as the key determinants of what will happen. Accordingly, futurist methodology tends to be more creative and artistic rather than mechanistic. Great emphasis is placed on the ability to imagine many different possible scenarios within the context of certain constraints.

Futures studies are not necessarily quantitatively weak. What they do is integrate quantitative socio-metric approaches in a larger interpretative framework. Yehezkel Dror (Dror 1974: 170ff.) summarized six features of good futures studies:

1. values sensitivity, explication and analysis;
2. creativity and imagination in prefiguring alternatives;
3. improving methodology (that is, clarifying and integrating the great variety of methodologies employed, from empirical to narrative, from historical to critical/rational);
4. multidimensional and combinational approaches (reflecting the various disciplines, the division of labor, and the need for integration);
5. a clinical attitude (i.e. unbiased towards favored outcomes) together with deep human concern;
6. respecting the dynamics of diverse outputs.

Within this setting, historical and cultural data are of fundamental importance. On the one hand they present a constraint and limit the range of probable future choices. On the other, they represent the resource base of imagination. Imagination is a key dynamic, for it is the catalyst of the creative and artistic representation of new possibilities within the constraints of resources, history, and culture. At the same time, because of the emphasis on history and culture, futurist scenarios contain within them the formative dynamism of institutions, structures, and values in collective choices. In this sense, they focus upon the actual psychosocial dynamics of a people and the types of choice such people would find meaningful and are in a sense predisposed to make. This is far richer than mere theoretical quantitative scenarios based on different technical possibilities inherent in a given set of resources. It also succeeds in circumventing the narrow and often mechanical notion of human motivation and action that underlies game theory and is evident in most models of economic rationality.

Eleanora Masini (1980) has summarized forecasting methodologies as *explorative* (opportunity or possibility oriented) and *normative* (mission or goal oriented). The former may be objective, using information about social indicators to extrapolate a possible future trend or pattern, or subjective, using panels, brainstorming techniques, and methods such as Delphi. Explorative forecasting prolongs events into the future; normative forecasting prolongs behavior into the future. The latter is not simply utopian; rather, it is purposeful and emphasizes perspectives and strategies to make such a future happen.

Futurist studies have much to contribute. But they are an art and their relevance depends to a great extent on the artistic qualities of the practitioners. Some of the proposals appearing under the guise of futurist studies amount to little because the practitioners have not taken the time to immerse themselves into the realities of resource constraints, human psychology, political interaction, history, and culture. An uncritical reliance upon futurist studies would be as disastrous as an uncritical reliance upon game theory. But as an element in a total decisionmaking process, the futurist forecasting methodologies can be very useful. They force observers to face up to the enormous number of future possible development paths and to all of the various dynamics that enter into human collective choice. If nothing else, they demonstrate that what exists now need not necessarily be and that the future is open-ended, not mechanistically determined. Such studies are more fruitful when they incorporate the type of quantitative models surveyed previously because such integration will force the forecaster to face up to implicit presuppositions and limitations of partial approaches regarding policy formulation and implementation.

A third type of model that one finds in the development literature is the historical model. Discussions of the Soviet Model, the Japanese Model, and the Chinese Model are well known. I personally believe that historical and institutional analysis is very powerful. It is of primary importance and its exclusion in many North American economics approaches is a very serious error. The identification of narrow econometric models with rigorous economic analysis is very shortsighted indeed (Kamarck 1983; Upton 1979). It is only in thorough historical and institutional analysis that one can grasp all of the dynamic elements of decisionmaking and gain a comprehensive and integrated perspective upon their interaction. The historical case studies of how development actually took place or was stymied within a particular country is of fundamental importance and cannot be substituted for either by restrictive quantitative models or by unmoored futurist speculations.

Nonetheless, such historical analysis is limited when one begins to ask what lessons can be drawn from the Japanese or Chinese experience, for example (Cline 1982; Sen 1983), because the economic development experience of Japan presupposes the history of Japan and the infrastructure, political institutions and culture of Japan. When one begins to think of applying the Japanese experience to Nigeria, one must be very careful in drawing lessons because the Nigerians are quite culturally diverse among themselves and certainly are not Japanese. The Japanese model has been applied with considerable success in both Taiwan and South Korea, but it must be remembered that those countries share many cultural similarities with Japan and, besides, they were Japanese colonies for a period of more than fifty years.

In assessing the viability of something like the Japanese model for other developing countries, an exhaustive evaluation of the sociocultural system and of human resources is indispensable. In addition, other factors come into play: (1) the prospects for technical resource preparation and utilization; (2) the accumulation and allocation of capital; (3) the strength, vision, honesty, and efficiency of government; (4) the viability of trade strategies (such as export-led growth or import substitution); (5) the potential for domestic markets; and (6) infrastructure development.

In the case of a country like Nigeria, one can take the Japanese experience as illustrative but not as normative. For historical analysis to be fruitful in terms of generating models of development, a wide number of case studies from different cultural and political backgrounds must be studied and compared. In this way it will be more possible to isolate factors that are recurrently important across countries and those that are more culturally specific. Further, among the recurrent factors it will be possible to rank their relative degrees of importance in differing local and international settings. None of these reflections will yield a blueprint that one could simply imitate. Rather, such analysis will be fruitful if it succeeds in suggesting critical areas of data overlooked and a series of questions to be reflected upon in one's proper historical context.

In principle, there can never be a satisfactory universal model of development. For any model is both an abstraction and a generalization. When compared to the flesh and blood of experience, it remains a lifeless skeleton. It cannot capture either personality or dynamics; it is without spirit, body, and stature. It is useful only in an illustrative way to highlight potentially important areas of experience and relevant questions. When used in such a creative fashion, the above models can be very helpful. But when one takes such a model as normative, rigor mortis sets into development analysis.

These models are not defined in an exclusive sense, for they obviously overlap. However, they do serve to underline the dominant orientation of various researchers. If economic development literature is troubled by problems today, one of the main reasons is found in the uncritical use of models, whether they be econometric, futurist, or historical. Economic policymaking is more an art than a science. Policy creation is similar to story telling. What is needed is the creative ability to imagine social alternatives and prefigure strategies to achieve them. Development policy is a narrative that imagines an alternative on the basis of resources, power, and values and also sets forth a plot with a cast of characters as a means to get there.

TOWARDS COMPREHENSIVE POLICY ANALYSIS

This chapter reflects upon development policy and models of social change. The types of development models I examined are actually models of social change. Social scientists have not yet come up with an adequate theory or laws of social change, although recurrent elements and important data have been identified.

Development policy is beset by problems. There is no completely satisfactory model detailing agents, ends and means, or the dynamics of social change. In addition, there is no secure way of modeling a policy and comparing it with alternatives once adopted. It is not easy to specify the elements or to create comprehensive and integrated development policy. The whole endeavor remains inherently experimental. Planners, administrators, and managers must take into account five key points: the realities of physical environment, the characteristics of the human resource endowment, the political environment, the business and economic milieu, and the sociocultural context (including values). In so doing the aim is to evolve good policies that give evidence of the criteria of being empirically comprehensive, value-critical, technologically feasible, and systems manageable.

Those four criteria, then, suggest a set of questions that are appropriate in the formulation of development policy. But frequently enough, even when one gives attention to the five areas of data and the four criteria listed above, different groups of experts will come up with fundamentally different sets of proposals for the same development context.

There is no easy way out of such an impasse. The data and the questions must be gone over again and again in order to discover false assumptions, lacunae, or errors in analysis. In policy formulation there always remains the unknown surd, which statistical models call random error or noise in the universe. Choice of an actual strategy depends very much on probabilities of success. Thus, policies must try to build in a certain amount of openendedness and flexibility that anticipate the possibility of change and reversals. Such flexibility recognizes the limits of modeling scenarios; after all, they represent nothing but rather severely circumscribed probabilities and are open to constant revisions.

The difficulties in determining social facts have already been discussed in Chapter 2. Both individual and collective bias remains a major obstacle to forging effective development policy. Development theories and models and their associated methodologies are all open to bias. In addition to the biases described in Chapter 2, I mention here three operational biases. There are frequently crucial behavioral assumptions made regarding the (1) poor, (2) governments, and (3) markets (FAO 1983; ILO 1983; Poats 1983).

Many development policies assume a certain homogeneity and solidarity among the poor. This proves to be the case often only in a very superficial sense, for there is considerable stratification among the impoverished, both in terms of social roles and cultural values as well as in terms of welfare and social inequalities. The poor are in many regions little more than a statistical grouping. Divided by social and cultural barriers, they possess little effective solidarity and do not constitute an effective political force. Good development policy must effectively address the concerns of all the different groups of the poor and also engage their participation. Effective development must at least in some way work from the bottom up. It is not a matter of simply doing things for the poor. Too often development literature portrays the poor as noble savage, leading to romantic visions of solidarity and participation that have little relevance for effective policy.

There also must be realistic assessment of the quality of political life and of local government, which after all has such an important role to play in designing and implementing policy. Is the state strong, honest, enlightened, and efficient (Biggs 1981; King 1981; Ergas 1982)? These are not indifferent matters and the fact that they are so frequently not explicitly discussed is disheartening. To the point, those calling for basic needs strategies frequently assign the government a central role. But when that government is Marcos in the Philippines, Duvalier in Haiti, or Mobutu in Zaire, the prospects of a basic needs strategy would be dim to say the least. Planning may be a logically coherent proposal—so much of planning literature epitomizes the "rationalist person." But pitfalls are frequently assumed away such as: (1) the quality of data and statistical systems, (2) the communication and processing of information, (3) the efficiency of the logistical infrastructure, and (4) the dynamics of organizational politics and turf battles.

Finally, in such strategies, the scope for private enterprise in development must be anticipated in terms of broader economic, social, and cultural dynamics. In each country one must assess the *quality* of the market and of the institutions (such as the law) intended to safeguard the integrity of the market. (U.S. Agency for International Development 1982; Evans 1979). It is a requirement of policy that the fair and efficient functioning of markets be ensured. This is not the case in many countries currently described as market economies. The realities of competition and power frequently contradict the prerequisites of market-based economic efficiency. Further, the operative assumptions regarding economic efficiency are frequently biased toward large-scale, capital-intensive operations. In addition, markets are often referred to as a univocal concepts, applying equally to Nestlé as to a tenant farmer in Brazil. The failure to articulate the qualities and characteristics of markets means that policy never spells out the type of markets that are desirable and the social conditions and institutions (such as law) that are necessary to preserve fairness.

To conclude, development policy implicitly contains a theory and model of social change. As such, there are multiple assumptions regarding what is realistic in terms of four main analytical variables I have employed: population/resources, technology, power, and culture. One of my main points is that these issues should not be left implicit but should be raised to the level of explicit discussion and analysis.

There is no blueprint for development policy. The following chapters discuss elements of strategy on the domestic and international levels. The aim of such discussion is to discover possibilities and assess their potential for implementation.

REFERENCES

"Better Than a Blindfold and a Pin." 1985. *The Economist* (November 9): 71.

Biggs, S.D. 1981. "The Implications of Bureaucratic Factors for Agricultural Policy Analysis." *Bangladesh Journal of Agricultural Economics* 4, no. 2: 35-50.

Bruton, Henry J. 1985. "The Search for a Development Economics." *World Development* 13, no. 10/11: 1099-1124.

Center for World Food Studies. 1980. "Global Modelling of Food and Agriculture." *Pakistan Development Review* 19, no. 3: 159-80.

Chenery, Hollis, et al. 1974. *Redistribution with Growth*. Baltimore: The Johns Hopkins University Press.

Cline, William K. 1982. "Can the East Asian Model of Development Be Generalized." *World Development* 10, no. 2: 81-90.

Cole, Samuel, and Henry Lucas, eds. 1982. *Models, Planning and Basic Needs.* New York: Pergamon Press.

Dror, Yehezkel. 1974. "Futures Studies-Quo Vadis?" In *Human Futures: Needs, Security, Technologies*, 169-76. Proceedings of the World Futures Conference, Paris.

Ergas, Zaki. 1982. "The State and Economic Deterioration: The Tanzanian Case." *Journal of Commonwealth and Comparative Politics* 20, no. 3: 286-308.

Evans, Peter. 1979. *Dependent Development: The Alliance of the Multinational, State and Local Capital in Brazil.* Princeton, N.J.: Princeton University Press.

Faenza, V. 1981. "Integrated Rural Development in African Countries." *Rivista di Agricoltura Subtropicale e Tropicale* 75, no. 1: 5-23.

Fasbender, Kal. 1982. "Strategy of Integrated Development." *Intereconomics* 17, no. 6: 291-95.

Food and Agricultural Organization (FAO), Committee on World Food Security, 1983. *Interim Report on Constraints on Food Production in Low-Income Food-Deficit Countries of Africa.* Rome, Italy: Food and Agricultural Organization.

Gran, Guy. 1983. *Development by People.* New York: Praeger Publishing Co.

Hall, L., and E. Thorbecke. 1982. "Agricultural Sector Models for Policy Planning in Developing Countries: A Critical Evaluation." Working Paper No. 95. Cornell International Agricultural Development Center, Department of Agricultural Economics.

International Labour Organisation. 1983. "Review of ILO Rural Development Activities Since 1979." Advisory Committee on Rural Development, Tenth Session. Geneva, 22 November to 1 December 1983. Geneva, Switzerland: International Labour Office.

Johnson, Frances. 1984. "Food for All Through Enterprise." U.S. AID, Washington, D.C. Unpublished papers.

Kamarck, Andrew M. 1983. *Economics and the Real World.* Philadelphia: University of Pennsylvania Press.

Kaneda, H. 1982. "Specification of Production Functions for Analyzing Technical Change and Factor Inputs in Agricultural Development." *Journal of Development Economics* 11, no. 1: 97-108.

King, Dwight Y. 1981. "Regime Type and Performance: Authoritarian Rule, Semi-Capitalist Development, and Rural Inequality in Asia." *Comparative Political Studies* 13, no. 4: 477-504.

Lakshmanan, T.R. 1982. A Systems Model of Rural Development. *World Development* 10, no. 10: 885-98.

Masini, Eleanora Barbieri. 1980. "Explorative and Normative Methodologies in Social Forecasting." Geneva, Switzerland: ISA Scientific Council.

_____. 1981. "Philosophical and Ethical Foundations of Future Studies: A Discussion." *World Future Studies* 17, no. 1: 1-14.

Poats, R.M. 1983. "Towards More Effective Campaigns Against Poverty." *OECD Observer* 12, no. 5: 5-11.

"Power To Organize, The." 1982. *Ceres* 15, no. 3: 15-38.

Rein, Martin. 1976. *Public Policy.* New York: Penguin.

Ruttan, V.W. 1982. "Perspectives on Agrarian Reform and Rural Development." *Quarterly Journal of International Agriculture* 21, no. 3: 240–49.

Sen, Asim. 1983. "Lessons for Development from the Japanese Experience." *Journal of Economic Issues* 17, no. 2: 415–22.

Szal, Richard. 1980. "Operationalising the Concept of Basic Needs." *The Pakistan Development Review* 19, no. 3: 237–46.

UNIAPAC Conference. 1981. *Proceedings.* Wolfsberg, Switzerland: UNIAPAC.

Upton, Martin. 1979. "The Unproductive Production Function." *Journal of Agricultural Economics* 30, no. 2: 34–49.

U.S. Agency for International Development, Bureau for Private Enterprise. 1982. *Policy Paper.* Washington, D.C.: U.S. Agency for International Development.

Weeks, J., and E. Dore. 1982. "Basic Needs: Journey of a Concept." In *Human Rights and Basic Needs in the Americas*, ed. Margaret E. Crahan, 131–49. Washington, D.C.: Georgetown University Press.

8 DOMESTIC DEVELOPMENT

The literature in the policy area is vast; much of it remains untested. I know of no easy solutions. I restrict myself to addressing lines of action that, taken together, address in a promising way the issues brought out in the preceding chapters. The primary goal of development is to overcome absolute poverty. Policy must, therefore, directly address the problems of the urban unemployed, the rural landless, the social position of women, and the plight of dependent children. In so doing, development policy must explicitly face issues of demography and natural resource management, technical transformation of the economy, the realities of power and the dynamics of culture.

In my approach to poverty and development, politics and social structures occupy central stage. In this chapter, I confine myself to domestic issues and discuss in turn the politics of development, private enterprise and market strategies, and private voluntary organizations. I conclude with some remarks on social efficiency in the management of the political economy. Throughout, my emphasis is on a social market economy model of development.

THE POLITICS OF DEVELOPMENT

In discussions of development, the major emphasis falls upon the nation-state. This is more than a convenience; it underscores the fact that the civil authority system is the pivotal social unit in assessing the prospects of development. The prospects for development are far brighter when a government is enlightened, benevolent, efficient, and honest. The government is expected to achieve two principal goals in its legislative, executive, and judicial functions; namely, to establish and preserve public order and to positively foster the social well-being of its citizens. When those objectives are not approached with integrity, it is clear that international interests and domestic elites can easily wreak havoc upon the body politic.

The major problems in development today are all somewhat political in nature. The dynamics of population, resources, science, and technology are all complicated by politics. Feasible demographic and natural resource policies, technical proposals, and scientific research plans, can become absolutely intractable once they enter the political arena. At the same time, political systems have a cultural base as well as a power base, which workable and effective development policies must respect. In speaking of the politics of development in this section, I purposely confine myself to the roles of national and local government (leaving the consideration of other participants to later sections).

That the quality of a particular country's governmental institutions receives so little attention in the development literature is a serious shortcoming. Part of the reason for this neglect is political: the nation-states have become sacred cows. Although the euphemism of "nation building" is used, United Nations and other government documents rarely seriously analyze the quality of political institutions. Rather, they content themselves with expatiating on the population time bomb or the sins of the transnationals. These same government-based groups have taken up the rhetoric of the new international economic order, self-reliance, interdependence, and development by people, without adequately addressing the fact that none of this can or will happen without a fundamental transformation of politics, both domestically and internationally.

The nation-state today frequently presents a sorry picture. Many governments are in the hands of unrepresentative elites who invoke the sacred scripture of national sovereignty and the sanctity of internal affairs to mask every sort of excess. This is true of administrations of the so-called vanguard parties of the left as well as of the national security-state ideologues of the right.

The poor quality of governments has provoked an extended philosophical debate over the nature and function of the state in concrete cultural contexts; for example, African socialism and the Chinese road. These issues are both theoretically and historically complex and cannot be adequately addressed here. The point I wish to make is that "the state" does not represent a univocal reality throughout the world. The nature, function, and limits of the state are differentiated from place to place on the basis of social structure, the formal objective tasks of the government, and the constraints and social crises it faces. The potential role of the state in development between Thailand and Nigeria, for example, differs widely because the quality of government and sociopolitical institutions differs.

A significant number of governments hardly even represent viable nation-states, in terms of resources, population, administrative efficiency, or legitimacy. Yet governments today are key actors on the development stage. This is the case for many reasons. Chief among them is the fact that most governments are economic producers and public enterprises represent a significant portion of GNP. They are also makers and enforcers of many of rules of the game, the guarantors of order, the sources of finance, the architects and implementors of planning, and the arbitrators of disputes. They may do these things even-handedly or on behalf of special interests. No significant study of development today can omit the primacy of governments and the pivotal importance of the public sector (cf. Figure 8-1).

It soon becomes clear that the building of benevolent, enlightened, honest, efficient, and stable political institutions is itself a necessary condition of economic development and of social justice. If the history of Europe and North America is any guide, it is clear that such an evolution is a rough-and-tumble process that takes generations. Cultural stability cannot be fairly expected of states that only broke away from colonialism in the 1960s, and whose national borders and very national identity are still taking shape. The primary long-term goal for development, and the one that fiercely conditions the prospects of all other goals, is the building of just and otherwise adequate legislative, judicial, and administrative governmental structures on both local, national, and international levels. This being said, I confine my remarks in the rest of this section to the more specifically economic responsibilities of government in development. I begin with local government.

The role of local government is often neglected. But it is very important in development and calls for explicit examination. Frequently enough, local government is the primary level of government that most people encounter. It is also the only level at which national programs have any realistic chance of being implemented. There is no reliable formula for properly determining patterns of decentralization (Rondinelli et al., 1984) or for improving the qualities of local governments (Cochrane 1983, Gould and Amaro-Reyes 1983). So much depends on historical and cultural analysis that global generalizations say little.

Figure 8–1. The Role of Government in Development (Desired qualities: benevolent, enlightened, honest, stable, efficient).

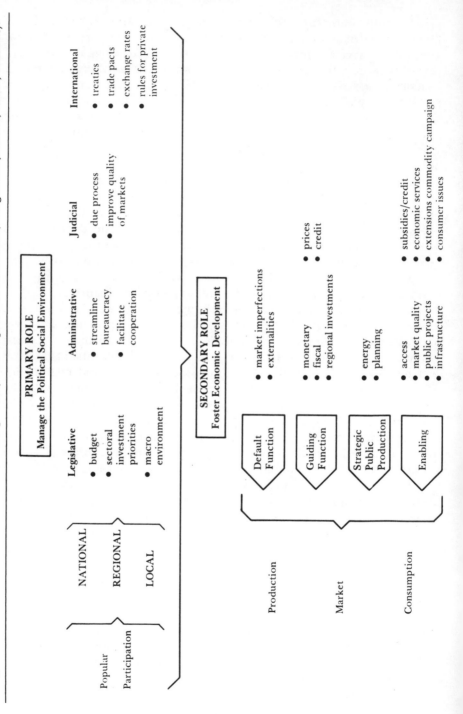

The main priority would seem to be to build up grassroots structures of participation. Participation is a necessary condition for credibility as well as for responsibility, but it has proven extremely difficult to achieve. Peasants have always been unwilling clients of academics, government bureaucrats, party cadres, development consultants, and others in the national and international planning communities. Even the halcyon days of Mao's cultural revolution, during which bureaucrats and academicians were sent to the countryside to learn from the peasants, failed to turn the situation around. The last decades have witnessed a spate of articles on eliciting the cooperation of the peasants rather than forcing development down their throats. Repeated failures have spawned slogans calling for "self-reliance" and "development from below." Like all slogans, they possess a kernal of truth. Development is not something to be done for or to the peasants but with them. The key note of such development is not merely the active participation of peasants but their self-determination.

The heart of the matter is grassroots community organizing, where outside catalysts (such as technicians and government representatives) collaborate with local people who take the principal role in articulating their needs, the means to meet them, and the strategies to be followed. Such organization does not preclude outside agents, but it builds off of local values, leadership patterns, and resources. The primary component is local. Leonard Joy and associates have evolved an interesting social development management workbook (Joy 1983). It represents an approach to popular participation and empowerment that recasts the role of central government, the character of bureaucracies, and the dynamics of planning. In the process of decentralization and increasing popular participation, the role of government and bureaucracies should encourage others to act for themselves. Planning emerges more as a process of social learning and experimental unfolding of choices rather than a precise blueprint.

The starting point is found in traditional and oftentimes informal organizations and structures that, for very little capital expenditure, can be transformed into development institutions. Included here are traditions of resource management, processes of decisionmaking and leadership, and the role of women. The focus is on taking the next step that the local people desire and are capable of taking primarily with their own resources. Such development breeds small successes and further development. The criteria of participation are not necessarily the criteria of liberal Western democracy, which are often individualist, conflictual, and rationalist. The participative dynamics of the local culture will dictate the course of action. Although it is to be expected that new forms will evolve, the most fruitful starting point in a particular village is the question: How does anything get done here?

Within this context, innovations can be introduced. For example, Winrock International has for some years been involved in projects to improve the breeding stock of goats (Winrock International 1983: 82–85). The project brings technical experts to the outlying rural villages and puts them into direct contact with the people who raise or can raise goats. Government bureaucracies are bypassed. It is a model of technological innovation introduced at the grassroots level and adapted to the local milieu.

The role of government is to facilitate not dominate. Glynn Cochrane (1983) has effectively demonstrated that central government must work efficiently with local governments if public sector policies are to be effective. His argument is delineated in terms of fiscal relations, personnel management, and the clear allocation of functions (including service delivery functions). What is needed is central government commitment to stabilizing the role and improving the quality of local governments. Too often they are in competition, leading to overcentralization of development policy.

Regarding regional and national government, my position is that the first task of these levels of government is to *foster* development. "Foster" definitely does not mean that the government holds all the reins of power, controls all initiatives, or eliminates the private sector and markets. It means that it facilitates the cooperative interaction (in its legislative, administrative, and legal functions) of all participants in society (including households, private voluntary organizations, and economic organizations ranging from small enterprises to large corporations). Its task is to move the development process forward, to facilitate and support development processes rather than exercise absolute control. The more a government is enlightened, benevolent, honest, stable, and efficient, the more it will be able to do this. Bad governments mean bad development. Even when there are good people in government (for example, in Tanzania) such good intentions cannot effectively substitute for other qualities (Ergas 1982; Yeager and Miller 1982).

What is the responsibility of the public sector? I envision two related functions (Figure 8–1). The first is administrative—including maintaining public order, setting public priorities, achieving efficient coordination in legislation and management of the budget. The second is productive—whether direct production by the public sector or "enabling" activities that facilitate production by the private sector. All of this can be summarized under the rubric of planning.

There is, however, a considerable amount of confusion about the word "planning" itself. It is not a univocal concept. For some it means primarily research, forecasting, and communication of information; for others it means dismantling the market system; others still see it as a device for rescuing and controlling certain segments of the economy.

In the context of modern economies, it is senseless to ask whether or not to plan. The automatically self-regulating market is a utopian dream. The basic question is what kind of planning is appropriate to enhance the positive functions of markets. Secondly, all planning is inherently political: It uses the legislative, judicial, and executive functions of government to change the political–economic rules of the game. In and of itself, planning is neither left wing nor right wing. Planning in its most general sense stands in distinction to markets. It amounts to guiding markets by political choice.

Planning can be advocated for a variety of reasons. Much of the literature has been devoted to providing an economic rationale, in terms of efficient management of supply and demand to meet social priorities. This view has been sharply disputed by market theorists. It is important, however, to point out that central planning and public ownership are often advocated for political rather than economic reasons. Strong central authority is often seen as the only effective means to hold powerful elites in check. The argument is based more on practical power politics than on economic ideology. The decentralization of markets would allow strong families and elite factions too much power and social control. Only a well-organized public sector, it is argued, can effectively counter-balance entrenched classes; centralized planning is one useful instrument in this struggle.

Market solutions to sectoral, regional, and trade strategies are today more and more circumscribed by political processes on both domestic and international levels. Good political planning is seen as necessary to provide a hedge against sectoral poverty, harmful patterns of urbanization, and other economic uncertainties. If well done, it can help provide for orderly marketing procedures. But there are many problems involved, not the least of which is bureaucracy.

In planning, economics and politics fuse. As a working definition, I use planning in the sense of public political choices that set rules of the game for markets. It is only in the concrete details of the law and the budget that actual planning priorities are really grasped. The principal role of government in development is to exercise its primary functions efficiently. It is effective laws that make the rules of the game clear; only a fair legal system ensures that they function correctly. Further, only in the budget process do sources of revenue and patterns of outlay become concrete in terms of prices, fiscal and monetary policy, and exchange rates so that their combined effect upon production, income distribution, investment, and various sectors and regions of the economy may be assessed. It is noteworthy that the World Bank Report on agriculture in Sub-Sahara Africa (World Bank 1981) singled out government price policy as a major factor in the lack of agricultural development. Furthermore, it is through governmental policy that the local economy is linked to the world economy. Legislative, budgetary, and administrative processes as well as international accords pit competing interests against each other in a complex political and bureaucratic interplay. The honesty and efficiency of the politicians, civil service, and interest groups can never be taken for granted (Gould and Amaro-Reyes 1983). No market is insulated from these processes.

Whether its planning be more direct or indicative, the state plays an indispensable coordinating role in the economy. There are four aspects of planning that are primary: sectoral, regional, international, and social class relations. Ideally, legislation and budgetary planning represent practical coordination between agriculture, industry, and services, between various geographic regions of the country, and between import and export strategies. These are usually discussed with production and marketing orientations. Yet an equally important aspect of contemporary planning is the management of the characteristics of relations between social classes. Generally this takes the form of producer incentives, consumer policy, and market adjustments, although it can include class warfare and the radical redistribution of wealth and resources (e.g., land reform). Each area is fraught with problems, yet a certain common wisdom has evolved since 1945. My initial remarks concentrate on production and marketing policies. Consumer policy is treated later.

In my approach, the government has a secondary function to foster economic development. Fostering development involves four types of activities, which will vary from place to place according to concrete conditions. Firstly, fostering development includes a *default function*. That is, public policy is called for when markets do not work properly, as in the case of externalities and market imperfections. Secondly, there is a *guiding function* that derives from government's primary role. The key points here are monetary and fiscal policy and budgetary matters of regional investments, price policy, and credit. Thirdly, there are various *enabling functions* that a government undertakes. This function clearly overlaps with the preceding functions. Also, in concrete detail it varies widely from place to place. But it includes ensuring access to inputs and markets, ensuring market quality (e.g., by grading quality), and providing necessary infrastructure and public projects (e.g., a transport system). It also includes attention to economic services (e.g., weather and price information), extension programs, consumer issues and certain subsidies and credits for target groups. Finally, there is a *strategic function* where government may undertake public production (e.g., in areas of postal and telecommunication services, energy, and vital commodities such as steel). As noted, the reasons for this may be more political than economic.

There is no global answer to what sort of concrete secondary functions a government should undertake. Historically, however, those countries that have given priority to agriculture have fared the best. In recent development experience, countries like Kenya, Malawi, the Ivory Coast, and Thailand outperformed countries like Ghana, Zambia, Tanzania, and Burma primarily because of the attention paid to agriculutre.

Sectorally, for a variety of both economic, demographic, and social reasons, most developmentalists advocate an "agriculture first" policy as a foundation both for expanding industry as well as services. An adequate sectoral policy towards agriculture includes positive investment and nonexploitive price and tax policies (Clute 1983; Johnston and Kilby 1976; Krishna 1982). It is the rural sector— agriculture and the types of industry and services that complement agriculture—that holds the best prospects for the production of an economic surplus, the provision of jobs for the growing labor force, and the development of local markets. How to achieve this is not immediately evident. But a number of possibilities are increasingly found in the literature. (Latremoliere 1981; Conde 1981; Ruttan 1985). These include:

1. Focusing upon the small farm household, with special attention to price policy, credit, appropriate input supply, marketing of output, and rural industry that complements agriculture.
2. Harmonizing the simultaneous development of cash and subsistence crops, as well as animal and crop production.
3. Ecological management of natural resources.
4. Transforming the rural technology set to raise production and increase jobs by focusing on agriculture's scientific technical base.
5. Focusing upon "commodity campaigns" to exploit present opportunities to increase production of x or y commodity and to employ "farming district programs" to adapt public programs to local resource potential.
6. Managing the quality of the economic environment (especially factor prices) which are conducive to technical change.
7. Improving the quality of labor and management through education and extension, as well as health and nutrition.

Most developing countries are involved in agricultural development. Figure 8-2 presents an overview of percentage distribution of official commitments to agriculture. Land and water projects have commanded nearly 22 percent of funding, while research has received a little less than 5 percent. All of the investment categories are important. The main constraint is the amount of funds to invest. As a practical matter, as will be discussed in the following chapter, most developing countries rely heavily on outside aid and foreign direct investment.

Much of this has become common wisdom in the past twenty-five years. Two particular types of policies emerge as having very special problems: credit and prices (Bates 1982; Havnevik and Skarstein 1983; Vermeer 1982; Fasbender 1982).

Commercial lenders often find agricultural loans unattractive in developing countries. In some areas, the rate of repayment by both large and small borrowers in farm loans has been poor; in practice, this means loss of liquidity for credit institutions and additional costs for collecting payments in arrears. The population is often illiterate, which makes it difficult to deal with formal credit institutions. In addition, rural population is generally dispersed and the size of holdings is small; the costs associated with processing a large number of small mixed loans is very high and also the collateral that a small farmer may offer is inadequate. Because of these problems it has been estimated that only about 5 percent of small farmers in Africa and 15 percent in Asia and Latin America have effective access to commercial institutional credit. It seems imperative, therefore, that local governments facilitate suitable credit mechanisms.

Such government activity might take the form of organizing cooperatives for credit, for purchasing production inputs, or for marketing final products. Further government activity could either guarantee agricultural loans, subsidize the interest rates on farm production loans, or otherwise provide profit incentives to lenders and borrowers. Governments frequently seek to control interest rates. The combination of low rates of return with high risk of losses, however, generally make small holder agriculture unattractive to private financial institutions. Dennis Anderson and Farida Khambata (1985) have argued for a two-fold approach: (1) relaxing regulations of interest rates and (2) a sharing of administrative costs and risks between public and private sectors. The latter is, in effect, a subsidy to suppliers of credit, who (it is presumed) would be more efficient managers. That is problematic, and in addition, there are many problems with peasants participating in formal credit institutions. As was argued in Chapter 6, explicit attention should be paid to traditional

Figure 8–2. Percentage Distribution of Official Commitments to Agriculture (Excluding Technical Assistance Grants) by Purpose, 1976–1983.

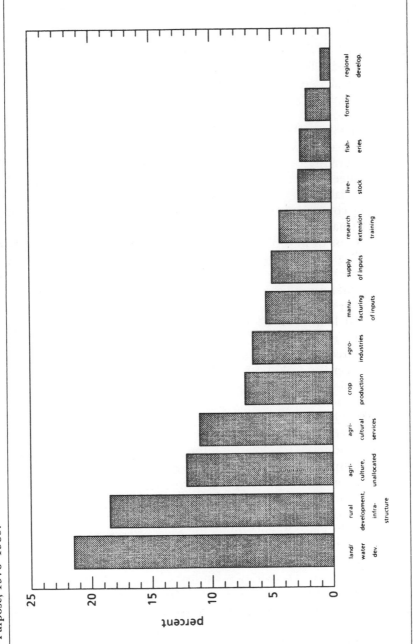

Source: Based on Food and Agriculture Organization (1985: 183).

nonformal institutions. Bennett Obioma (1983) has demonstrated that in Nigeria traditional savings groups could provide workable channels for credit if slightly improved.

Recently, World Bank lending to small farmers has come to emphasize a "package" approach, which includes not only credit but other inputs required for agricultural production. Often distribution in kind (e.g., fertilizer and small tractors) has proven to be the most effective means of distributing production credits. Problems with such an approach cannot be underestimated. In a cross-national study, Richard Vengroff and Ali Farah (1985) have found reason for caution. Their preliminary findings indicate that the use of government services to distribute agricultural inputs in Africa have largely failed. At the same time private sector sources are not well-developed. The project and package approaches have received considerable attention: The key variable in whether they work on the local level seems to be the quality of leadership and management. Secondly, it must be emphasized that, however fine credit and package approaches may be for the small farmer with land, they do not reach the landless who form a sizeable proportion of rural population and who are the worst off.

One of the most significant areas (and one of the most mismanaged) in which government can influence the accumulation of capital in certain sectors of the economy is through price policy (World Bank 1981). A sensible price policy allows farmers to make profits and mitigates the credit problems. The terms of trade should favor farmers by keeping prices of farm inputs low and prices for farm outputs high enough to guarantee the farmer a good profit. Capital is accumulated via the market in a way that provides an incentive and stimulates further production. As this process continues, not only is the production side of the development equation improved, but the marketing side is also. As the rural population moves beyond subsistence and accumulates profits, savings will increase, on the one hand, and the rural population will enter the market as purchasers, on the other.

If investment in industry is of the type that serves agriculture and rural population, then it can be seen that a great push will be given to development and the flow of capital by building up and tapping the internal market potential for a country. But all of this takes time to unfold. For example, in raising agricultural prices since 1979, China has experienced a sustained surge in agricultural production (over 10%) as well as in agricultural based light industry (over 15%). However, the government has found that the economic burden of higher prices on the urban sector was politically explosive. So it continued heavy subsidies (30% of the budget) with the hope of an eventual resolution. In late 1985 and early 1986 it moved even further toward markets prices both for farmers as well as for consumers. But substantial controls remain.

In addition to credit and price policies, a number of other issues deserve comment: regional development, trade, public production priorities, and consumer policy. Regional development within a country presents many special problems. One of the reasons for this is that the start-up costs in terms of providing infrastructure in a number of economic centers rather than one or two are formidable. Yet there are powerful arguments for some sort of regional balance in development, mostly stemming from efficiencies in resource use, the military advantages that many centers afford, and the necessity to stem certain negative patterns of urbanization. Achieving this involves improving administrative coordination (Leach 1982) and stimulating appropriate institutional changes. These institutional changes call for implementing national and regional development strategies together with local governments and for extending infrastructure in a balanced way (Kopp 1983).

Trade presents a very difficult problem for most developing countries. The difficulty is primarily in developing markets rather than in merely determining a comparative production advantage in x or y commodity. The history of ill-conceived import substitution strategies is well-known. And the export led strategies that have been viewed in more promising terms (e.g., in East Asia) have of late been stymied by shrinking market prospects both for raw materials (especially in terms of volatile commodity prices) as well as for exports of semi-processed and industrial products. This otherwise promising element of the "East Asian model" is not always a real possibility for many developing countries today (Cline 1982). If trade is to be a catalyst of development, its domestic and regional potential (South–South trade) must be built up, since first-world markets are becoming saturated. The prosperous small-farmer emphasis can help in this regard in developing domestic markets as can economic integration (regarding tariffs and currency) regionally. Such an approach demands a reassessment of comparative advantage in terms of market potential and a concomitant restructuring of output. Again all this is easier said than done.

What should the public sector produce, and what should be left to private enterprise? This is a very thorny question for which there is no clear answer. A convenient economic reference point (in distinction to public sector arguments based upon the necessity to contain the power of local elites) is found in the notion of social goods. The government should produce goods and services that are deemed socially necessary but that private enterprise would not provide for economic reasons. This corresponds to the default and enabling functions noted above.

Increasingly the production of economic infrastructure figures as a social good. This is true of a transport system and water and energy projects. It also applies to information and communication systems (including extension).

Governments are usually active not only in transport, water, and energy projects but also in providing economic services. Governments generate many economic services in providing for basic research, macro assessments of the economy, commodity supply and demand outlooks, weather and natural resource surveys, identifying and quantifying new economic opportunities, and management of constraints and resource limits. Increasingly, governments play important roles in the transfer of management and technology.

This transfer of management and technology skills is more than simply giving advice. It means educational and organizational change and the building up of an infrastructure capable of generating management skills and research capacity in areas where it is either nonexistent or at a very low level. At the basis of any technology transfer is the creation of the ability to absorb, adapt, and diffuse it. Governments are prime agents in developing human capital. Education as a form of investment in human capital is an absolute prerequisite of any development program. The viability of technology transfer also depends on public health and nutrition, which affect the learning process so profoundly. Unless attention is given to these basics, little else can be done. These aspects of management and technology transfer tend to be broadbased, with a low return in immediate market terms. As such, they generally fall into the public policy realm.

There are many other suggestions for public sector production in the literature, including developing rural village industries that have an agricultural base (Padmanabhan 1983; Gray 1983) and sponsoring rural works policy (Schumacher 1981). Their appropriateness, however, must be evaluated in terms of the local context.

Finally, a word on consumer policy. Increasingly development policy is taking on a specifically consumer focus. Basic needs strategies provide a case in point. As with production and market policies, the main political task in this area is to harness market forces to politically determined social objectives so as to achieve the common good of human social development. It is not surprising that in the "Basic Human Needs" approaches there has been considerable discussion of public programs to remedy the defects and malfunctions of the food market system. The discussion has centered upon the economic variables observed in the *consumption* function: (1) to guarantee the quantity supplied through food reserves, feeding programs, rations, and so forth, (2) to control prices, and (3) to subsidize incomes through measures such as food stamps.

In socialist countries, the main tools used to ensure supplies of basic food to people are price controls and rations. Rationing seems to provide a simple solution, yet the administrative requirements and the policing of "underground markets" can be quite formidable. To get around this, in many countries efforts have been made to solve the hunger problem through feeding programs, which focus upon children in schools and public health outlets. One advantage of such programs is that quality control can be ensured nutritionally and that waste can be minimized. Administrative costs can be quite high, however. The main targets and the most success has been with school populations. But in the poorest countries many of the school age population are not in school, and so the program falls short.

As with rationing, price controls seem to be a simple way to solve the hunger problem. But such controls are notoriously difficult and costly to administer. In addition, low prices tend to have disastrous effects upon production incentives, even in socialist economies. In the case of China, where socialist rationing and price controls have had some success, one has found during the years of tightest controls repeated warnings to peasants to plant the essential staple crops (where economic return is low) rather than shifting planting to more lucrative nonstaple items. That is, low prices induced people to ignore public production plans. Finally, with the policy of Deng Xiao-ping, prices were raised to provide incentives to farmers. Yet subsidies to the urban sector consumed over 30 percent of the state budget (Lardy 1983). In a market economy, control over farmer decisions is even worse because farmers will shift away from the areas of low economic return to either plant other things or to plant only for their own needs and engage in other occupations. Rural underground market trade and hoarding has proven historically difficult to police, even in a tightly organized society such as China. In theory, differentially controlled pricing and a tax policy may be used to (1) change consumer tastes away from more affluent to simpler patterns and (2) reward food production and distribution, making it more profitable to producers by providing incentives. There are, however, tremendous administrative problems as well as enormous transaction costs.

Finally, income. In a study of the effects of income distribution on nutrition in parts of Colombia, Per Pinstrup-Andersen and Elizabeth Caicedo (1978) convincingly show the interrelationship between income distribution and nutrition, arguing that programs to overcome hunger that focus upon increasing production, while neglecting income distribution really fail to get to the heart of the matter. In their study, the bottom 18 percent of the population, who received 5 percent of the income, managed to fulfill only 89 percent of their caloric and 72 percent of their protein requirements. If one considers the bottom 36 percent, which received 13.6 percent of the income, they fulfilled 99 percent of calories and 83 percent of protein requirements. The middle third of the income groups and, of course, the top third, were found to overfulfill basic requirements by increasing amounts.

In most countries, commodities needed to meet basic human needs, such as health, housing, clothing, and food, are purchased. The single most important policy to counteract hunger in developing market economies, and to a considerable degree in socialist economies, is providing for employment, which would guarantee income adequate for basic needs. Technology choice and tax plans must be explicitly examined with this in mind. A second income policy, and perhaps more short term, is an income supplement that provides direct cash grants or income aids such as food stamps. In countries where a market exchange system is found, income supplements are considered less distortive of the market.

The most serious problem facing development economists is that of redistribution. Although much of the literature continues with a single-minded focus on growth in output, it is by itself insufficient. While it is true that there must be something to distribute for people to be better off, a simple trickle-down effect cannot be assumed. This brings the discussion back to power. Public policy is the key arbitrator of public power. Public development policy must explicitly address power in natural resource distribution, in access to and participation in public procedures, and in effective voice in shaping policy priorities.

PRIVATE ENTERPRISE AND MARKET STRATEGIES

Agribusiness firms have been highly criticized for abuses and lack of concern for the poor. In many cases the criticism is justified. But it is difficult to imagine any solution to the hunger problem that does not elicit the creative support of agribusiness. A completely adversarial position toward business interests is not necessarily helpful, although, of course, one should not abdicate either critical judgment or conditional participation.

In a traditional market-type economy, where the small family farm is still the dominant unit, one finds both nomadic and stable agriculture together with both subsistence farming and varying degrees of market orientation. Agricultural history attests that the small traditional farms possess technology sets that are quite diverse regionally and only now are beginning to make wider use of new biochemical and industrial inputs. The traditional farmer is basically found in an extended family structure; income averages less than $500 per year. One finds low productivity and only a limited market orientation. The potential exists, however, for employing new inputs, once the barriers of lack of capital and lack of know-how can be overcome. In many places the type of tenure system is both a social and an economic problem.

In many market economies the family farm or small farm enterprises have been supplemented by cooperatives, whether for the acquisition of production resources (such as credit), for production itself, or for marketing. Numerous forms of cooperatives are obviously possible. In taking advantage of economies of scale and enhanced bargaining power, they hold out the potential of being more efficient in resource use. The biggest problems are found with management.

Over the past twenty-five years, large-scale farming has emerged in market economies in the form of corporate farming, whether national or international. Many farms in the United States now earn more than $100,000 a year. These farms are marked by a high degree of specialization and division of labor, extensive use of modern mechanical and biochemical inputs, and a small labor force that exhibits very high productivity. Often a unit of less than 2,500 acres is not considered a reasonable unit given the level of overhead associated with this type of operation. Many types of corporate farms are becoming increasingly international as they scan the globe not only for new markets but also for natural resources and cheaper inputs, such as labor. As these new types of agribusiness corporations expand around the world, they can increasingly compete or conflict with the small family farm in the battle for resources. Many contend that the small family farm faces extinction at the hands of modern corporate farming. In practice, the survival of the small farm depends on the government's commitment in this area. There is also the possibility of organizing small farmers around a corporate nucleus, as will be discussed below.

A Small Farm Household Model

In recent years, discussions of the transformation of traditional agriculture have been polarized by the conflict between small farmers and modern agribusiness. Discussions have been heated and protagonists on both sides have tended to be utopian regarding their own positions while excoriating their adversaries.

One can only enter the debate with a certain amount of trepidation. In what follows, I argue for a form of private enterprise based on the small farm household yet incorporating a potential role for larger agribusiness concerns.

Considerable evidence has emerged in recent years to suggest that it is essential to concentrate on the small farm household. Rather than treating the small farm as a production unit or firm, the simultaneous interaction of household production and consumption decisions are stressed (Singh, Squire, and Strauss 1985). Production and consumption decisions interact through farm profits. There is a certain simultaneity to small farm household decisionmaking that looks to security in overall well-being and the quality of life.

Can the small farm household survive in a modern and increasingly international market system? There is no reason in theory why small farmer market strategies cannot work. In fact, the reasons why they often do not work in practice is that the free-market presuppositions regarding resource control, market entry, information, and power are violated in reality. Frequently rural markets suffer from lack of infrastructure in areas of input supply, legal framework of resource control, transport, warehousing, processing, and information. More often than not, they are distorted by unfair uses of power.

Since the late 1960s an impressive amount of evidence has been marshalled that development strategy based upon the small farmer holds out bright prospects for success (Johnston and Kilby 1976). At the same time, increasing amounts of research have been done on overcoming the discord in farm systems between crops and animals. Poor people have been depicted struggling in a system where there is competition between resources for cash export crops rather than food, in addition to competition between feed for animals and food.

Such scenarios are possible, but they need not be. The first dilemma has already been discussed in Chapter 5. Regarding the second, Winrock International has done some very interesting work on integrated small farm systems (cf. Figure 8-3), which stress plant, animal, and human complementarities (Winrock 1978; 1983). Their research emphasizes not only the ecological and technical rationale of such systems but also the positive cultural components. These farming systems are clearly compatible with traditional agriculture and small-scale enterprise. Further, they diversify the farmers' output, they make good economic sense and add further weight to a small farmer approach.

Figure 8-3.   Winrock Small Farm System Model.

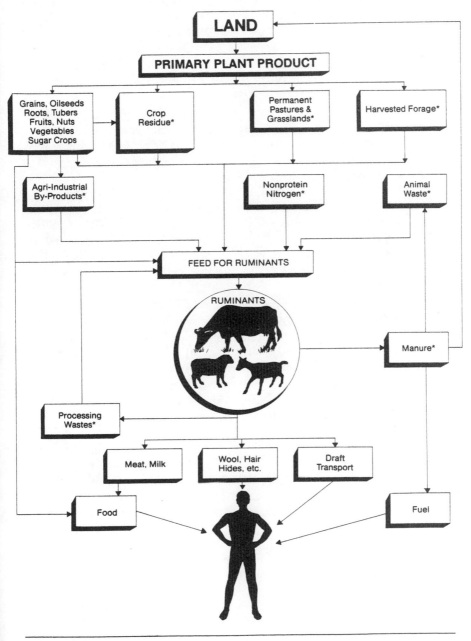

*Products not normally consumed by man.
Source: Fitzhugh et al. (1978).

I think a small farmer policy is the most fruitful path to follow for a number of reasons. Firstly, it is based on the family. This makes sense both sociologically and economically. In traditional societies the family is the fundamental social unit. Such a strategy builds off of existing social organization, thereby reducing administrative problems. Further, family-based farming is adaptable to cooperatives and incorporates the possibility of developing a sound approach to incentives.

Secondly, there is no longer doubt that with proper training and support the small farmer can be efficient. The small farmer knows how to manage resources to some degree, is capable of being trained to adopt improvements, and generally understands and responds to prices, risks, and other economic motivations.

Thirdly, a small farmer policy will best serve the multiple goals of increasing production, improving rural income, and stimulating domestic markets.

Fourthly, a small farmer policy is vital to political and social stability. It often turns out that it actually leads to political stability and strengthens the interests of existing capitalist groups (Dunham 1982).

For all that, it is not easy to enlist the collaboration of small farmers in conventional planning procedures for reasons of economic costs, political realities, the rigidity of social patterns, the mind-set of the poor, and administrative difficulties (Hunter 1982). Discussions of small farmer strategies are frequently associated with the "East Asian Model" (Japan, Taiwan, and South Korea).

In the light of the tasks of government in achieving redistribution, much has been made of the historical results in East Asia. It is a fruitful historical example that is worth examining in more detail. The nature and specific causes of poverty change and shift as one moves from country to country and from region to region. Yet of all the problems noted, the one that stands out in almost every context is that of income distribution and the ability to enter the market, whether for final food products or for the means to produce them. A development strategy must have as its objective the improvement of production conditions and the augmentation of output in aggregate terms. Growth alone will not necessarily benefit the poor. Development must nevertheless be targeted at building domestic markets and getting income into the hands of the poor by adopting a set of policies focused on small producers and using a labor-intensive technology set.

The governments of Taiwan and South Korea have succeeded in getting income into the hands of the rural poor, who could then enter the market to satisfy their consumer needs. Such a strategy was followed up by a sequence of innovations whereby a type of industry was developed that served the needs of the rural economy. A step-by-step development of agriculture and industry took place and the infrastructure associated with marketing and resource flows between the two sectors was gradually established. As the economy expanded and different employment opportunities opened up in industrial, services, and public sectors, labor itself was drained from agriculture and the rural technology set was gradually transformed. Taiwan and Korea have had a certain amount of success regarding both economic growth and material well-being. East Asian growth was led by exports. The same market opportunities however, do not necessarily exist for other countries. New markets (both domestic and regional) must be found (Cline 1982).

The East Asian model is generally touted as one of the more successful approaches of the last twenty-five years. But it is not without its problems. What is generally lacking is access to economic inputs as well as access to markets and services that are part of positive interaction with other sectors of the economy. In a small farmer market strategy, the two most critical issues are price policy, both for inputs and outputs, and participation (FAO 1981).

To put it simply, farmers should be allowed to make a profit. In this way their direct contribution to rural welfare as well as to other sectors will increase as production and productivity increase. Also, the indirect contribution to the general economy will show itself in transfers via market purchases from other sectors and via savings mechanisms and resource transfers.

The biggest problem is found in the dynamics of participation. Recent years have seen a large number of articles appear on the subject (Bryant and White 1982; Gow and Vansant 1983; Uphoff 1982). It means actively involving the farmers in (1) project design (focusing on their goals), (2) implementation (both building off of existing organizations and leaders and linking local groups to external collaborators), and (3) evaluation.

The "Core/Satellite" Model of Agribusiness—
Small Farmer Cooperation

In an integrated social-market approach to development (designed to provide employment to the poor in the cities, as well as improve the standard of living of the peasants), corporate agribusiness activity is not crucial in the production sector. As Johnston and others have shown, with an "unimodal strategy" the production technology set of traditional agriculture can be transformed by adapting the structures of that agriculture and supplementing them with new forms of agricultural technology (Johnston and Kilby 1976). To capture economies of scale, there is considerable scope here and perhaps even a necessity for cooperatives, provided they could be properly managed.

Determining the role of agribusiness is not easy. There are four actors on the scene: agribusiness enterprise (either local or transnational), the home country, the donor country (in the case of TNC's or international agreements), and the small farmers. As noted in Chapter 5, observers such as Joseph Collins, Frances Lappe and Susan George generally view agribusiness as predatory and exploitive, placing narrow corporate interests over people's needs. Barbara Dinham and Colin Hines (1984) note that agribusiness historically has been an extractive industry (in terms of plantations and cash crops) in Africa. As it increasingly becomes involved in African food crops, they see great difficulty in harmonizing the goals of corporate profits with human development. On the other side, Arthur Goldsmith (1985) sees agribusiness as possessing attractive features when specific technical, economic, and social conditions prevail. And Simon Williams and Ruth Karen (1985) see agribusiness as a leading change agent, while at the same time they call for a specific human development framework. There are also other corporate typologies that very much identify agribusiness with economic growth and social progress and recognize little social responsibility for development.

All of the typologies are beset with certain assumptions. Interestingly enough, there is little evidence in the writings I have seen that the various authors have had much interaction or, indeed, take each other seriously. One assumption worth noting is found in attitudes toward government. The first two groups cited above see government in a more benevolent light, attributing many of the problems to powerful classes. Goldsmith, Williams, and Karen generally see government as weak and somewhat ineffectual regarding rural development programs. Secondly, the former have a proclivity for communal-based economies, while the latter are more private. Thirdly, the former take more of a local self-reliant emphasis while the latter see it necessary to become far more integrated into the global economy. Finally, all of these observers base their remarks on cases and examples—sometimes even the same companies—but they have different methodologies in assessing benefits and costs.

The Williams/Karen work is more extensive and based on first-hand research. Linked to the observation that government is often weak and ineffectual, they see the corporation (whether domestic or transnational) as the most dynamic change agent on the scene. It is distinguished in terms of cash flow generation, risk absorption, management training, market development, and research capability. It can also facilitate ties between the peasants and government as well as integrate both into the international community.

They provide a role for local government similar to many aspects of what I mentioned above: tax policy, prices, exchange rate management, infrastructure, land distribution, improvement of the bureaucracy, and generating positive private sector policies.

The corporation is seen as the one institution best suited to provide farmers with what they want and need; namely, assistance with inputs, advice on production techniques, and access to markets. In this line, they make a number of very concrete suggestions. The first set is a triad: to intensify the search for investment opportunities, to set up an investment corporation to finance long-term and/or risky investment, and to foster the role of private agro-industrial enterprise in rural development. Coupled with this they propose another set of recommendations: to establish a center to train professional managers for such rural development projects, to compile an active registry of such professionals, to improve the methodology of assessing benefits and costs of rural development projects, and to create a permanent center of information and exchange. Many of the items in the second set seem to have the character of "social goods" and tacitly imply government or joint public/private financing.

Williams and Karen have compiled an inventory of some fifty cases, with many more in the works. Oddly enough, the data most difficult to come by are profits. This area is "sensitive"; but the lack of explicit information about the one thing everyone most wants to know—the amount and distribution of profits—leaves their work incomplete and open to the accusations against agribusiness that others make. Nonetheless, there is potential. The main question is what kind of corporate core is suitable, and what social conditions are called for? I begin with the small farm household.

The small farm household's aspirations are for the most part family-related: housing, medical care, education for children, transport, meeting consumption needs, and overall security. The farmers' main problems revolve around low and unstable income. Governments balk at raising prices because of related urban and export problems. The possibility to increase revenues by expanding the area of cultivated land is limited by both natural and social factors. There are two ways out: (1) social reorganization of productive resources (via land reform *together* with access to other production inputs and markets and (2) reorganization into more efficient economic units (taking advantage of scale as well as of integrated operations such as cash/food crops and crops/ruminants.

Theoretically, these objectives could be reached via government collectives or by small farmer cooperatives. Yet the quality of governments is so poor in most areas that historically and practically they have not proven to be effective agents. The development terrain is littered with the carcasses of top-down, technology-oriented, highly visible, and highly cross-sectional programs where production choices, development, and distribution take place only by logical assumption. In some cases, government bit off more than they could chew; in others, programs were ruined by corruption. My argument is historical: the record of governments is spotty, ranging from poor in most of Africa and Latin America to fairly good in East Asia. Farmer cooperatives are more promising in many respects. What the farmers have to offer are suitable land and the capacity to produce. Yet the inability to finance inputs, the low level of technological know-how, the lack of access to markets, as well as the lack of management skills represent *historically* (not logically) insurmountable problems.

In this case the organization of small farmers around a corporate nucleus has potential in both modular and integrated area approaches. In principle I favor local agribusiness over foreign and production and marketing approaches skewed in favor of the small farmer over large landholders. This is the case not simply for production reasons but for reasons of domestic industrialization, market development and the achievement of larger social objectives. In many ways I think actual production should remain as much as possible if not completely in the hands of the small farmers. In setting a contract with a corporation the farmers gain (1) assistance with inputs, (2) technologies and management production advice, and (3) a secure (and hopefully fair) market for their products. If contracts are fair, the corporation can be an effective agent of development.

To summarize, the first potential contribution of agribusiness is to provide inputs to farmers at low costs and, in conjunction with this process, to supply some new management techniques. It has already been pointed out in Chapter 4 that much of the new biotechnology is corporate controlled and will not come cheaply. A corporate alignment is one way to provide small farmers with access.

Another major potential contribution of agribusiness firms is in the area of food engineering, which comprises formulation, processing, and packaging of foods. Food formulation is extremely important in developing countries and involves fortifying and otherwise supplementing basic traditional food commodities (such as cassava) to increase their nutritional value. Processing is vital both in preserving foods and transforming them into more readily usable forms. It also helps to prevent waste, which is historically high. According to Conference Board estimates, on small farms of one to ten hectares (where 80 percent of the food produced is retained for home consumption (Conference Board 1976). Of that which goes beyond the farm gate, anywhere from 20-50 percent is wasted. According to present world consumption patterns about 80-85 percent of food is purchased in retail outlets for home consumption, while the rest is consumed in institutions such as hospitals, industrial facilities, and schools.

The third major potential contribution of agribusiness firms is in the area of marketing and distribution of product. The food delivery system is of two types: delivery of food ingredients to the consumer in forms that the consumer can readily prepare to be consumed, and the delivery of food already prepared and ready to eat, whether in school cafeterias or hospitals.

My position is that agribusiness potentially can make a contribution to development. Why does it often fail to do so in practice? When will business undertake an investment in the food sector? Firstly, there must be a market with a promise of a profitable return on investment that compares favorably with other investment opportunities. Through such investment, special contributions may be made in the areas of food processing and distribution, where now so much is wasted. But the food sector must offer the corporation an attractive market (whether nationally or internationally).

Secondly, the company looks for a hospitable social and political climate. Above all, this means that the government take a positive approach to the private sector and set up policies that make private enterprise viable; stability of the government is also very important.

Thirdly, a hospitable economic climate is expected. This basically means that a government accept the concept of profitability (and, in the case of transnationals, the repatriation of profits). The Conference Board report states that the government either must pay to feed the poorest of the poor, or they must generate a process that brings the poorest of the poor from the noncash into the cash economy, enabling them to pay for themselves. In this position, one grasps clearly the suggested division of responsibilities in overcoming poverty.

Fourthly, a company does not want to be viewed as a development agency, but as an agent in the development process. The general business view is that overall development and attainment of public welfare are the responsibility of the local host government. The corporation's business is business. On this point the Williams' take the corporations to task and call for a new approach to management that takes more account of the corporations' actual social power and position.

A number of problems emerge. For example, if a country sets priorities that benefit the poorest in the country, it may thereby set up a climate that agribusiness considers inhospitable to business. As a result, further investment—together with management and technology—are simply lost.

There are frequently conflicts between agribusiness and social priorities in answering the questions of what to produce, how, and for whom. To give an example, there has been a considerable controversy over affluence in food consumption patterns (Dinham and Hines 1984: chs. 1, 6, 7). The argument has focused on moving away from consumption of "luxury foods," which are basically animal products that in their present-day production processes consume large quantities of cereal and vegetable products. Simpler diets are possible. Pulses and oil crops, for example, compare quite well with animal products in terms of nutritional potential. While some intake of animal protein remains quite necessary for a balanced diet, there are certain low-cost dietary combinations that are possible and also attractive as food. Yet in production decisions there is a consistent pattern of producing to meet wants, while needs remain unsatisfied. The more lucrative affluent markets are emphasized over consumer welfare.

Another controversy has focused upon the use of mother's milk rather than milk substitutes (Berg 1973: 230 ff.). There are a number of benefits to be derived from breast feeding: optimal nutritional mix, which mother's milk holds over cow's milk, the rather chancy preparations of milk formula by local, often illiterate people, the effects upon fertility of breast feeding, the lack of sanitary conditions, the physiological development of the child, and the psycho-personal relation between mother and child. In a sense, all of this seems so obvious that one may wonder where the problem lies. The problem has been a socio-cultural one, wherein "modernity" and higher social position came to be associated—partially through aggressive advertising—with not breast feeding one's own children.

Such difficulties notwithstanding, I advocate a potential role for private enterprise forms of agribusiness in the development process. It would be naive to presuppose that agribusiness automatically harmonizes either with development plans or the needs of the poor. There is no shortage of cases showing the horrendous sides of international agribusiness, but there are also positive cases as Goldsmith and the Williams' show. Clearly, the issue cannot be decided upon the basis of generalizations from cases and anecdotes. What is needed is some attention to structures that might guarantee fair play.

Firstly, while arguing for the development and potential of agri-business, it should not be automatically assumed that I mean large-scale transnational conglomerates. In fact, the most promising path for local industrialization to pursue might well be the development of local agribusiness. Some input industries (e.g., machinery and fertilizers) might well call for multinational involvement for reasons of technology, scale, and management. Yet there is a range of choice on the menu, from wholly owned subsidiaries to joint ventures to licensing agreements. Many other agribusiness activities, however, could be performed by small-scale, intermediate technology industries, and cooperatives (Harper and Kavura 1982). This is true, for example, of the supply of farm implements, canning, transport, and marketing.

Secondly, agribusiness industries generally deal with farmers in a contract system. Frequently it is objected that the agribusiness enterprises hold such power that they can easily exploit the farmers in such a system. That may be—cases are not lacking. Yet there are also instances where the contract system has worked more favorably (Buch–Hansen and Secher Marcussen 1982). There is no reason in theory that contracts cannot be structured fairly, as they are pretty much done in the first world. The issue is power and here there is a crucial role for the government. What is needed is a legal system to ensure fairness in the conditions of contracts. Lacking the political legal infrastructure, it is likely that exploitive power will dominate.

The market exchange system is based on supply, demand, and the mutual profits (or utility) of buyers and sellers. Socialists would ideally distribute the world's goods and services on a different basis: from each according to ability and to each according to need. In this ideal sense, socialism is very attractive, particularly to one whose roots are firmly planted in a communitarian ethic. But there are two items to note: (1) while socialism is very attractive, actual socialists (and their so-called vanguard parties) are not; at best they turn the capitalist jungle into a zoo; and (2) there is little probability that private enterprise, based upon making maximum profits in the exchange system will pass away.

These factors call for a broader social analysis of private investment projects. A system of financial and social accountability must be set in place so that a rural development's profit/loss as well as social benefit/cost profiles are clear rather than assumed. For example, what is the hunger impact in Mexico to produce vegetables and fruit on Mexican soil for North America? What is the hunger impact in Brazil to produce soybeans for export rather than black beans for domestic consumption? And so on with tea in Sri Lanka, coffee in Uganda, and avocados in the Ivory Coast. The social benefits and costs of private investment and development plans must be properly assessed. It is obvious that the market takes no account of the poor unless they enter it, either as buyers or sellers, which, precisely because they are poor, is unlikely. There is no purely market solution to poverty and world hunger; the market by its very nature responds to purchasing power, not needs. There are allocation efficiencies in the market exchange system, but market exchange functions must be subordinated to the common good and people's needs. It requires a fair budgetary and legal framework.

If a business comes to a country and exploits land for cash crops, (rather than food crops) or processes food crops for foreign rather than domestic markets, or pushes subsistence farmers and their families further into the relentless suffering of poverty, there is a problem with business. In addition, the problem may well lie either with government elites who, for all the talk, actually care little for the welfare of the people; or with the efficiency of a government that has failed to design its development plans in a manner to simultaneously provide for the welfare of the people as well as the exigencies of development (e.g., capital accumulation).

If the government operates by and for the people and is also efficient in its development plans and execution, it may still have significant problems in attracting foreign private investment in terms of not offering a package which is profitable enough. It may be worth the effort to come up with an attractive package for international business; for, as even many socialist countries have discovered, the agribusiness systems approach has much to recommend it in terms of management and efficiency. Up to now, only the private enterprise concerns have, in fact, been able to deliver the system functioning well (in terms of technical and allocative efficiency). But private enterprise will not automatically produce satisfactory welfare results in its normal course of operations. A government that is enlightened, honest, efficient, and benevolently committed to the welfare of the people is an absolute prerequisite to insure positive development. Such conditions are notoriously difficult to ensure.

The social contract between business and other elements in society must be refashioned so that it matches today's technology and institutions as well as the aspirations of people for justice and peace. What is called for is a type of corporate management that, while pursuing its own proper interests, is socioeconomically efficient and is both socially accountable and socially responsive. There are dilemmas in the marketplace. Is the market self-regulating? Regarding some aspects of technical and price efficiency it may seem that it is. But for overall socioeconomic efficiency a more visible hand is called for. When business causes harm, it is to be held *accountable*, making compensation where appropriate. Where it does not cause harm, but might alleviate it, it is to be socially *responsive*; i.e., willing to help provided there is an equitable bearing of the social costs.

PRIVATE VOLUNTARY ORGANIZATIONS

In addition to government and business organizations there are many organizations and interest groups that have a direct impact on development policy because they occupy positions of persuasion in society. Such groups are families and kinship units, religions, universities and research groups, the arts and mass media, and interest groups (organized around issues such as environment and ecology, population control, or nuclear energy). Before examining the potential of these groups, it is important to clarify a general role for private voluntary organizations.

In the preceding section I outlined a potential role for private enterprises and markets in the rural economy in terms of the small farm household and also of corporate agribusiness. But, many of the rural poor are landless women and children. They have few productive assets. The corporate-nucleus scenario is not likely to include members of such households. Some suggest that the only effective redistributive agent is the government. Yet the governments in question are frequently inept, tools of repression or responsive only to special interests with clout.

The poor are often enough voiceless. Frequently, only private voluntary organizations can exercise influence upon governments and corporations on their behalf. What private voluntary organizations have to contribute varies according to their nature and purposes. Frequently enough they are indigenous to the local scene and possess an aura of political acceptability. Secondly, they generally possess some grassroots structures and can elicit popular participation. Finally, their administrative structures are often quite efficient due to small scale of organization, high motivation of members, and low costs of delivery associated with volunteers and relatively unencumbered procedures.

Family and kinship organizations are unique, for they are not voluntary organizations in the sense that other groups are. The main social structure in most third-world countries is the extended family.

In many countries the sense of nationhood is weak. People's primary identity is that of family and clan or tribe. Their loyalties are to these groups and their "policies" rather than to government and its policies. This reality is perhaps more important in Africa than anywhere else. If development planners neglect these dynamics, their prospects of success are bleak indeed, since family elders and other guardians of tradition have tremendous persuasive power over attitudes regarding outside agents of change and innovations. All of this makes nation building and related national development policies very difficult. There is an important institutional conclusion to be drawn from this. In many countries individual based representative democracy may not be appropriate. More important on the national level is perhaps a clan/tribe and faction-based democracy where all significant groupings have an appropriate share in the larger national order. Within the groups themselves more traditional patterns of decisionmaking may predominate. In this sense it may be that the one-party states that dominate so much of the developing world are not as bad as they are portrayed. There are excesses to be sure, but in many ways they have more potential of forging participatory coalitions between groups than conflictive party politics.

Next to family and kinship systems, religious groupings are social institutions of major importance. They deserve special comment because so often they are seen as tradition-bound and major obstacles to development. Buddhism in South and East Asia, Hinduism in India, Catholicism in Latin America, and Islam from the Middle East to Indonesia have all been perceived in this light. In each case, there is historical evidence of religious groups being so bent on achieving institutional aims of social power and privilege (in terms of property, funding, authority, and control of the peasantry in religious business) that they work against the true interests of the people. Marx was not entirely wrong in characterizing much religion as opium. What Marx missed is that religion can also have a liberating and prophetic side. Indeed, some of the most biting critiques of development models emanate from religious values regarding human community and concomitant norms of justice in profits, prices, and overall distribution.

I am more familiar with ecumenical Christian groups, so I confine my remarks to them. Most of their church work has been in the realm of aid, not development. Even these efforts have been criticized as masking designs of proselytization. Such motives of conversion are not absent, but they are less the case in the past twenty years. For example, if one examines recent work among refugees, there is little evidence of conversion motives.

The point that interests me more is whether religious groups can be development agents. Whether for good or ill, they do, in fact, have tremendous social power. More important, against oppressive regimes the churches are often the only institution strong enough to oppose the regime and speak for the poor. Christian churches currently have strong presence and social organization in Latin America and Africa; In most of Asia they have significant social organization despite remaining a small minority. I think they can become important development agents, but for them to do so requires some changes in order to overcome institutional rigidity.

There are a number of specific areas of development cooperation that suggest themselves in light of the above remarks. Because of the actual structures and activities of many churches, there are four that are more important: health, education, community organization, and media.

In the area of health, it is well-known that churches have developed a significant network of hospitals, infirmaries, and out-patient programs over the past centuries. While in developed countries many of their functions have been overtaken by the state or other agencies, churches in developing countries generally have some sort of health-care system in place and their role is vital. Points for dialogue with the governments would be how to develop these facilities so as to more adequately provide for primary health care. The various peoples of the world and the churches surely share a commitment to put an end to the fact that millions of children die needlessly each year and to alleviate chronic, disabling diseases that sap energy and limit human aspirations. A number of steps can be taken to improve rural health services. Structures already in place could be transformed with relatively little effort by channeling efforts towards nutrition and preventive medicine, by employing oral rehydration therapy (ORT), and by improving birth control information, maternal training, child care, and sanitation practices.

Education provides a second major area of focus. The churchs' educational network is even more extensive than its health-care network. It is often of major importance in developing countries where the state system may not be so well developed and where church school systems provide the major part of the available schooling. In most cases the church school systems are separately administered but receive substantial direct and indirect public subsidies. There is considerable scope for cooperation in areas of teacher training and curriculum development and the reshaping of educational endeavors so that they directly serve development needs. What is needed, therefore, is both financial aid and technical cooperation to expand and improve the basic educational system already in place.

A number of other related themes might at the same time be usefully explored: schooling for girls and disadvantaged minority groups and the use of nonformal education (such as the case of "INADES" in francophone Africa) to improve adult literacy and to impart technical skills, refugee education, and preschool education and child care. In all of these areas, the churches already have some structures in place. With the proper technical and financial assistance, they could be improved and targeted upon certain priority objectives and groups in the development scene.

A third area of church activity is community development projects. Admittedly the term is nebulous and is used to cover anything from housing and water projects, to sewage, rural electrification, roads, and warehouses. Clearly, church leaders as such are not particularly trained in the technical aspects that such projects call for, nor do they possess the necessary raw materials. What they do have to offer, however, is a respected forum for public discussions, a somewhat efficient social organization that can help in getting things done, and a social system beyond family or clan that is trusted. These qualities are of fundamental importance for community development projects, and the scope for their utilization in development is quite positive. Church organizations can provide a venue for popular participation in development, enabling the people to identify their needs, help design a project, implement it, and then evaluate it.

A fourth area of specific cooperation involves the church activities in the mass media. In most parts of the world the churches have developed considerable capacity in the print and radio media. In some places there are television facilities. They are usually under diocesan or regional auspices and in some parts of the world reach vast audiences. These media are of considerable interest in the development context. In fact, they could rather easily be harmonized with efforts in the health, education, and community development spheres. Of course, media activities serve many purposes, and education and communication about development are only two of them. They are nonetheless vitally important.

I have concentrated my remarks on Christian churches. Analogous remarks could be made of other religions—Judaism, Islam, Buddhism, and Hinduism—all of which have profound social connotations. A profound and inspirational spirit endures in each one as well as tremendous social persuasive power that provides the basis of a critique of "development" and the potential to galvanize political will.

In addition to kinship and religious institutions, a third major set of voluntary organizations are found in educational institutions and research centers. To what extent these institutions are private and voluntary is debatable. So often they are controlled by government or business circles, either directly or through funding mechanisms. Nonetheless, the personnel of these institutions manifest a certain independence of thought and action. A case in point is how much the governments of developing countries fear student activism.

One point worth special attention is the type of pedagogy that characterizes such institutions and to what extent it is related to research projects geared to development. Almost all experts agree that it is fundamental that all developing countries create basic research capacities, especially in tropical agriculture. To help in this end, it is important that researchers, teachers, and students become integrated into the international intellectual community by sending students abroad and participating in conferences and joint research projects. Such activities are fundamental to both the general transfer of technology and the genesis of new technologies. They are also important in assisting the management of concrete rural development projects.

Educational associations and personnel are not only technical agents of change. They are also very important in effecting changes in kinship, religious traditions, and values and, in this way, forging new cultural forms and institutions.

The arts and mass media are likewise of pivotal importance. More than any other medium, the fine arts are capable of creating a new sociocultural vision. For their part, the communication arts are powerful tools to transcend narrow kinship, religious, and other traditional bias. Some of the greatest problems in development are in galvanizing political will. The arts and mass media have tremendous persuasive power in transforming values and building social unity. They also have enormous educational potential in areas of extension and the diffusion of technology.

To be sure, the arts and mass media are subject to government and business influence. Most governments seek outright control of the media and exercise heavy political censorship. Corporations for their part can exercise comparable economic censorship. Yet the very fear such entities have of the arts and media emphasizes their powerful potential. Even when the arts are forced underground, as they so often are, they manage to survive. In fact, they not only survive but keep alive what most regimes find the most dangerous of all: an alternative vision of the good society.

Finally, there are numerous potential roles for private voluntary associations and other interested groups in shaping development. The free association, which both transcends family and clan ties and is free of government or business domination, is a central feature of Western social thought. But similar entities exist in other settings. For example, secret societies have long played an influential role in Chinese history. In the development scene today, many such groups have proliferated; a significant number are international. The focus of interest ranges from population and ecological resource management to technology transfer, scientific exchanges, and international *fora* on development. These groups tend to be small and low-cost, with a dedicated core focused on achieving very specific results. Hence, they can be quite efficient on a small scale. They can also not only give voice to the disenfranchised but help organize them into effective social participants. They have great potential in galvanizing public opinion.

The conclusion to be drawn from this brief survey of private organizations is that development is too important to be left merely to government and business circles. In fact, such narrow approaches will not work as they lack the capacity to galvanize political will.

CONCLUSION: A SOCIAL MARKET ECONOMY

The sketch of domestic public development policy presented in the preceding pages is cast in terms of the interplay between government leaders and civil servants, market agents, and private voluntary organizations.

My position entails a social vision. As such it is predicated upon the tenets of some form of participatory society (if not representative democracy) that would allow for the fair participation of all in public institutions and processes. It also explicitly considers normative criteria of social ethics and cultural appropriateness in evaluating a set of public policy priorities.

In addition to social vision, I argue for a fundamentally market economy. The issue is the *quality* of markets and the social nature of private enterprise associated with it. Private decisions have profoundly public effects. There are many issues of fairness in setting social priorities and in delineating a set of rules of the game that correspond to a fair sharing of social benefits and costs. The social efficiency of a market economy presupposes fair political and legal institutions as a framework in which markets are guided by public choice based on and consistent with a coherent worldview and set of values.

REFERENCES

Anderson, Dennis, and Farida Khambata. 1985. "Financing Small Scale Industry and Agriculture in Developing Countries: The Merits and Limitations of 'Commercial' Policies." *Economic Development and Cultural Change* 33, no. 2: 349–71.

Bates, R.H. 1982. "The Regulation of Rural Markets in Africa." Social Science Working Paper No. 451, Division of the Humanities and Social Sciences. Pasadena, Calif.: California Institute of Technology.

Berg, Alan. 1973. *The Nutrition Factor.* Washington, D.C.: The Brookings Institution.

Bryant, C., and L.G. White. 1982. "Managing Rural Development: Peasant Participation in Rural Development." *Research and Development Abstracts* 10, no. 1/2: 25–26.

Buch-Hansen, M., and Secher Marcussen. 1982. "Contract Farming and the Peasantry-Case Studies from Western Kenya." *Review of African Political Economy* 23, no. 1: 9–36.

Cline, William. 1982. "Can the East Asian Model Be Generalized?" *World Development* 10, no. 2: 81–90.

Clute, R.E. "The Role of Agriculture in African Development." *African Studies Review* 25, no. 4: 1–20.

Cochrane, Glynn. 1983. *Policies for Strengthening Local Government in Developing Countries.* Staff Working Paper No. 582. Washington, D.C.: World Bank.

Conde, S. 1981. "Agriculture d'exportation et agriculture viviere dans de developpement economique de la Cote d'Ivoire." *Annales de l'Universite d'Abidjan* Serie K., no. 4: 5–17.

Conference Board, The. 1976. *Partners in Agroeconomic Development.* New York: The Conference Board.

Dinham, Barbara, and Colin Hines. 1984. *Agribusiness in Africa.* Trenton, N.J.: Africa World Press.

Dunham, D. 1982. "On the History and Political Economy of Small-Farmer Policies." *CEPAL Review* 18, no. 1: 139–69.

Ergas, Z. 1982. "The State and Economic Deterioration: The Tanzanian Case." *Journal of Commonwealth and Comparative Politics* 20, no. 3: 286–308.

Fasbender, K. 1982. "Strategy of Integrated Development. Some Remarks on the Development of Rural Areas in Developing Countries. *Intereconomics* 17, no. 6: 291–95.

Fitzhugh, H.A.; H.J. Hodgson; O.J. Scoville; T.D. Nguyan; and T.C. Byerly. 1978. *The Role of Ruminants in the Support of Man.* Morrilton, Ark.: Winrock International.

Food and Agriculture Organization (FAO). 1981. *The Declaration of Principles and Program of Action of the World Conference on Agrarian Reform and Rural Development.* Rome, Italy: Food and Agriculture Organization.

_____. 1985. *The State of Food and Agriculture.* Rome, Italy: Food and Agriculture Organization.

Goldsmith, Arthur. 1985. "The Private Sector and Rural Development: Can Agribusiness Help the Small Farmer?" *World Development* 113, no. 10/11: 1125–38.

Gould, David J., and Jose A. Amaro-Reyes. 1983. *The Effects of Corruption on Administrative Performance: Illustrations from Developing Countries.* Staff Working Paper No. 580. Washington, D.C.: World Bank.

Gow, D., and J. Vansant. 1983. "Beyond the Rhetoric of Rural Development Participation: How Can It Be Done?" *World Development* 11, no. 5: 427–46.

Gray, J. 1983. "How the Chinese Channel Rural Industry's Profits into Agriculture." *Ceres* 16, no. 1: 20–27.

Harper, M., and R. Kavura, eds. 1982. *The Private Marketing Entrepreneurs.* Agricultural Services Bulletin No. 51. Rome, Italy: Food and Agricultural Organization.

Havnevik, K., and R. Skarstein. 1983. "Agricultural Backwardness and Foreign Aid in Tanzania." *Journal of Social Studies* 22, no. 1: 57–68.

Hunter, G., ed. 1982. *Enlisting the Small Farmer: The Range of Requirements.* Occasional Paper No. 4. Agricultural Administration Unit, Overseas Development Institute.

Johnston, Bruce F., and Peter Kilby. 1976. *The Role of Agriculture in Structural Transformation.* New York: Oxford University Press.

Joy, Leonard. 1983. *Report on Responses to a Workbook on Social Development Management.* Working Paper No. 10. Washington, D.C.: National Association of Schools of Public Affairs and Administration.

Kopp, A. 1983. "Regional Policy in Third World Countries." *Intereconomics* 18, no. 4: 185–90.

Krishna, T. 1982. "Some Aspects of Agricultural Growth, Price Policy and Equity in Developing Countries." *Food Research Institute Studies* 18, no. 3: 219–60.

Lardy, Nicholas. 1983. *Agricultural Prices in China.* Staff Working Paper No. 606. Washington, D.C.: World Bank.

Latremoliere, J. 1981. "Pour une seule agriculture africaine: cultures vivrieres et culture de rente." *Marches Tropicaux et Mediterraneens* 37, no. 1883: 3281–83.

Leach, J. 1982. "Administrative Co-ordination in African Rural Development." *Agricultural Administration* 11, no. 4: 295–302.

Obioma, Bennett. 1983. "Traditional Financial Group Markets—Lessons from the Nigerian Experience." Ph.D. diss., Pontifical Gregorian University, Rome, Italy.

Padmanabhan, K.P. 1983. "Village Industries as an Element of Rural Development: The Indian Strategy." *Ceres* 16, no. 1: 15–19.

Pinstrup-Anderson, Per, and Elizabeth Caicedo. 1978. "The Potential Impact of Changes in Income Distribution on Food Demand and Human Nutrition." *American Journal of Agricultural Economics* 60, no. 3: 402–15.

Rondinelli, Dennis A., John R. Nellis, and G. Shabbir Cheema. 1984. *Decentralization in Developing Countries, A Review of Recent Experience.* Staff Working Paper No. 581. Washington, D.C.: World Bank.

Ruttan, Vernon W. 1985. "Technical and Institutional Change in Agricultural Development: Two Lectures." Bulletin No. 851. Economic Development Center, University of Minnesota.

Schumacher, A. 1981. *Agricultural Development and Rural Employment: A Mexican Dilemma.* Working Papers in U.S.-Mexican Studies, No. 21. University of California, San Diego.

Singh, Inderjit, Lyn Squire, and John Strauss. 1985. "Agricultural Household Models: A Survey of Recent Findings and Their Policy Implications." Economic Growth Center Discussion Paper No. 474. New Haven, Conn.: Yale University.

Uphoff, N. 1982. "Farmer Participation in Project Formulation, Design, and Operation." In *Promoting Increased Food Production in the 1980's—Proceedings of the Second Annual Agricultural Sector Symposia,* 231–90. Washington, D.C.: World Bank.

Vengroff, Richard, and Ali Farah. 1985. "State Intervention and Agricultural Development in Africa: A Cross-National Study." *Journal of African Studies* 25, no. 1: 75–85.

Vermeer, E.B. 1982. "Rural Economic Change and the Role of the State in China, 1962–1978." *Asian Survey* 22, no. 9: 823–42.

Williams, Simon, and Ruth Karen. 1985. "Agribusiness and the Small-Scale Farmer—A Dynamic Partnership for Development." Boulder, Colo. Mimeo.

Winrock International. 1978. *The Role of Ruminants in the Support of Man.* Morrilton, Ark.: Winrock International.

_____. 1983. *Sheep and Goats in Developing Countries: Their Present and Potential Role.* Washington, D.C.: Winrock International.

World Bank. 1981. *Accelerated Development in Sub-Saharan Africa.* Washington, D.C.: World Bank.

Yeager, R., and N. Miller. 1982. "Food Policy in Tazania: Issues of Production, Distribution and Sufficiency." Report, No. 17. Universities Field Staff International.

9 INTERNATIONAL POLICIES FOR DEVELOPMENT

In recent years there has been increasing discussion of interdependence between nations and peoples in the world. Talk of interdependence underscores the fact that it is no longer feasible for nations to pursue isolationist policies of narrow self-interest. I begin by examining this concept in terms of technological, geopolitical, and cultural implications.

More than anything else, the new interdependence is a function of new means of transport and communication. The development period following World War II has witnessed an explosion of the technology of interaction between peoples. Firstly, the means of travel have been revolutionized. By air, it is possible to reach any other country in a few hours; surface transportation is only a matter of days. These means of transport have radically altered the search for resources and the choice of localities of economic production as well as the area of markets.

In addition to changes in travel there have been startling changes in the ability to scan the globe and accumulate and process information on natural resources as well as most other socioeconomic factors. Satellite systems have made it possible to catalogue and monitor the world's agricultural and natural resource picture. These vast amounts of data can be analyzed, cross-referenced, and interrelated by means of electronic information processing systems.

Finally, all this information can be continually updated and communicated around the world within seconds. The scope of business activity is now more than ever before truly transnational. The economic notion of comparative advantage is no longer circumscribed by either geographic or national frontiers.

Interdependence has both a technical and scientific base. It goes without saying that those persons or nations who control this modern technology automatically occupy a superior position in relations of interdependence. The world political economic order is now more international than ever before. The geopolitical economy of interdependence is fraught with problems, because nation-states are still operating within the framework of nineteenth-century politics. Adequate international institutions and structures of interdependence, such as truly effective international law, do not yet exist.

Three points of the historical legacy are important. Firstly, the nineteenth-century legacy is that of overemphasized nationalism. When it comes to interdependence, nationalism breeds a spirit of group egoism. National self-interest remains the overriding category of "realistic" politics. As such, there is no truly international sense of solidarity and of the common good. For many nation-states, moral responsibility frequently stops at the national borders.

At the same time, the colonial heritage or the historical vassal status of most third-world countries has locked them into new patterns of unequal participation if not dependence. This phenomenon has been characterized by many observers as the phenomenon of center/periphery international economic structures (Prebisch 1964; de Janvry 1981: ch. 1). This more radical view maintains that the economies of the developing countries are still frequently locked into, dependent on, and exploited by the developed countries. As mentioned in Chapter 5, I am not convinced of the necessity of such a scenario. But I do think there is an "exploitive interdependence" that is responsible for what many observers call the development of underdevelopment. It is important that such a status frequently serves both the economic and political interests of the dominant states as well as those of local elites. To maintain that sphere of influence the more powerful states will often install and maintain corrupt elites in power.

A third point of the historical legacy to consider is that many newly independent nations are not viable states either politically or economically, because of either poor resource endowment, population characteristics, geographical position, or infrastructure. Such circumstances lead to such nonviable states being locked into cycles of poverty and exploitation and to an exacerbated dualism wherein the plight of the masses becomes more miserable and the small elites prosper.

When all is said and done, I do not think the historical legacy is deterministic regarding dependency. As will be discussed later, there is much that developing countries themselves can do to break the pattern. But at the very least, their starting point is one of unequal participation or partial dependence.

Thus far I have been discussing the North/South aspects of geo-political interdependence. But there is another aspect: the East/West struggle and the relation between the superpowers. This problem has had one immediate and very damaging effect in terms of resource accumulation and use: the prolonged and escalating arms race. Furthermore, the world must live in the constant tension of a fragile peace. This tension has made it seemingly more important than ever for the superpowers to secure their spheres of influence throughout the world, whether Afghanistan or Central America. Third-world countries have a very difficult time remaining nonaligned; furthermore, they themselves are drawn into the arms race.

Finally, there is a culture of interdependence. This has been seen in discussions over the new international information order (Mac-Bride 1981) and in the internationalization of mass media especially in musical and visual forms of entertainment. Such mass culture can only questionably be considered as art. No one, however, would deny that it represents a vast potential of indirect social control. It plays an undeniable role in the stimulation of market demand as well as in the manipulation of political allegiance in the face of so-called enemies who would destroy the current way of life. More and more, mass culture is manipulated by both political and economic interests in a manner that socializes people into the present system and legitimates it. In so doing, it also challenges the survival of local traditional cultures and the identity of minority ethnic groups. More material aspects of cultural interdependence are seen in technology and its diffusion. The spiritual aspect is seen in the battle over ideologies. This latter struggle has been so dominated by the superpowers that other voices suggesting alternatives to actual patterns of capitalism and socialism receive scant hearing.

Interdependence is beginning to permeate all levels of contemporary life: technical, political, economic, and cultural. What is at issue is the quality of interdependence. What types of structures and institutions should be evolved to improve the quality of interdependence? How can that be done? There are wide ranging debates on these questions underway today. In the political economic sphere the central issues revolve around resources and in particular, capital, management, and technology.

On the capitalist side, points of view range from free market fundamentalism and the pursuit of narrow self-interest to the more enlightened position of groups such as the Trilateral Commission, which goes beyond narrow self-interest to public policies based upon mutual self-interest. Regarding explanations of the word "mutual," however, such positions remain strangely silent. There are few specifics about what would constitute just patterns of distribution of benefits and costs.

Socialists talk of solidarity. But they range from a solidarity dominated by the national interest of the dominant socialist state and the party to new forms of Marxism that seek to allow more social participation—what Mr. Dubcek called socialism with a human face. Despite the rhetoric of solidarity, socialist parties have not succeeded in going beyond group self-interest.

There are many diverse private voluntary groups calling for a new quality of interdependence based upon human rights at both individual and social levels of experience. They are raising the right issue, for the question is what type of interdependence do people want and what types of strategies are appropriate for it. Much of today's interdependence is in fact, a form of dependence. But dependency theory only partially accounts for the poor quality of interdependence, notably by neglecting local alternatives and responsibilities. Modern dependency is not an inevitable result of historical forces. It is a choice that can be avoided. In the rest of this chapter, I discuss the international protagonists in the drama of development and then take up a consideration of some short-term issues, some long-term strategies, and a reconsideration of the central problem of galvanizing the political will to move forward.

INTERNATIONAL PROTAGONISTS

In this section, I review the major international policy-making organizations active in the development arena, I discuss in turn government, business, and sociocultural organizations (MacBean and Snowden 1981).

Government organizations are of various types both in terms of forms, functions, limits, and significance. First are the various United Nations organizations: the UN itself, its commission on trade and development—UNCTAD, its agricultural organization—FAO, its labor organization—ILO, its health organization—WHO, and its educational and social organization—UNESCO. The UN organizations have very little real power, either to formulate finance, or implement policy. They function primarily as centers of debate, education, and information. They gather and disseminate information and frequently serve as *fora* for public debate on international issues of interest. There is, however, one enduring problem that they run into by their very structure and charter: They are biased in favor of governments. In UN studies of poverty, hunger, and development, for example, one can find detailed studies on the activities of the multinationals, the role of women in development, and appropriate technology. One hardly ever encounters a critical evaluation of the nation-states—corruption, bureaucratic bungling, and power struggles. As has been seen, the civil authority system is frequently the main problem in development; this omission in UN documents renders their material considerably less useful. For similar reasons, also, they rarely undertake critical evaluations of cultural preferences and traditions. All in all, the UN bodies generate useful statistics; if one knows how to read their documentation, some profit can be derived from it.

The international governmental organizations with the most power are associated with the governments of the eastern and western blocs. The first-world governments are loosely organized in the Organization for Economic Cooperation and Development (OECD). Twelve European nations are organized into the Common Market (EEC) as well. The first world also has common defense arrangements under the terms of the North Atlantic Treaty Organization (NATO). The political economy of these nations tends to be some form of constitutional democracy with a clear market orientation. The purpose of the OECD and EEC is to foster economic cooperation in resource use, investments, and market development.

The Soviet bloc is well organized in terms of COMECON and its defense arm of the Warsaw Pact. COMECON comprises the USSR, the socialist nations of Eastern Europe, as well as Afghanistan, Cuba, and Vietnam. They have financial and trade rules that govern their relations among themselves. They tend to deal with the capitalist world by way of state trading companies and bilateral agreements. Relations with third-world countries also tend to be bilateral, although there is at times considerable coordination of efforts, as, for example, in the southern spheres of Africa and in the Middle East. India and some countries in Africa have derived some benefits from COMECON, yet overall, what it can and does give to the third world is limited by its own development needs and geopolitical priorities.

The third-world countries also are organized into various regional groups, such as the Organization for African Unity (OAU), the ASEAN countries of Southeast Asia, and the Islamic countries. In addition, there is the "Group of 77," the group of officially nonaligned countries (which now numbers some 110 members). These groups serve as *fora* for the exchange of information and debate and as a stimulus to the awakening of public opinion; but they have few resources of their own to draw upon and little power to effect international monetary and financial policies.

The two pillars upon which the system rests are the International Monetary Fund (IMF) and the General Agreement on Tariffs and Trade (GATT): international organizations with many members. In their bylaws and policy they have been clearly dominated by the first world since their inception at the 1944 Bretton Woods Conference and during the negotiations of the postwar years.

In these two organizations the *locus* of real power of the international economy is apparent. In a very real sense the above organizations, which are largely controlled by the first world, set the terms for the world economy because they set the terms for international monetary and trade agreements. Quite understandably, they are the focus of the debate in proposals calling for a new international economic order. I return to them in the policy discussions which follow.

In addition to these governmental organizations, the business world features many protagonists on the international scene. Foremost among these are the transnational corporations. There is a lot of discussion surrounding the role of transnationals in development, but there is no one who doubts that they have tremendous power. The primary source of their power lies in their control of capital, management, and technology. The transnationals are leaders in research and development in almost every field. Their research and development capacities often surpass those of the various nation states. They also have a well-developed scanning capability, which enables them to survey the world for resources and to spot production, marketing, and trade opportunities.

In addition to the resource/product-oriented transnationals, an increasing role is being played by transnational banks. Third-world debt has surpassed $600 billion; the vast majority of that debt is held by private banks through syndicated loans.

The transnationals have tremendous clout. They have powerful voice with their own governments, which often subsidize them and shield them from risks, as through the Overseas Private Investment Corporation (OPIC) in the United States. They have tremendous power with international organizations. And they have considerable power over local third world governments, with respect to local resource development, trade potential, and transfers of management and technological skills. This position of power is frequently further enhanced through corrupt dealings with local elites. In addition, the transnationals are well plugged into the military industrial complexes, both in their own countries as well as internationally. Thus, the transnationals are very active political lobbyists on both the national and international scene as they seek to forge what they call a positive environment in which to do business.

A third set of international groups involved in the process of international development policy are found in the sociocultural persuasion system. These groups play many roles ranging from doing research and modeling policy alternatives to consulting and communicating analysis and information and transferring resources. They are of particular importance in galvanizing political will.

Universities and private research institutions play a leading role in development policy. The universities of OECD countries as well as of COMECON train thousands of third-world researchers and scholars. They send many of their professors and students into the field in order to assess conditions and to function as advisors. Also, the various professional associations and academies of science are major agents in the transfer of technology. Numerous foundations (such as the Ford and Rockefeller foundations) have long been active in funding such activities. In this way, all these organizations play a very valuable role in the transfer of technology and in building the educational and research infrastructure in third-world countries that long-term development calls for.

A second major type of participant is found in the circles of the arts and media. As noted in Chapter 8, these agents are very powerful in shaping people's aspirations, attitudes, and concrete expectations regarding development. As the "New International Information Order" movement attests, attempts to control them are intense. International publishing houses—and even the mass pirating of printed and taped works—play a vital role in transforming local economies. The potential of new satellite and video technologies is only beginning to be tapped. The pervasiveness of U.S. recordings, films, and television programming throughout the third world presents a concrete vision of different life possibilities and (for better or worse) a stark challenge to traditional ways.

Thirdly, religious groups are very active in trying to shape development policy. The Islamic revolution is very strong in the Middle East, parts of Africa, South Asia, Malaysia, Indonesia, and (to a lesser extent) in the Philippine Islands. The reflection of Buddhist scholars on the ethics of development was outlined in Chapter 6. Both the World Council of Churches and the Catholic Church have grown increasingly active in the poverty/development debate. On the one hand, this has given birth to liberation theologies; on the other, national churches such as Lutheran (Bread for the World) and Catholic (Misereor) in West Germany have long sponsored development projects (financed out of the German church tax). Many other groups, ranging from Baptists to the Society of Friends to Jewish groups and ecumenical groups such as CODEL are also very active in concrete development work as well as the battle over public opinion.

Finally, there are a number of interest groups active in development work and public policy. Oxfam International, Planned Parenthood, Amnesty International, the Green Movement, and countless other groups work vigorously on development issues from widely differing perspective. They finance their work from donations and private and public grants, as do the religious groups.

I conclude these reflections with some observations on organizational politics in the international arena. I have briefly outlined some of the main types of groups presently active in the area of international policy and indicated their power base either in the civil authority system, the economic exchange system, or the sociocultural persuasion system. It must be emphasized that such systems and their corresponding groups do not operate in isolation. In fact, they not only go about pursuing their own purposes, but they are actively involved in trying to co-opt other groups into being fellow travelers. For example, managers of a transnational corporation spend a great deal of time precisely trying to manage the social milieu. They know that they must deal with governments, other corporations, and various coalitions of interest groups. It is clearly in their self-interest to lobby governments and local elites, reach agreements with other corporations, and win over whatever interest groups possible. Governments also spend a great deal of time and resources rationalizing their behavior to the people and presenting themselves as guardians of the public interests.

A key strategy in such approaches is spelled out in terms of social incentives and sanctions. For example, the Nobel Prize or the Order of Lenin are given out to scholars of distinction but also to persons who are fundamentally supportive of the system. To co-opt others, corporations may try outright bribery and corruption. But that is sometimes a risky strategy that may backfire. It is easier to confine oneself to campaign contributions, awards, signs of prestige, provision of perquisites, and offers of grants, funding, and help in aiding a particular interest group to attain a particular goal. In this sense, government funding and business philanthropy have become very big matters indeed in shaping the social environment.

The purpose of such organizational politics is to build coalitions that are founded upon mutual self-interest rather than outright domination. When a corporation or the Pentagon channels research or scholarship money to a university, they are involved in both setting up social priorities of research and cementing some political friendships that will serve them well in terms of future support.

The importance of organizational politics cannot be overemphasized in the arena of international development policy. These dynamics characterize not only how people relate to each other within organizations but how organizations and bureaucracies relate to each other in terms of international policy formulation and implementation.

SHORT-TERM POLICIES

In this and the following section, I discuss some concrete policy proposals. I have divided them into short-term and long-term measures. As a prelude to this discussion, I want to relate these remarks to the context of the 1983 meeting of UNCTAD VI in Belgrade. From the background papers for this meeting (UNCTAD 1983) it is clear that almost all the main problems in the crisis of resources revolve around capital. Furthermore, there is little evidence to suggest that, given present structures alone, a way out of the crisis can be found. The UNCTAD proposals call for some sort of market adjustment: (1) opening them up in the case of overcoming protectionism and (2) stabilizing their prices in the case of raw materials. In this section, I do not intend to go over the suggestions listed in the preparatory documents for UNCTAD VI. Rather I begin with two observations regarding the problem of international capital.

Firstly, it is important that something be done because the present state of things constitutes not only an economic crisis but an injustice, especially when it is realized that the main problem is not the absolute scarcity of resources or technology, but a lack of control and political will. Secondly, it is granted that there are many feasible solutions to any of the given problems mentioned by the UNCTAD documents, that is, a number of different packages could be put together. I confine my remarks in what follows to short-term and long-term policy measures. The short-term measures are necessary over the next six to ten years while the long-term measures are being set in place.

One of the first short-term measures that is called for is aid. The amount of aid from OECD and OPEC countries was around $35 billion in 1984. This is not an insignificant amount of money in itself, but it is small in terms of both need and percent of donor country GNP. With the fall in oil prices the OPEC contributions will surely diminish. Most important is the aid given to agriculture. Official assistance from 1981–83 was a little over $12 billion (Table 9–1). Roughly 60 percent was on concessional terms. Roughly one-third of all aid is going to agriculture. Yet it is not sufficient to meet requirements.

There is a built-in political preference for bilateral aid because in that sort of agreement the donor country can lock in a set of benefits for itself. Multilateral aid channeled through public agencies such as the World Bank is more respectful of the legitimate interests of the recipient countries. Also, due to the fact that such aid is not tied to the markets of the donor countries through purchasing and shipping requirements, it enables the recipient countries to get the most for their money in purchases. Other forms of aid, which must be increasingly considered in light of growing world debt, are found in canceling of debt obligations or in renegotiating the terms of loans (at least those held by the public sector).

In addition to aid in cash, aid in kind is also very important. Since the World Food Conference of 1974, there has been considerable discussion about creating a system of international reserves, which would function as a sort of food bank and would be used to cover food shortfalls in times of emergency. This sort of aid has been more forthcoming (Figure 9–1) and has been instrumental in staving off disaster in Africa. It is also easier for OECD governments to give as they have agricultural surpluses.

The United States would figure prominently in such a scheme as it effectively controls the majority of the grain stocks and is a major exporter of grain (either bought commercially or through PL 480). Canada, Australia, and Argentina, with relatively large amounts of land and small populations, are also major grain exporters. Little progress has been made towards establishing the international reserve fund since the World Food Conference of 1974. Figure 9–1 illustrates the problem of food aid to Africa, which is the area worst off. Promised aid does not match needs. Furthermore only 12 percent comes from the World Food Program. Most countries prefer to hold onto the supposed political advantages of bilateral aid; others, notably the COMECON countries, are striving to meet the demands of increased domestic affluence and show little interest in making such contributions. In addition to the problem of who would contribute, there is the problem of where these reserves would be stored, who would pay for the costs, and who would control them.

There is also considerable discussion of how much grain should be held in such a stock. The discussion focuses upon the potential shortfall in any given year and how much of this potential should be cov-

Table 9–1. Official Total Commitments to Agriculture (Broad Definition), Three-year Moving Averages.

	1974–76	1975–77	1976–78	1977–79	1978–80	1979–81	1980–82	1981–83
				$ millions				
Total at 1980 prices	8,219	9,138	10,044	10,994	11,326	11,825	12,730	13,426
Total at current prices	5,002	5,963	7,146	8,752	10,149	11,204	12,100	12,235
Multilateral sources	2,811	3,406	4,084	4,788	5,680	6,297	7,005	7,254
Bilateral sources	2,191	2,557	3,062	3,964	4,469	4,907	5,095	4,981
OFFICIAL CONCESSIONAL COMMITMENTS								
Total at current prices	3,244	3,816	4,682	5,935	7,049	7,753	8,029	7,583
Multilateral sources	1,355	1,553	1,945	2,300	2,939	3,263	3,424	3,163
Bilateral sources	1,889	2,264	2,736	3,635	4,110	4,490	4,605	4,420
OFFICIAL NONCONCESSIONAL COMMITMENTS								
Total at current prices	1,757	2,147	2,465	2,417	3,100	3,451	4,071	4,651
Multilateral sources	1,456	1,854	2,139	2,488	2,741	3,034	3,581	4,091
Bilateral sources	301	293	326	329	359	417	490	561

Note: The broad definition of agriculture includes forestry, agro-industries, and rural infrastructure and development.
Source: Food and Agriculture Organization (1985: Table 1–21, p. 60).

Figure 9–1.   Food Aid to Africa, 1985 (in thousand tons).

Total Import Needs in Principal Food Deficit Countries

Cape Verde: 65
Burundi: 50
Rwanda: 60

Grand Total

  needs: 9690
  promised: 6065.5

Aid Promised By Donor Countries (to 21 African Countries)

United States	3,075
Common Market, Total	1,780
multilateral	795
West Germany	195
France	150
Italy	130
United Kingdom	85
World Food Program	730
China	155
Japan	120
Australia	115
Sweden	35
Zimbabwe	25
Saudi Arabia	20
Soviet Union	7.5

Source: "Aid to Africa" (1985: 29–32).

ered. The world maximum shortfall historically has been and may be expected to be in the neighborhood of 25 million tons of food grain. Many experts believe that 68 percent coverage would provide adequate food protection against a shortfall, that is, a reserve of some 15 million tons would seem to be adequate. The United States has already pledged 6 million toward this end, but after ten years of talks the problem is yet unresolved.

The second set of short-term measures designed to help developing countries overcome their capital problems calls for increasing the amount of credit and easing the conditions that surround the extension of credit. In addition to trade difficulties, the developing countries are locked into patterns of debt that are increasingly difficult to manage (UNCTAD 1983). Sources of loans are the private banking industry, foreign governments, and international organizations such as the World Bank. The private banking industry naturally follows lending rules based on profit, avoidance of risk, and so forth. Accordingly, the funds are not generally channeled to the poorest countries. Aid from individual countries to another country is often tied to political or other economic conditions. Funds from an entity such as the World Bank may be preferable because of lower interest rates and lack of other restraints, but they are limited to only about $15 billion a year while developing country debt is around $700 billion. Debt servicing becomes an even greater burden upon the poor countries when productivity of planned development fails to materialize (cf. Chapter 5, Table 5-2). The poorest countries then become locked into debilitating cycles of debt and poverty.

The debt crisis must be put in proper perspective. As Darrell Delamaide has pointed out, the international bankers are responsible for making an enormous number of bad loans (1984; cited in Crittenden 1984: 7, 8). Bank managers have not always been economically efficient. At the same time, developing countries were also very poor debt managers (Adedeji 1985: 65-67). The debt results not from the necessity of world capitalism, as some dependency theorists would maintain, but from poor market decisions by the suppliers and demanders of loans.

It has become axiomatic that sources of loanable funds must be increased. Private lending, however, is always on market terms. Furthermore, it tends to go to the most credit-worthy in terms of resources and prospective earnings (cf. Figure 9-2).

In Africa, since 1978 the majority of disbursed funds were from private sources in contrast to 1971 when official creditors accounted for 67.5 percent. In addition, the amount of African debt grew at an annual rate of 16.2 percent between 1971 and 1982 (Adedeji 1985:

54–55). Recently, however, even many of these countries have run into a repayments crisis that threatens both their own financial stability as well as the health of the lending institutions.

It is important in this context to attempt to minimize the risks of loans. One means of doing this, which is actually widely practiced, is to diversify the number of banks participating in the loans made to a particular country. Another method that has been suggested, but is not operating in a significant way, holds that concerned governments should sponsor a system of loan insurance. This would at least lessen the risk of loaning funds to countries that are not financially stable. This is another form of establishing concessional terms for countries most in need of credit and amounts to softening market terms, while nonetheless maintaining a basic market framework.

On the international scene, both private investment and commercial lending tend to flow to the favored LDCs that are resource-rich. In the late 1970s, fifteen countries were receiving more than 75 percent of Euro-currency bank credits, including Mexico, Brazil, Indonesia, Algeria, Iran, Peru, the Philippines, Argentina, South Korea, and Hong Kong (Wionczek 1979; United Nations Conference on Trade and Development 1983). The poorest countries are not attractive and must rely on aid and meager domestic savings. Based on agriculture and trade, their past has been tortured and their future is bleak (McNamara 1979). The resource-rich LDCs have faced rather brighter prospects, yet poor planning, corruption, the world recession, and unstable markets have also left them in a precarious position ("Poor Outlook for Poor Nations" 1985).

There are many other concessional frameworks that have been suggested in the context of the various "special loan facilities" set up to deal with fluctuations and instabilities connected with energy prices, the foreign exchange markets, and food supplies. All of these facilities amount to modified market frameworks or insurance against the irregular fluctuations of vital markets, which could undermine the development and growth of the economy. Of course, the establishment of all of these facilities implies that public credit funds be increased by donations from the well-off countries, that somehow something like the fulfillment of the famed goal of transferring 0.7 percent of GNP be implemented by the developed countries (see Table 9-1).

The debt crisis is difficult to tackle in the short term because it arises from so many diverse causes. William Cline (1984: ch. 1) has cited shifting oil prices, high interest rates, decreasing volumes and prices of third-world exports, domestic economic management problems, and adverse psychology. More radical observers link the crisis to the U.S. deficit and trade policies (Castro 1985). In addition, there is corruption and the flight of capital from poor countries (Getschow, Moffett, Solis 1985; Lohr 1985). The above articles cite examples from Mexico, the Philippines, and Zaire, where local government and capital elites export large capital holdings.

Solutions are not easy. Suggestions abound, ranging from Castro's call for default to Peruvian President Alan Garcia's call to link repayment schedules in a formal way to export earnings (Martin 1985). In addition, the IMF proposes a series of high conditionality measures (cf. Chapter 5). Others still speak of establishing an International Debt Discount Corporation (Cline 1984: 114). There is logic to all of these proposals but also a certain impracticality. The corrupt elite will not reform themselves, the banks will withdraw any future cooperation in the face of default or limited repayment, IMF belt tightening is related to domestic political instability, and discount or other development assistance corporations must be financed by deficit-ridden OECD countries. In the end, most OECD countries tend to favor economic rather than political solutions. The most effective way to acquire foreign exchanges is trade, but trade is itself a problem area.

The third short-term measure suggested in UNCTAD preparatory discussions touches upon export earnings. The economic discussions center upon three main points: market entry, price stability, and foreign exchange. As may be seen from the data presented in the general report of UNCTAD VI, poor countries are major importers of first world goods (United Nations Conference on Trade and Development 1983). (The value of manufactured goods trade is $123 billion or 30 percent of the total.) Yet LDC exports of manufactured goods to the first world is only $26 billion. Total LDC exports have not been on all that vast a scale and have been mainly in primary products. Furthermore, commodity prices have been notably unstable; this together with the fact that foreign exchange is scarce and subject to both inflation and exchange rate volatility (80 percent is in U.S. dollars) make it difficult for poor countries to both accumulate capital in desired amounts and plan effectively. Both the relative size of earnings as well as stability are important if development planning is to have a solid basis. Various formulas are possible, such as specific commodity agreements (e.g., for bananas and sugars) or a general program such as the Common Market's "Stabex" or the general system of preferences suggested by previous UNCTAD meetings. But it is clear that in the short-term something must be done to face the deteriorating terms of trade that the developing countries find themselves facing (see Chapter 5, Table 5-1).

Export earnings derive primarily from two sources: the trade of commodities and raw materials and the trade of semiprocessed and industrial goods. For some countries tourism is also important. Regarding commodities and primary materials, there are two types of problems (Ahmod 1985). Either the third-world commodity is competing with other third-world producers or it competes with first-world domestic production. In the latter case it is more subject to tariffs, quotas, and other trade barriers for it threatens domestic producers and thus leads to political problems (Nogues 1985). Third-world products competing among themselves, e.g., coffee or cocoa, are more subject to the dynamics of supply and demand. The point is that for a variety of reasons, ranging from oversupply to the existence of substitutes and changes of tastes, third-world prices and earnings have fluctuated widely over the past twenty years (Food and Agriculture Organization 1981; Dinham and Hines 1984: 187–99). In addition, prices of the items they import have risen so that their net terms of trade in real terms has steadily declined. All of this makes planning much more difficult. Some sort of price stability is very important, but it is not easy to bring about, either for reasons of fluctuation of supply and demand or for reasons of exchange rate instability. What is called for are trade agreements that lead to the stabilization of import purchasing power. Many observers think that some sort of expansion of the EEC's Stabex Scheme would be appropriate, at least in the short run. In the long run, of course, subsidies for overproduction only stimulate the continued production of surpluses and inappropriate patterns of supply.

The poor countries are caught in a squeeze in two markets: the export markets for their semi-processed and industrial goods are severely restricted and the market for foreign exchange, which is at the bottom of import strategies, is unstable. As Robert McNamara and many others have argued, overcoming protectionism and improving trade possibilities is vital to the health of the poor countries and to the world economy as well. Yet the political will to do so is practically nonexistent (McNamara 1979).

In the above capital malaise, direct foreign private investment often appears as an attractive way out. Benefits derived from foreign investment take many forms and include new technology, managerial know-how, marketing skills, and contact with foreign markets. It may even stimulate local savings and domestic investment and make possible the use of local manpower, raw materials, and other resources that might otherwise remain idle or be used considerably less efficiently. Benefits from such investment can show up in higher wage receipts for local labor, domestic market development, and higher tax revenues for local governments.

Problems continue to arise because private enterprise demands an "attractive" investment that is competitive or comparable with alternatives in the international business settling. It also seeks political economic stability so that the investment not be jeopardized by a political uprising or a government takeover of foreign investments. Furthermore, private investors seek a "positive infrastructure," whether it be in the realm of efficient bureaucracy and noncumbersome regulation or in the area of transport, labor force skills, and communications networks. For these reasons, most corporations find the countries most seriously affected by poverty (see Chapter 1) unattractive areas of investment. In addition, a corporation generally seeks as much freedom of movement as possible regarding production decisions, movement of capital, technology development, and marketing; in addition, it seeks a favorable tax position, including concessions, exemptions from tariffs, import restrictions on equipment and materials, and protection from competing imports. Corporations may also mop up local credit and other resources, leaving indigenous entrepreneurs bereft of opportunity. Thus, private foreign investment frequently imposes costs that many host countries are reluctant to incur.

All of the above three short-term measures focus on the transfer of capital from the developed to the developing countries. Together with such capital transfers, one sees calls for immediate transfers of technology and management.

Technology transfers raise complex issues of international law and intellectual property. Technology is protected by patents and licensing agreements as well as by the contract conditions surrounding joint ventures or transnational wholly owned subsidiaries in the developing world. The case of IBM in India or of the Apple Computer Co. in parts of East Asia are well-known. These points are further complicated by the whole debate over appropriate technology, which suggests that some of the high-level technology that third-world countries are seeking is actually not suitable in a socioeconomic sense of providing more jobs and raising rural incomes. Corporations play by market rules and developing countries have little hope of acquiring technology from them other than by paying for it or entering into one of the above forms of agreement. There is considerable scope, however, for government institutions, such as the U.S. Department of Agriculture or university faculties to be quite active in the transfer of technology both by training foreign nationals and by sending their own experts to the field. This issue will be taken up again when discussing long-term policies to set up appropriate development infrastructure.

This kind of technology transfer can be set in place with fairly low costs. It goes together with the developing countries demand for transfers of management and training skills. Along these lines, voluntary associations such as Oxfam International have long been active in technology and management (as well as some capital) transfers. Many church organizations have also cooperated in this way for development. In the present context, however, the resources that such private voluntary organizations command are severely limited. Regarding cooperating with governments of developed countries, these private organizations are wary of being coopted by the interest of "the center" in the guise of helping the poor (Henriot 1981).

All of the above measures call for significant transfers of capital, management, and technology. They are needed, but they are not sufficient. For the primary development problems are not technical but sociological. In particular, the problem of corruption by local elites must be addressed. The well-known investigation of Zairean copper provides a case in point. President Mobutu reportedly stashed away $5 billion in Swiss banks, an amount equal to the country's entire foreign debt (Crittenden 1985)! In the sales of Zaire's copper, local elites established a holding company in Switzerland that enabled them to funnel funds outside the country to add to their own personal wealth. Without coming to terms with such systematic power abuses, all the transfers in the world will do little to help overcome poverty and hunger.

LONG-TERM MEASURES

More than short-term thinking is required. Specific attention must be given to four long-term measures: the setting of development priorities, restructuring of the economy, diversification, and development of infrastructure.

Local and international development priorities must be recast in terms of overall human development. Some of the more important issues are (1) educating people for development so that they become more active and responsible participants, (2) establishing in planning and budget expenditures the priority of needs over wants, and (3) reducing the waste of capital used for military expenditures (LDCs spend more than $20 billion a year in the international weapons market (Sivard 1985). These are matters of immediate concern but nonetheless difficult. Powerful elites interfere with such orientations in development policy. Any results will tend to be more long-term than instantaneous. But unless measures are taken to cure the endemic mismanagement of developing country economies, little else will change. Tragedies such as the Sudan's starvation are caused primarily by human error (Putka 1985).

The budgetary process is at the bottom of setting national priorities, but those priorities will represent little more than the interests of a small elite if attention is not given to educating people to become responsible social participants. Education for development implies a transition from people being treated as passive objects of development to becoming subjects of development, who have a sense of responsibly shaping their own destiny. The path of that transition must first take root in a society's traditional modes of organization and action on local, regional, and national levels.

In the face of power abuse by both traditional and new international elites, such pedagogy is a slow painstaking process from conscientization to significant action, but it is not impossible. Moreover, there is considerable scope for leaders and educated persons in persuasion groups to articulate the issues in a manner to give voice to the people. In Latin America and in many parts of Africa and Asia, private voluntary organizations frequently run great risks in being an alternative voice in society as they raise issues of priorities in planning and budget expenditures and counteract the selfishness of elites and the national security state ideology. Setting valid public priorities is necessarily a long-term process of education and dialogue. It is particularly difficult in totalitarian and nonparticipatory societies. Some of the grasroots organizing strategies reviewed in Chapter 7 are promising in several respects.

Restructuring of both developing and developed country economies is widely recognized as being necessary, but it is a very long-term operation. The first area of restructuring is resource control. Unless resource control is addressed, no amount of "development" will reach the poor. Rather, local elites will continue to pursue their own narrow interests. This issue of access to productive resources—land, water, credit, and other inputs—as well as access to markets and other services has been underlined by a wide variety of observers (Food and Agriculture Organization 1981; Wortman 1978, ch. 6).

The obstacle to such restructuring of resources is power on the part of those who actually control those resources. This has prompted those on the left to suggest that the only effective strategy is armed struggle to throw out the oppressors. In some cases that may in fact be true. But for all that, armed struggle is not a quick and easy path to social change. One of the reasons that the elite is the elite is that they are quite capable and know how to take care of themselves. Armed struggle would likely be protracted and could also draw in outside powers who seek to protect their geopolitical interests.

Secondly, solidarity in opposition to an enemy very often does not translate into solidarity in positive government and programs after the revolution. A surprising amount of historical evidence suggests that the shake-out that occurs after the revolution frequently leaves another oppressive elite in power.

Reform is slow, but not necessarily much slower than revolution when all is totaled up. When there is a just and efficient legal system in a country, it represents the preferred path of social change. But such is not the case in many parts of the developing world. There is, however, still some room for persuasion. Enlightened elites will perceive that unless they give something and move toward reform they run the risk of losing it all. In fact, they have much to gain in terms of civil order and in terms of new customers and markets that the poor would constitute once they became better off. Such points are lost on many local elites who answer poverty and hunger with more repression. Such institutionally violent behavior can hardly end in any manner other than armed violence. Changing patterns of resource control remains very difficult. I know of no genuine land reform, for example, that was brought about by other than a coercive authoritarian government.

Secondly, the institutional framework must be restructured. Development loans must adapt to rather than ignore or suppress traditional forms of organization and management. For example, systems of informal credit and traditional markets can be important institutions. Also, education should be transformed to serve development needs, a measure that would also be of some help in curbing the brain drain.

In development thinking during the 1950s and 1960s, it was often assumed that modernization meant Westernization of institutions. Thus, democracy and forms of economic administration and management were frequently thrust upon developing countries. Even third-world people who studied abroad came to be Westernized and even to disdain their own traditional ways or feel inferior about them. In the postcolonial period, the European forms of civil service, law, and decisionmaking that had been set up in the former colonies soon proved to be inadequate. More and more it came to be realized that domestic institutions should build off local culture and traditions. But there still remains a conflict between such ways of doing things and the way business is conducted in the international political economy.

Two types of institutions are needed. On the local level, domestic administrative policy should harmonize with local cultures and traditions. When international organizations enter a country to cooperate in development projects, they should not import their own ways but should plan strategy around local resources for planning and decisionmaking.

At the same time, developing countries should develop their international expertise in terms of dealing with futures markets, international corporations, and other governments. To do this, most developing countries need to reform legal institutions, streamline bureaucracy, and achieve international standards in trade practices, customs inspections, and licensing. A country's financial and trade administration is often a cumbersome impediment in the development of more positive international relations. Adebayo Adedeji (1985: 60) clearly makes this point when assessing the internal factors underlying African debt.

Finally, the input–output composition of the economy should be restructured. In the long run, production should be in view of a securely defined market. The greatest future market potential for most developing countries is domestic and regional rather than in the first world, where markets (e.g., for textiles) are often glutted. As was seen in Chapter 8, the development of a domestic market means harmonizing agriculture and industry and the fostering of an income policy that lets the poor make money. Such an approach means that strategies to produce growth must also produce jobs; appropriate (intermediate, labor-intensive) technology must be used. What is produced and how must be simultaneously decided in terms of markets that actually exist as well as in terms of comparative advantages in production.

Such restructuring of the composition of input and output is a very complicated issue internationally. As usually presented, the theory of comparative advantage is a straightforward issue of deciding, on the basis of resource endowment, what to produce for oneself, what to export, and what to import. The textbook exposition of the theory can be deceptively simple. The issue is far more complex when one tries to simultaneously estimate which set of the thousands of possible outputs from a country's resource endowment should be selected.

What is more important, however, is the fact that comparative advantage is not just a production issue but a market issue. One must anticipate the supply and demand decisions of all the other potential compettitors as well as the tastes of consumers, their income picture, and the movements of prices. One of the main problems in the area of agricultural commodities is that too many producers are in the market for a limited demand. While short-term strategies to limit supply or to fix prices may possess some logic, in the long run such policy is inefficient. The long-term prospects for the growth of these raw material and commodity markets is limited. While commodity contracts can help in introducing order into supply and demand, new customers and markets must be sought in terms of output diversification and in regional cooperation. As it is, many of these countries are producing the same things and trying to sell to the same people. They must restructure in order to develop complementary economies. This leads to diversification.

Diversification of the economies of the developing countries would seem to be necessary if risks associated with market fluctuations are to be reduced. There are three areas of diversification that should enter into long-range planning. The first is to diversify what is produced so as not to be exclusively dependent on one or two commodities or industrial products for one's export earnings. Over fifteen African countries depend upon one or two commodities for the majority of their export earnings. The idea is to shift to a relatively more stable product mix. This point is tied to the preceding one of restructuring, but diversification of the product mix adds to the idea of restructuring the notion that it is dangerous to depend on a few products. Market fluctuations are inevitable. When there is a dependency on a few products, such fluctuations will be accompanied by wide swings in revenue that will disrupt development planning.

Countries dependent on raw materials for exports grow at considerably slower rates than those exporting semi-processed goods and manufactured goods. This is true even of OPEC countries that were thought to be in an unassailable position five years ago. For Mexico each one dollar drop in oil price has meant a loss of one-half billion dollars in revenue (Stockton 1986). The IMF has estimated that OPEC economies grew by only 1 percent in 1985. At the same time, countries that are exporters of primary products are estimated to have grown at about a 2.7 percent rate. Exporters of manufactures, on the others hand, have seen the volume of their exports grow by 10 percent during the 1970s, and they are estimated to have grown by about 7 percent in 1985, with 6 percent projected for 1986 ("Poor Outlook for Poor Nations" 1985: 81). Most of the so-called Newly Industrialized Countries (NICs) are in Asia and have followed a positive agricultural policy.

As noted, production decisions cannot rely on a calculation of comparative advantage based upon resource potential alone. Far more important in today's context is to correctly anticipate market conditions. Some of the guesswork can be taken out of market estimates by entering into regional planning with other countries who may be producing the same things. Another alternative would be to enter into long-term trade contracts with one's trading partners so as to guarantee an outlet for supply over a significant period.

In agriculture there is also considerable scope for import substitution strategies. Cash export crops can be expected to bring in diminished amounts of foreign exchange because their markets are becoming glutted. It is wise to cut down on food imports by producing what the country needs. This is important because such imports also drain foreign exchange and at times act as a damper upon the development of local agriculture.

In industrial goods, there is perhaps considerably more scope for export substitution diversification, particularly in the processing of agricultural raw materials, handicrafts, and light industrial goods.

Secondly, it is important to diversify trading partners so that markets do not collapse when a recession hits one country, consumption patterns change, or the country turns to either domestic production or to synthetics. This diversification could well be associated with longer term trading contracts, which would specify an assured level of demand and, thus, could be used as a basis to rationalize production.

The government of India has long aimed to pursue such a diversified policy. Because of its population, geopolitical position, and influence in the third world, India has important international stature. This fact has made it easier to follow the strategy of milking more than one cow, as Mrs. Gandhi put it. In so doing, India has simultaneously reaped benefits from the Soviet Bloc, Europe, and North America. The ASEAN Countries and China have given signs of following a similar strategy of diversifying both sources of supply as well as markets for exported goods and services.

In simultaneously dealing with Japan, Europe, the United States, and the Soviet Union, there is the possibility that a country could miss out on some of the benefits it might get if it allied itself more exclusively with one or the other. But it is important to remember that the increased benefits in that case bring much more political control and leave one with much less room for maneuver. Furthermore, in such a case, a country is more subject to the vicissitudes of negative economic events in the partner country, such as changes in consumption patterns or recession.

Diversification carries with it the advantages of managing risk in a more stabilized way, and it also fosters the development of specialization and division of labor with one's domestic economy. This

Table 9-2.   Origin and Destination of Merchandise Exports, Selected
Developing Countries, 1965, 1983.

Country of Origin	Destination			
	Industrial Market Economies		Developing Economies	
	1965	1983	1965	1983
Chad	64	72	34	28
Congo	86	98	13	2
Ghana	74	47	9	20
Ivory Coast	84	70	13	27
Kenya	69	47	28	51
Malawi	69	68	30	31
Nigeria	91	74	6	26
Tanzania	66	59	32	37
Zaire	93	89	7	10
Zambia	87	65	11	34
Bangladesh	—	43	—	47
China	47	42	40	52
India	58	55	23	26
Indonesia	72	73	23	26
Korea (South)	75	65	25	25
Malaysia	56	50	36	47
Philippines	95	77	5	20
Thailand	44	56	53	37
Argentina	67	40	26	30
Bolivia	97	41	3	58
Brazil	77	66	18	26
Colombia	86	78	12	18
Ecuador	89	61	11	38
Mexico	82	85	13	14
Peru	86	76	12	21
Uruguay	76	34	19	55
Venezuela	63	60	37	39

Note: The remaining percentage of trade is destined to either the East European non-market economies or high-income oil exporters.

Source: World Bank (1985: Table 12, pp. 196–197).

process itself is very important and will foster the further growth of domestic markets.

Thirdly, it is important to attempt to diversify both production and trade through regional (South–South) cooperation. As Table 9-2 indicates, the majority of developing countries are locked into trade patterns destined toward the first world. Furthermore, the single nation-state is not always economically viable or optimal in terms of either production resources or markets. Current patterns of over-dependency on the first and second worlds offer rather bleak long-term prospects. Such cooperation between developing countries is sometimes blocked because of political difficulties or because their economies do not mesh (e.g., they may all want to sell textiles). In the long term, the economic incompatibilities are amenable to restructuring and diversification.

The more serious problem is political. While no ready blueprint is to be found, the potential of technical and economic cooperation and trade and monetary accords between developing countries should provide some incentive for entering on the difficult road of negotiations. Simply looking to the developed countries is not sufficient in the long run; a certain measure of regional self-reliance (rather than merely national) emerges as an absolutely necessary ingredient of a more just and efficient international economy.

There are not many examples of successful regional cooperation in the world today. South–South cooperation has received a lot of attention in recent years, yet it is beset by difficulties on political, economic, and broader social grounds (Pavlic et al., 1983; Laszlo 1983: ch. 4). Ervin Laszlo has listed six major obstacles ranging from shortsighted nationalism and self-centeredness to disparity in development levels, cultural biases, dependency relations, and lack of complementarities in size and location. Solutions along these lines are definitely long term. Third world countries from LAFTA and the Andes Pact in Latin America, to the East African Community and ASEAN in Southeast Asia have had only very limited success, if they have not ended up in ruins altogether. But there are many potential advantages to be gained. The third world cannot expect the first world to undergo radical changes in present structures and institutions. Within the context of restructuring and diversification mentioned above, it is in the interest of poorer countries to develop new alliances. Developing countries such as India and Brazil are also quite sophisticated in terms of industry and technology. Conceivably, they could supply developing countries with necessary industrial technology and inputs at lower prices than first-world countries could.

A final area of long-term strategy is the development of the infrastructure necessary for development. Most important of all are energy, transport, storage, and communications, without which it is difficult for agricultural and industrial growth to take place. The public sector most often assumes leadership in this regard. This is one area, however, where multinational corporations can be intelligently integrated into development plans if the financing of such projects can be worked out. As pointed out in Chapter 4, these are the primary leaders in biotechnology, for example.

Public services are part of the economic infrastructure. The development of an efficient civil service and bureaucracy ranging from the setting up of a statistical system, gathering and processing information, analyzing all such material, and bringing it to bear upon planning, budgeting, and financial and fiscal policies is essential (Adedeji 1985: 67-68). Many governments that dream of scientific planning seem to take such an infrastructure for granted. Historically, in fact, in many cases it has proven to be a major obstacle to making any progress (Waterston 1976).

Another infrastructure element of fundamental importance is to develop within developing countries structures of scientific research and experiments that would be devoted to fundamental economic and social issues rather than to military purposes. This is far easier said than done. At present, world research expenditures run at about $150 billion a year. There are some 3 million scientists and engineers. Only 3-5 percent of present research is in the third world (mostly in India, Brazil, and Mexico). Furthermore, only 3 percent of world research goes for agriculture while military research gets 24 percent (50 percent in the United States). Thus both the location and nature of research has to be transformed. The surest long-run measure to overcome dependency and deficits in technology is to set in place domestic research and to facilitate the production of indigenous technologies. How to do it is not clear. As was indicated, universities and governments can play a larger role in transferring not only technology but *research capacity*. The scope for regional cooperation between third-world countries as well as with first-world countries should be clear enough, although frequently the political obstacles are not overcome.

POLITICAL WILL: SOME REFLECTIONS ON PRESENT PROSPECTS

When all of the above measures are analyzed in terms of their resource requirements, it becomes patently clear that the main obstacles to development are not resource scarcity and technological difficulties but sociopolitical factors.

I have pointed out that various persuasion groups as well as transnational corporations are guilty of many transgressions in the development arena. But I lay major responsibility and accountability at the door of governments throughout the world because the primary problems are political and can be traced to the failure to galvanize the political will to overcome the problems. None of the measures discussed above is impossible, either on the basis of resource endowment, demography, or technology. The main issue is politics and power. This does not mean that the solution to underdevelopment is to be found in some sort of political voluntarism. Rather, some political agreements are necessary to open the door so that other potential solutions stemming from new technology and management might be allowed to work.

The point is that the world has become increasingly interdependent, but it has not developed the mentality, the structures, or the political institutions to manage that interdependence. Many discussions are underway and that at least is a hopeful sign. A beginning has been made, even though it will take a few generations to develop adequate international structures. Political will remains the chief problem.

There are many different motives for overcoming poverty. Some people are motivated primarily by a sense of solidarity with the poor and a thirst for social justice. Others are moved by the new markets, which the more than a billion poor people would represent, if they were to move to a level of adequate welfare and income. Still others see that poverty is inherently destabilizing and perceive that, if something is not done now to alleviate it, those who are well off run the risk of losing everything in the end. All these motives can be brought to bear on program design and be helpful in forging some sort of policy coalition.

Each protagonist mentioned above represents a certain potential as well as certain deficiencies when we think of their role regarding poverty in the world today. The dynamics of organizational politics frequently becomes quite complex and various forms of sanctions come into play. For instance, to control the policy of an international organization, such as UNESCO or the IMF, a rich country, such as the United States, will manipulate its budget contribution, which is often of critical importance. Corporations will use philanthropy and grants to churches and universities to steer those organizations toward their own interests. Yet, at the same time, as movements for honest and participatory government, the Islamic revolution, and other groups show, there are socially prophetic voices that call for justice in development. They will not be stifled or co-opted.

Those advocating justice in economic development are accused of being utopian. They do not even completely agree among themselves on the criteria of justice. Yet this level of discourse is highly important, for it alone attacks the dominant values and ideologies which underpin the persistance of poverty (i.e., the sociocultural base of poverty). It is here that one finds the visions expressed by Gandhi, Mao, the Islamic revival, and those who are promoting liberation theology and a "preferential option for the poor" in Latin America.

The "realists" frequently ignore such concerns. They do not appeal to the dispossessed but to those in power. In this view, many of the powerful elites today follow a short-term strategy of grabbing and running, rather than undertake a long-term strategy of mutual self-interests (as advocated by the Brandt Report). The latter approach is considered realistic and will avoid losing everything in a revolution. It will also reap the benefits of new stability and expanded markets.

The gambit of political will turns on persuasion. Here it is clear that the persuasion going on among the dispossessed turns on justice and the persuasion going on among the principalities and powers turns upon self-interest. A realist recognizes both of these points.

On the domestic level the galvanizing of political will is stymied by misgovernment, as well as by oppressive elites, narrow factionalism and interest groups, and the lack of adequate political institutions and processes.

On the international level, discussion has focused upon forging a "new international economic order" and "managing interdependence." Talk of interdependence implies that it is no longer feasible or desirable for nations to pursue policies of narrow self-interest. Even though development is usually discussed in terms of the nation-state, what is implied is that nationalism, after all, provides too narrow a base for overcoming poverty. Interdependence is an ever-increasing reality at all levels of contemporary life. What is at issue is improving the quality of interdependence in a way that would assure the dignity of all persons and of all peoples.

The forging of political will is a complex social process that goes forward on many levels at once. It is shaped by great leaders and innovative elites who act as catalysts, by conscientization regarding values and overall human development, by confrontation and social conflict, and by new possibilities of human community ushered in by technology and material innovations.

Why has no effective political will materialized to overcome poverty? Surely a major reason is the pervading spirit of group egoism and the eroding of communitarian values that dominates most countries and social classes. But it is also being undermined by the deteriorating quality of political economic institutions. Increasingly the legitimacy of such institutions is being questioned, for they systematically work against the poor even when individuals within them mean well. It is clear that "development" does not reach the poor nor will it do so without radical change not only within the existing institutions but of the institutions themselves (that is, altering the rules of the game in governments, the IMF, and GATT).

At the same time, the well-off countries have only recently emerged from one of the worst recessions in fifty years. Poverty itself is even growing in the first world. Increasingly the developed countries are in deficit and cannot fund their own welfare programs. Domestic concerns rather than the more glaring international needs garner the attention of politicians.

If one compares 1975 with 1985, it is difficult to see a lot of progress. But if one compares 1985 with 1945, it is easy to see a considerable change for the better. One of the most positive things that has happened is, firstly, poverty is clearly seen as avoidable. Secondly, it is really in no one's interest to maintain a system that produces poverty. Governments recognize this, corporations do, and so does the public at large. The problem now is not in perceiving the benefits. The problem is that no one is willing to pay the costs. These realities undermine political will.

REFERENCES

Adedeji, Adebayo. 1985. "Foreign Debt in Africa During the 1980's." *The Journal of Modern African Studies* 23, no. 1: 53–74.

Ahmod, J. 1985. "Prospects of Trade Liberalization Between the Developed and Developing Countries." *World Development* 13, no. 9: 77–86.

"Aid to Africa." 1985. *The Economist*, July 20, 29–32.

Castro, Fidel. 1985. "Avoiding a 'Crash'—A Radical Proposal for Solving the Debt Crisis." *World Press Review*, August 23–16.

Cline, William R. 1984. *International Debt: Systemic Risk and Policy Response.* Washington, D.C.: Institute for International Economics.

Crittenden, Ann. 1984. "In for a Dime, In for a Dollar." *New York Times*, 8 July 1984.

de Janvry, Alain. 1981. *The Agrarian Question—Reformism in Latin America.* Baltimore: The Johns Hopkins University Press.

Delamaide, Darrell. 1984. *Debt Shock: The Real Story of the World Credit Crisis.* New York: Doubleday and Co.

Dinham, Barbara, and Colin Hines. 1984. *Agribusiness in Africa.* Trenton, N.J.: Africa World Press.

Food and Agriculture Organization (FAO). 1981. *The Peasants' Charter.* Rome, Italy: Food and Agriculture Organization.

_____. 1985. *The State of Food and Agriculture, 1984*. Rome, Italy: Food and Agriculture Organization.

Getschow, George, Matt Moffett, and Dianna Solis. 1985. "Nation in Jeopardy: Mexico's Crisis Grows as Money and the Rich Both Seek Safer Places." *Wall Street Journal*, 11 October, sec. I.

Henriot, Peter, ed. 1981. *Private Voluntary Organizations and Government Aid*. Occasional Paper. Washington, D.C.: Center of Concern.

Laszlo, Ervin. 1983. "Regional Cooperation Among Developing Countries: The Operational Modality of ECDC." In *The Challenge of South–South Cooperation*, ed. Breda Pavlic et al., 93–105. Boulder, Colo.: Westview Press.

Lohr, Steve. "Philippine Capitalist Looks Overseas." 1985. *New York Times*, 29 July, p. D4.

MacBean, A.I., and P.N. Snowden. 1981. *International Institutions in Trade and Finance*. London: George Allen and Unwin.

MacBride, Sean, ed. 1981. *The MacBride Report on the New International Information Order*. Geneva: UNESCO.

Martin, Everett G. 1985. "Peruvian President's Push on World Debt Gains Him Visibility and Public Approval." *Wall Street Journal*, 25 September, p. 34.

McNamara, Robert. 1979. "Address to the Board of Governors." Washington, D.C.: World Bank.

Nogues, Julio J. 1985. "Agriculture and Developing Countries in the GATT." *The World Economy* 8, no. 2: 119–33.

Pavlic, Breda; Boris Cizelj; Marjan Svetlicic; and Raul Uranga. 1983. *The Challenge of South–South Cooperation*. Boulder, Colo: Westview Press.

"Poor Outlook for Poor Nations." 1985. *The Economist*, November 9, 21.

Prebisch, Raul. 1964. *Towards a New Trade Policy for Development*. Report by the Secretary General of UNCTAD. New York: United Nations.

Putka, Gary. 1985. "The Tragedy of Sudan's Spreading Starvation Is That It Is Caused by Man's Errors, Not Nature's." *Wall Street Journal*, 22 January, p. 35.

Sivard, Ruth Leger. 1985. *World Military and Social Expenditures*. Leesburg, Va.: WMSE Institute.

Stockton, William. 1986. "Mexico Trims the Price of Its Crude." *New York Times*, 31 January, pp. 33–35.

United Nations Conference on Trade and Development (UNCTAD). 1983. *Background Papers on the International Economy for UNCTAD VI*. Geneva, Switzerland: United Nations.

Waterston, Leon. 1976. *Lessons from Development Experience*. Baltimore: The Johns Hopkins University Press.

Wionczek, Miguel S. 1979. "Debt in Less Developed Countries." *World Development* 6, no. 6: 779–82.

World Bank. 1983. *World Development Report*. Washington, D.C.: World Bank.

Wortman, Sterling. 1978. *To Feed This World*. Baltimore: The Johns Hopkins University Press.

AUTHOR INDEX

305

SUBJECT INDEX

ABOUT THE AUTHOR

Paul Steidlmeier teaches at the School of Management of the State University of New York, Binghamton. He is a specialist in international economic development and management. He received his Ph.D. in 1975 from the Stanford University Food Research Institute, where he specialized in Chinese agriculture. He has previously taught at the Santa Clara University Institute of Agribusiness, the Gregorian University in Rome, and Loyola Marymount University. Dr. Steidlmeier has written several articles on Chinese development as well as on business and society. His present research focuses on management strategies in developing countries and the coordination of the initiatives of private enterprise, governments, and other social organizations in development policy.